PRAISE FOR *EMMA'S LAUGH:*
THE GIFT OF SECOND CHANCES

"*Emma's Laugh* traces the author's moving, exhilarating, and devastating journey as a parent. Told with humor, humility, and grace, it is filled with deep sentiment but never falls into sentimentality. This moving family story had me at the edge of my seat, clutching a box of tissues, never wanting it to end."

—MARIA KUZNETSOVA, author of *Oksana Behave!*

"*Emma's Laugh* is an honest and beautiful look at parental love. From her early rejection of her special-needs child to her gradual falling in love with her daughter, Kupershmit shows us how much a mother is willing to give of herself for the sake of her child. I read with my heart in my throat all the way to the end."

—MONICA WESOLOWSKA, author of *Holding Silvan: A Brief Life*

"Diana Kupershmit's innate gift of storytelling and astute observations carefully invite the reader to bear witness to a heartbreaking journey toward acceptance. This gorgeous and honest memoir holds up the lens to motherhood and dares to address the profound grief that is capable of burying us or propelling us. Emma's Laugh is a mother's love letter to a remarkable child and a beautiful reminder to each of us that in life, the two most valuable things are time and laughter—everything else is simply details."

—JESSICA CIENCIN HENRIQUEZ, author of *If You Loved Me, You Would Know*

"*Emma's Laugh* made me laugh, and cry, and smile, and cry again. Kupershmit delivers literary love with a capital L. This is what motherhood is. This is what love is. Just as Kupershmit climbs into a crib to 'mold herself' around her daughter when she suffers headaches and pain, I felt myself molding to this story, ever involved, rooting for mother and daughter and this family all the way."
—ELIZABETH COHEN, author of *The House on Beartown Road: A Memoir of Learning and Forgetting*

"Diana Kupershmit has written a remarkably honest and unflinching account of her journey from rejection to acceptance raising a special-needs child. A heartbreaking and heartwarming tribute—and a testimony to one mother's endless love for her extraordinary child."
—HEATHER SIEGEL, author of *The King and the Quirky*

"With a voice that is crisp and clear, Kupershmit shares the story of her daughter, Emma, and the earthshaking decisions that came with parenting such an exceptional girl. Faced with situations that most parents are spared, Kupershmit takes us into her darkest moments with tenderness and grace. What shines the brightest is the joy that is set free when we accept that instead of controlling outcomes perhaps our greatest responsibility is in surrendering to the possibility that our children come with their own plan for how they will live and what they will teach."
—ASHLEIGH RENARD, author of *Swing: A Memoir of Doing it All*

"The author effectively shows how she learned lessons from raising Emma that allowed her to draw on a wellspring of love for other members of her family. . . . An engaging work about how the tenacity of a young girl changes her parents' lives."
—*KIRKUS REVIEWS*

EMMA'S LAUGH

A MEMOIR

EMMA'S LAUGH

THE GIFT OF SECOND CHANCES

DIANA KUPERSHMIT

SHE WRITES PRESS

Published 2021
Printed in the United States of America
Print ISBN: 978-1-64742-112-0
E-ISBN: 978-1-64742-113-7
Library of Congress Control Number: 2020922825

For information, address:
She Writes Press
1569 Solano Ave #546
Berkeley, CA 94707

Interior design by Tabitha Lahr

She Writes Press is a division of SparkPoint Studio, LLC.

Any views expressed therein, are mine and mine alone and not necessarily those of the City and DOHMH.

Names and identifying characteristics have been changed to protect the privacy of certain individuals.

for Emma

CHAPTER 1

I PEELED MY BODY AWAY from the wetness of the sheets and heaved myself out of bed. My eyes landed on the plastic diaper pail that occupied the corner of our bedroom, like some sentry on the lookout for an incoming baby. Next to it stood a cake fashioned out of Pampers that balanced a basket filled with baby paraphernalia: lotions, creams, shampoo, gender-neutral onesies. I laughed to myself at the absurdity of the situation. Here I was, rolling out of bed where my water had just broken, with the baby right on schedule, and nothing to show for preparedness other than the gifts from the baby shower my coworkers had surprised me with just weeks before.

This was not my choice. Had I had the energy to challenge my mother's old-world, cultural superstitions, which dictated that one does not celebrate a baby's arrival prematurely—to avoid tempting fate, messing with the universe—I would have had the spare room of our three-bedroom duplex apartment fully equipped, with all the bells and whistles, furnishings, and requisite five-foot plush giraffe, ready to receive its new tiny tenant. Had my perfectionist tendencies been given full rein to wield the control that I brought to all situations, I would have thrown *myself* the baby shower, and feigned surprise. My mother didn't care to know that at twenty-six, having spent more than half my life in this country, I considered myself an American, or at least more American than Ukrainian.

"Let's do this!" my husband, Anatoly (Tolya, as I called him), announced with the inappropriate glee of one not expected to shortly push a human out of their privates. *He* was not doing this. "Technicality," I could imagine him answering if I were to point this out.

I forgave him. Because the truth was, we were doing this together, and things were largely moving according to plan. We were both gainfully employed professionals. I'd completed graduate school and worked my dream job as a family therapist. Though many days I felt ill equipped to be helping others while battling my own demons of anxiety and self-doubt, I learned quickly to act the part of the qualified clinician—to fake it till you make it.

Because on the surface, things checked off. We were confident in our parenting abilities, having had the benefit of "playing house" with my thirteen's-year-old sister, Holly, who had come to live with us three years prior. New baby worries were dwarfed by typical teen angst. I believed we were at an advantage, some might even say ahead of the game.

I grabbed the stair rail and stepped down, taking one last sweeping glance at our open living room area—arguably my favorite space. Contemporary but comfortable furniture in the bright color palette of a Kandinsky painting was arranged just so. The red leather sleep sofa that had withstood so much adolescent action when still in Tolya's parents' home now anchored our living room. Adjacent to it stood the sexy, steel-framed, round open shelf unit—a serendipitous Soho furniture store find—on whose beech shelves lived my extensive collection of books. A jolt of excitement moved through me as I imagined myself on the couch, nursing, and *my* favorite books sharing shelf space with puzzles and Dr. Seuss books.

Tolya held the door open for me as I made one final scan of the space I would be returning to with a baby in my arms. Ashes, our Russian Blue cat, sat perched on the faux Le Corbusier Chaise, like a Bastet statue—the Egyptian goddess of cats, the home, family, and motherhood. Perfect.

I tried not to dwell on the notion that he was possibly still grieving the loss of his partner in crime—our cocker spaniel, Jules—who died unexpectedly just a few months earlier. Had I been superstitious like my mother, I would have worried about this foreboding event. But I had not lived long enough for the mystical world to threaten me or impinge on my sensibilities. I believed in science and medicine and playing by the rules for the best outcomes. What could possibly go wrong?

I straightened the tilted hallway mirror and walked out the door.

In the car, I strained to tune in to what was happening in my body; no sign of contractions, only the flutter of butterfly nerves that accompanied all new and anxiety-provoking situations in my life. As I watched my husband's hands gripping the steering wheel, I told myself that before long, those hands I loved so much would be holding our newborn baby. Tolya's hands were my favorite of his physical attributes. Though not long-limbed, Tolya boasted long, tapering fingers that seemed to have evolved directly from the pronounced veins that ran like a multilane highway, with protruding knuckles serving as speed bumps. Hands defined but smooth, as if years on the tennis team chiseled them, and the years on the swim team tamed them into soft ripples.

I wondered who the baby would look like. Would it have its father's generous forehead? —an attribute my mother always insisted characterized intelligence; "*Beeg head to hold a beeg breyn,*" I could hear her saying. I never dared ask what my small, flat, unimpressive forehead signified. I hoped the baby would inherit Tolya's large deep-set eyes—brown pools of kindness—and not my beady ones, as he once called them, teasingly.

"Do you think it's a boy or a girl?" I asked, more to dispel my nervous energy than anything else.

Months ago, when the sonogram technician asked if we wanted to know the sex, Tolya had said, "I don't want technology announcing to me the most natural, momentous event in life." This was coming from a computer programmer, someone who stared at a screen day in and day out. He was not about to allow a machine to dispense foreknowledge and therefore control of the uncontrollable.

Now he said, "I don't know." I thought he would reveal his hopes, but he joked, "It's one or the other."

I secretly wished for a girl.

In the hospital, a nurse wheeled me into a room where a handsome intern was waiting to help things along. "We're going to break your water fully, to speed things up," he said matter-of-factly. I cursed the timing of his youth and good looks. *Why did I have to get the hot doctor in these embarrassing circumstances?* I was suspicious of the reasons male medical students settled on obstetrics and gynecology as a specialty. The real question was why I was even entertaining those musings. It's not like we were on a first date and I'd suddenly realized I'd forgotten to shave my legs.

Before I could finish my thought, I felt a flood of wetness. The contractions heralded a tsunami of pain that washed over me, then ebbed. Drugs seemed the obvious answer. My mother's war story of how she labored with me for twenty-four hours without pain medication surfaced briefly at the rim of my awareness. I felt a tinge of sympathy for her and said a mental prayer of thanks that I was delivering my baby in the United States, where drugs were plentiful. This was 1996 and not the backwards 1969 of Soviet Ukraine.

I awoke from a blissful epidural-induced sleep, savoring the quiet and peace. Though it only lasted a moment before the delivering doctor turned on the bright overhead light and announced that it was time to push. Encouraged by him, I sat up to a practically upright position to see my baby make an entrance into the world. One last push, and a tiny grayish being emerged almost effortlessly and then was placed on my chest.

"It's a girl," the doctor said.

My skin bristled in a warm afterglow, and as I clutched my baby, one hand on her head, the other on her bottom, all I could think was, *I did it*—wholly convinced I had produced something truly singular and original, my greatest creation. I felt completely at one with her and apart from the world. My husband, the doctor, the nurse ceased to exist—receding into the peripheral darkness of the delivery room. And it was just me and my baby—my slight, ashen, still baby.

The doctor made his way to us, Tolya at our side. He lifted the baby and placed her face up into the crook of my arm. I looked down at her, and that's when I saw it.

"Something's wrong," I said.

I looked to Tolya. Fear was engraved into his face, in the widening of his eyes. I mined my brain for the maternally correct words. "She doesn't . . . look like either of us." I fixed my desperate gaze to the doctor.

That's what I said. What I *thought* was critical, ugly, and completely unacceptable. What I thought as I cradled this small, greenish, alien-looking baby, my daughter, Emma, was that she looked sick. Abnormal. Imperfect.

Of course, I had no experience with what a newborn looked like seconds after entering the world. I expected to see a balding, cherubic infant, with features that suggested some future version of what could evolve into my thick straight hair, my husband's aquiline nose, my grandmother's hazel eyes. What I saw was low-set ears; wide-set eyes; a flat, practically nonexistent nose bridge; tiny lips; and a small head. She was visually striking, but not in the way I had expected.

I lowered my eyes to survey my baby's face again. Emma's mouth grimaced at no one in particular, as if she were preparing to howl in protest at being so rudely disturbed— evicted from her warm cocoon of a home and thrust under the offensive, sterile light of the overhead examination lamp. Yet no sound of protest escaped the twisted gash that was her mouth. It was then I realized that she hadn't yet cried. There was no piercing sound that is the expected rite of passage of one just initiated into the world.

She didn't announce her presence. She arrived much too quietly.

The doctor stepped forward, and I waited for his reassuring words—for him to tell me I was overreacting. Instead, his downturned mouth and furrowed brow mirrored mine. I felt my eyes well with sadness and imagined that the mascara I had vainly and hurriedly applied at home after my water broke was leaving a dark trail of despair on my face.

My baby was seconds old, and already she was flawed.

"We'll have to run some tests," the doctor said. He removed Emma's soft body from mine and handed her to the nurse, who whisked her away to administer the Apgar test.

The Apgar test, we later learned, was designed to quickly evaluate a baby's physical condition shortly after birth. The higher the score, the healthier the baby. Sometime later, Tolya and I would recall the numbers and laugh at the absurdity and improbability of her 8 out of a possible 10 score. She couldn't have gotten much credit for being greenish-gray instead of pink, floppy in tone, with an absent response to stimulation and an immediate need for supplemental oxygen. Perhaps the nurse was trying to be hopeful.

I turned to Tolya. "What's happening?"

"I don't know." He shook his head.

It seemed impossible. We were young and healthy. I'd been so careful. I'd exercised during my pregnancy, took the horse-tranquilizer-sized prenatal vitamins religiously. I'd even excused myself from helping transcribe a book my social work school professor recruited me for, so I wouldn't expose my belly to the radiation.

I attacked the task of conceiving like a zealot—graphing my morning temperature so I could track my ovulation and do the deed on just the right days, and no others. "Tolya, get up," I would say, shaking my husband awake on those days. "I'm ovulating. Let's get to work."

"Oh my god," he would moan and try to roll over. But I persisted. The naturally pleasurable act morphed into a scheduled chore, a to-do list, bereft of color and passion, but not humor. The end justified the means in my mind, and I was not to be distracted from my mission.

I had loved being pregnant. Loved the doting and the extra attention—the knowledge I'd always be able to get a seat on the train if I opened my coat, stood tall, and thrust my pelvis out just enough. I didn't even mind so much strangers touching my belly as if they knew me intimately, gushing as if I were carrying their child. "Aww, how far along are you?" a woman on a train asked once, her foreign hand making its way over my roundness. Life as a human incubator had been lovely.

The next several hours were a blur. It was as if someone had taken an eraser to the "Assignment of the Day" carefully written out on the blackboard and obliterated the words, leaving behind a messy residue of chalk.

I left the delivery room in a wheelchair, ignoring my mother and sister-in-law's tirade of panicked questions: "What's wrong? Why are you crying? Where's the baby?"

I cried the length of the hospital corridor on my way to the recovery room. *Don't look at me. Don't pity me.* People's glances landed like punches to the gut. Something about seeing another person cry is intriguing, like slowing down to take in a five-car pileup on the highway. I've known the feeling of wanting to come up to a stranger and ask to hear their story.

Someone helped me onto the hospital bed, I heard a baby cry, and then there was blackness.

I think I slept. Snippets of a baby crying, nurses moving in and out, talking, lights behind the curtain separating my world from another's left tracks on my dreams.

The crying baby was not a dream. But the crying baby was not mine. The cries belonged to a healthy baby born to the lucky woman with whom I was sharing the recovery room. I vaguely recalled her complaining about being asked to nurse her child in the middle of the night when all she wanted to do was sleep.

I glimpsed day from beyond the curtain separating me from my neighbor, her bed closest to the windows. Despite the morning light seeping in from above and below, my corner of the room felt painfully dark.

My baby was missing from my arms. My breasts did not know her touch.

I stirred and turned to see Tolya sleeping in the chair by the foot of my bed.

"You okay?" he asked, opening his eyes. Loaded question. I could not reach for the words. All I could do was shake my head as the familiar sting of tears from the night before resumed. A pain emanated from below. I could feel blood staining my pad and imagined my bleeding heart the source.

Sometime later that morning, my delivering doctor paid me a visit. He was joined by another obstetrician. They stood at the foot of my bed and asked questions. They spoke dryly, their voices solemn, but they were not devastated. I expected them to look stricken, like I felt inside.

They asked how I was feeling. I may have answered. I may not have with words. My tear-stained, swollen face spoke volumes for me.

In my head I bellowed, *How could you let this happen?*
You were supposed to take care of us! I trusted you!

They may have mentioned that Emma was undergoing
genetic testing. They may have suggested the possibility of a
congenital disorder. They said I could see her in the NICU
when I was ready. I said I wanted to go home.

I asked to see the baby. It seemed the maternal thing to
do, though fear of what I would find whispered I stay safely
in bed.

"Do you need help?" Tolya offered as he watched me
get out of bed. I was grateful for his concern, registering
briefly that I was not the only one this was happening to,
but at that moment I was too deep inside my own swamp to
acknowledge it.

The clothes I arrived in the day before felt absurdly large.
My stretchy wool pants barely held on to my hips, threatening
to slide off. I felt insignificant in my oversized sweater, which
had hours before disguised my belly, now already half its
former size.

Outside the door to the NICU a nurse handed us paper
hospital gowns to don, instructing us to wash our hands in the
deep sink before going in. *What is this world we have entered?*

Nothing prepares a parent for the NICU. No book we
could have ever read, no movie we could have watched could
help make this ordeal less of a nightmare. Emma lay sleeping
in a Plexiglas incubator. If we didn't know any better, she
could have passed for a preemie, like the ones that flanked
the room, their visible veins beneath diaphanous, paper-
thin skin—almost translucent. At a full-term weight of four
pounds, twelve ounces, she looked even smaller. Tubes and
wires circled her body. The beeps and lights reminded me
of a horrific movie I could have seen on the Sci-Fi channel. I
stared at her sleeping form. *How could the sky outside be so*
blue? How could this be my baby?

"Can I hold her?" I turned to the nurse, noting her pink uniform with playful bunnies in a pattern, which I assumed was meant to be consoling to new parents. Instead, it saddened me. It was not cute. It sliced through my heart—the reality of just how not cute our situation was.

It wasn't until the nurse gently removed Emma from the incubator and placed her in my arms that I realized just how dependent she was on the wires and tubes sustaining her. My flesh gave her life, but that wasn't enough.

A sense of incompetence and failure assaulted me.

I surveyed her body. Something, I'd later learn called a pulse oximeter, was attached to her toe that kept track of her oxygen levels. Little round stickers all over her slight body gauged her heart rate. A nasal cannula delivered the supplemental oxygen. But most disturbing of all was the white plastic tube filled with formula inserted into her nose and directed toward her esophagus. The wires composed a veritable petite octopus, its tentacles working to keep Emma alive.

"Why does she have the feeding tube?" I asked the nurse, trying to keep my voice from shaking.

"We tried giving her a bottle, but she didn't have a suck reflex. The feeding tube ensures that the milk doesn't go into her lungs and cause her to aspirate." *A baby that doesn't suck. A baby that doesn't cry. What have we done?*

I stared at Emma's funny face; wispy hair rose from her smallish head. She looked so fragile, felt so soft. Then she opened her eyes, her gaze the glassy surface of a lake. It beckoned me to embrace and protect her, but it frightened me also.

Not yet knowing whether she could see or hear, I whispered, "Hi, baby. Mama loves you."

I leaned down slowly to put my lips on her forehead. A tear landed on her chest, and her eyes darted back and forth in seeming acknowledgment. She didn't appear to look at me but past me—past my smiling tears, as if focused on a middle distance where a lifetime movie was playing, one I did not want to see.

Tolya draped his body over mine and reached to brush Emma's cheek with the back of his finger. I looked at him but didn't have to say anything—knowing his thoughts paralleled mine. A dark veil descended on us.

I refused to stay the extra night the hospital offered to all new moms. I yearned for my bed, the covers that would hide me from the rest of this cruel world that allowed babies to be born fighting for survival. I wanted to hide from my own maudlin thoughts that had already painted an ominous, alienating landscape of doctors, therapists, surgeries, medication.

Returning to the apartment that night, I saw our red leather couch as if it were a hot coal—burning, mocking. The cat did not come to greet us.

That first night back at the apartment, I couldn't sleep. Tolya woke to find me sitting up on the side of the bed, wailing. The sounds were unrecognizable even to me—a primal howl from somewhere deep I had never known existed. The mirrored doors of the wardrobe reflected a desperate figure, doubled over, face in hands.

Tolya wrapped his arms around me. It was all he could do. I was grateful for it.

CHAPTER 2

WE MET AT A FRIEND'S bar mitzvah, though *met* is not actually the right word. Each time I glanced at the table adjacent to mine, I first felt, then saw a pair of eyes boring a hole through my skull with a predatory intensity—that of a hormonal sixteen-year-old boy, as was the case.

"Who's that strange guy over there?" I asked Marianna, the girl I sat next to.

"Oh, that's my brother," she said, smiling without betraying the slightest offense. My face turned crimson.

"I'm s-s-o sorry," I said.

"It's fine, we don't look anything alike. I know, he's funny looking," she said and let out a rolling laugh. Tolya and I didn't speak that day. But our paths crossed again shortly after.

I was eight and Tolya eleven when we separately abandoned our respective corners of then-Soviet Ukraine. Our families joined the wave—an exodus of thousands—to freedom. It was the late 1970s, and the Soviet Union had just opened its doors to allow the Jewish population to get their unwelcome *tuchuses* out. We were political refugees, fleeing religious persecution. Communism was alive and well, atheism was the religion of the land, and Jews, as ever, were persona non grata.

We settled in Forest Hills, Queens, where I assimilated into the folds of the new country seamlessly, as the English language found its home in me as though I had always known it and it had merely been lounging in the corners of my brain, waiting to do its bidding. Queens, as it turned out—often referred to as the United Nations of boroughs—was the perfect place to land. My circle of friends ran the geographic and ethnic gamut: a Patel, a Lee, a Hernandez, a Jackson, and of course, Soviet immigrant kids. This was how Tolya and I met.

I was sixteen years old and Tolya was seventeen when we morphed into cliché high school sweethearts. Young and immature, we had little to talk about, but shared the history of immigrant childhoods and the burden of achievement that our family's sacrifice dictated.

Then my parents realized the ultimate immigrant's dream: they bought a house and moved the five of us (my two-year-old sister, Holly, and my paternal grandmother, Basya) from our humble one-bedroom in Queens to the suburb of Staten Island. Though a seemingly progressive step, for me it proved to be the tipping point and my unraveling. At the age of seventeen, I found myself brusquely uprooted and replanted in foreign soil—forced for the second time in my life to abandon everything familiar.

Paradoxically, the immigration from country to country felt less disruptive than the move from borough to borough. Much had to do with my age—teen existential angst, the act of relinquishing long-established friends compounded by the colossal struggle of breaking through high school cliques and negotiating new friendships.

Making it in high school as a new kid on the block became a social litmus test, which I failed miserably. "I can't do this," I would sob, dragging myself past my mother into the bathroom each school morning, leaning over the sink to splash cold water on my already red, tear-drenched face. "I can't go to school—I have no friends." I could feel my heartbeat break into a gallop, hijacking me as I said the word *friends*, which carried such significance then, as always.

"I don't belong," I tried to explain. My mother had an expression for this: *Ne vsoyey tarelkee*, meaning being out of your element, translated literally as not eating out of your own plate but out of someone else's—a nod, perhaps, to Goldilocks.

"You can do this," she would say with caution in her voice. "We are strong. We are survivors." This always seemed to open and close a conversation, no matter how improbable it was at the time. I suppose it was true; we had survived the rejection of our country of origin. Worse was dealing with peer rejection and my own rejection of my inchoate self.

So I fled at every opportunity.

My salvation came in the form of weekends, when I would make pilgrimages back to Queens, to my friends, and to Tolya. The Verrazano Bridge, with its tall, steel sail-like beams, was my lifeline. And thank god for it, because I was fully prepared to swim across the icy expanse to get to the other side—to the safety of the old familiar shore, to the concrete parking lot, flanked on all sides by the six-story apartment buildings that used to be home. This was where you could find the six to ten of us, hormones raging: leaning against cars, flirting, embracing, joking—Russian curse words rolling off our tongues, because English expletives had no chance of competing. If I listened hard enough, I could almost hear my father's melodic whistle signaling me home when the day receded into star-painted night. And if my father had already fallen asleep, my mother would assume his position at the third-floor window conveniently facing the lot and yell, "Deeana, damoy" (home), like a tenement woman gathering her children home.

The fault lines created by the move to Staten Island continued their trajectory into college. I spent my undergrad years in New York University, moving through a sea of people, feeling mostly alone. I shuffled from class to class on leaden feet. The metropolitan campus lent itself to getting easily lost in the maelstrom of anonymity, whether you intended to or not. It felt like a life on the periphery of life. I traversed the clustered blocks of NYU buildings, noting flyers attached to bulletin boards in the student center announcing comedy shows, musical performances, parties, and lectures on various social topics that idealistic college students pursued. And I walked past these, as if past a lavishly set table of exquisite foods I could not partake of, on my way to the express bus, Staten Island-bound.

As in high school, Tolya continued to be my safe harbor in college. With his arms around me, cloistered in the dark movie theater of NYU's Loeb's Student Center, we planned a future together—our own family.

I earned a bachelor's and then a master's degree, convinced that if I played by the rules, life's plans would materialize as imagined. I could control the outcome of things if I just applied the right degree of effort, at the right time, in the right place; if I colored inside the lines, as I was taught, the picture would emerge as perfect and harmonious as I intended it to be. We married right out of college.

An inveterate documentarian, Tolya could often be seen filling in his Franklin Day Planner, and was just as often heard saying, "If it's not on the calendar, it's not happening." He scheduled things weeks, months, years into the future and even had the recommended five-year plan in place. So, it was no shock to the people who knew him well that he would step out of the limousine on our wedding day with the planner under his arm. And when prompted, he proudly opened to the November 17, 1991, page, where in bold, crooked letters he had written: *Marry Diana.* As if, had it not been written, he might somehow forget to do it. As if, if he didn't specify me, then he could mistakenly marry someone else.

The prospect of children gave me hope—it was a star to shoot for, a beacon. Slowly life's knots seemed to be untying.

A child, I told myself, would mark a welcome, long anticipated new beginning. I was emerging into the Renaissance
of my life.

A perfect life beckoned on the horizon.

But nowhere in Tolya's actual planner or in my mental
one could we have anticipated Emma.

CHAPTER 3

"WHAT ARE YOU THINKING?" I asked, turning to look at Tolya. We had been on our daily trek to the hospital to see and hold Emma.

Silence.

This was the typical exchange, even before Emma's birth. I always hoped to get an answer to this burning question but instead continued playing the absurd game of repeating myself while expecting a different result. I could have offered him a winning lotto ticket for his thoughts—it would not have made a difference. And although I was never one to "search for words in my pocket," as the Russian saying went, this time neither of us had the vocabulary to describe what we were facing. There were no CliffsNotes for this story of a young couple forging a life with what we suspected would be a child with disabilities.

Tolya shook his head. "I don't know, or maybe I do. I just don't know how to put it into words."

This summarized our personalities neatly. Tolya was a computer science major, while I studied psychology. I often joked that he was a "numbers person" and I was a "words person." It is a wonder that we were ever able to carry on a conversation. I rarely missed the opportunity to rib him about his English-as-a-second-language status in college, especially when he would slyly brag about his higher SAT scores. "But remember, that was only because you took the TOEFL SAT for foreign students after being in the country for six years," I teased.

"Well, I feel like I'm on one of these amusement park rides. You know, the Tilt-A-Whirl," I said, "the one that spins at breakneck speed so that your back gets pinned to the wall, and then the floor drops unexpectedly."

My mental Rolodex of medical experiences was sparse. Other than the occasional childhood visits to a local clinic in Ukraine, either to get my ears pierced with a hot needle or receive the requisite vaccinations that left identifying cultural marks on my arms, white-coat phobia did not afflict me. It was with an innocent childhood wonder that I recalled the long wide steps of the clinic leading up to the painted mural at the top of the staircase, depicting bear cubs frolicking— some on see-saws, others on a swing. To my child self, the clinic felt inviting, friendly, even with the distinct scent of disinfectant cutting the air.

The NICU did not have the sanitary scent of a hospital. Instead, it smelled of sickness and despair. Perhaps it held hope for other moms whose babies were premature but otherwise healthy newborns who would ultimately thrive and live normal lives. I watched these moms daily, their comings and goings. I was envious of their knowledge—the promises I imagined they grasped and held close to their maternal chests. They were in an infinitely better place than where I found myself. I wanted to be them.

The wait to find out the results of the genetic testing seemed interminable. We knew that it would not be good news. In the interim, Tolya and I were also tested, to see if we were directly to blame for Emma's condition—if we were carriers of some- thing that would punish all future offspring we would try to bring into the world, as if for some past karmic transgression.

Of course, we were to blame. We made her this way, and the weight of the guilt and shame pressed relentlessly on our hearts. But wasn't she also made of the stuff of love? We wanted her. We planned for her. But can planning and coloring within the lines really insulate from life, from the inevitable grief and sadness that accompanies the living? Does playing by the rules guarantee a win? I believed so then.

Finally, the day arrived. The geneticist brought us into his office to explain the results of the test. We steeled ourselves.

"I'm afraid I don't have good news," he began. "Testing revealed that your daughter has a chromosomal anomaly." *I want to die.* "A translocation of the second and fourth chromosome." *I want to die.* "A fourth chromosome monosomy and second chromosome trisomy. Essentially, a piece of the genetic material detached from the fourth chromosome and attached itself to the second."

At least I think that's what he said. I listened, but barely understood, and immediately regretted not paying closer attention in high school biology class.

"The good news is that you're not carriers of anything that would prevent you from having healthy children in the future," he continued. "Emma is what we call a new mutation."

I couldn't breathe.

Did he just call my baby a mutant?

I heard a steel trap door slam shut in my brain, the door that had been held open to receive a healthy child.

"*How* did this happen?" I managed to ask.

"We have no way of knowing if the mutation occurred during conception or whether the genetic material was already in either of your sex cells, egg or sperm."

"What does that mean for Emma?" Tolya muttered, as if speaking to himself.

"Well, we don't exactly know. Unlike some of the more common chromosomal disorders, like Down syndrome or trisomy thirteen and eighteen, which have been studied extensively, Emma's particular genetic configuration is unique.

One of a kind, you might say." He went on to say that his
search in the database of a national organization of rare disorders revealed no matches to compare to.

"So, what you're saying is that you can't make any kind
of prognosis for her future?" I asked.

"I'm afraid not, but based on what we see now upon examination, the lack of basic sucking skills, her hypotonia or low
muscle tone, poor reflexes and lack of focus and tracking—
we can assume that she will live with moderate to profound
retardation."

Retard. You're such a retard. That's so retarded. How
many times had I heard that word growing up? How often
had I been guilty of saying it myself? How many times had I
used it casually to mock someone? Now I'd have to stop myself
before uttering it, because it would no longer be a term to use
lightly, but a description of my life, my child.

I would later learn that the word *retarded* originated from
the Latin *retardare*, first used to describe developmental delay in
the late 1800s. For many years after that it had a neutral conno-
tation and was used to describe people who were intellectually
slow. By the 1960s it took on a disparaging hue. That was also
when it entered public use and became the stuff of insult. The
irony was that I was a social worker, working in mental health,
a field that described my patients, and now my own child,
using precisely that word with the derogatory spin. It would
be more than a decade later, in October 2010, that Congress
would pass Rosa's Law, which would change the term "mental
retardation" in Federal laws to "intellectual disability."

Memories of working as a teacher's assistant at the Eden
II Autism Institute came flooding back. It was the summer of
1990, and diagnoses of autism were on the rise. The school
specialized in teaching autistic children. Working with a
group of profoundly delayed children and teens, I was in
direct contact with their families. One day, a mom of a

fourteen-year-old girl with severe scoliosis and autism asked me with tears in her eyes, "Who is going to take care of my daughter when I'm gone?"

Now I was that mom and Emma was that child.

I FELT USELESS. MY BREASTS had become engorged with milk, with no recipient in sight. At home, I'd gaze at myself in the mirror and stand in awe of them for the first time in my breast-challenged life. I had always been a mere A cup. Now I was a respectable B. I would often joke that my sister, immensely gifted in the bosom department, had inherited my mother's breasts while I got my father's. I felt more desirable—as a woman and now as a mother. These breasts were also for feeding and nurturing. Sadly, I felt both benefits lost on me. It was a cruel irony. "What a waste these are," I lamented.

"Stop," Tolya said.

Under different circumstances, my husband might have tried to dissuade me from self-criticism, maybe even dig up a compliment. But he was in his own quagmire of pain, and there were no warm fuzzy feelings to spare.

Emma's care in the hospital became more complicated, and the doctors approached us with plans for the next necessary form of treatment. Because of the serious diagnosis and poor prognosis, they didn't expect her to be able to eat normally by mouth anytime soon, if ever. She had already demonstrated an inability to coordinate sucking, breathing, and swallowing safely. Having aspirated the formula into her lungs meant she risked developing pneumonia.

"We need you to consider putting in a G-tube, a gastro-intestinal tube, as a means of feeding her," the doctor stated matter-of-factly. "It will replace the feeding tube that she currently has going into her nose, whose long-term use can cause irritation and is not advisable."

"I'm not following," I said. "What does this look like, and how do we use it? Is it forever?"

"It's reversible, if Emma ever learns to eat by mouth. We surgically create an opening in her belly, into which a tube is inserted, allowing food to be delivered directly into her stomach, bypassing the lungs and avoiding the risk of aspiration." He spoke with the grave tone of one accustomed to delivering bad news. I didn't envy his position, but I lamented my predicament more.

"Is this absolutely necessary?" Tolya asked. "Is there a way to avoid it?" It was a relief to hear him asking the difficult questions. I was still grappling with the prospect of Emma never being able to eat by mouth.

"Well, based on our experience, it would be ill-advised to leave things as they are." He went on to explain something about gastroesophageal reflux, which required a surgical procedure called a Nissen fundoplication that would prevent aspiration.

He was speaking a language I did not understand. Words I'd never heard before were embedded in sentences and being addressed to me, forcing me to make decisions the consequences of which I had no way of knowing.

EMMA WAS THREE WEEKS OLD when she underwent the first of her many surgeries. The next procedure would be one to correct frequent chronic urinary tract infections. Another opening was created, this time from the outside of her body to her bladder. This procedure was called a vesicostomy.

Today's Sesame Street program is brought to you by the letter V for vesicostomy.

As Tolya and I watched our baby being opened and put back together, I was reminded of the wooden Russian nesting dolls called *matryoshka* that I played with as a child in my grandmother's home in Ukraine. The doll would break open at the equator to reveal a smaller version of itself, until you reached the tiniest of dolls at the center. The smallest doll was whole. Were the doctors looking for my baby's wholeness?

Emma was poked and prodded incessantly, her tiny veins invisible to the naked eyes of the nurses, who with frustration mined them in the traditional places: hands, feet, arms. I cringed with each needle that went into her, felt her pain, and would have to turn away. She moaned with discomfort every time the needle was dug under her skin and moved about blindly in search of a source. The worst was when, with no success trying in the usual places, they would insert an IV into her head, at the temple, where the veins were blue and throbbing. That was when I'd have to leave the room for fear of losing it. Tolya stayed behind, comforting Emma with soft words and caresses. She was so little and had already endured so much pain.

The surgery for the reflux and insertion of the G-tube left Emma with a long scar that ran the length of her chest, starting at just under the breast and extending to her abdomen.

The foot-long tube, inserted into the opening in her belly, was an even more disturbing sight. For months, until it healed and was replaced by a smaller device, we resorted to dressing her in onesies with buttons or snaps running down the middle, to allow for easy access during her feedings. It was unsightly. The tube was attached to a longer tube that extended from a feeding bag. The bag hung from a stand above our heads and was set to an appropriately timed drip—like an IV bag, except delivering formula.

It seemed unnatural, outside of the world of medicine. I heard the doctor's words again: "one of a kind." Not only was Emma being kept alive in a way that felt foreign, but she was missing out on one of the most basic human pleasures— food. Not to mention the social implications of sitting at the dinner table, if there would ever be that opportunity as she got older.

I found myself pitched ten years into the future. Would she even be able to sit independently, or would her world continue to exist horizontally? Would she always be at the mercy of others to provide for her basic needs and ensure her survival? Would she be able to express herself in words? Would she ever be able to indicate hunger by uttering the most fundamental of declaratives, "I'm hungry, Mommy" or "I'm full"? Would she be able to let me know if someone had hurt her, or if she had a nightmare that woke her in the middle of the night? Would I ever hear, "I love you, Mama," or, from the mouth of a rebellious adolescent, "I hate you"? Would her singing voice reveal my ear for music or her father's deafness to tone? Would the name of a boy she liked ever leave her lips and land on my ears? Would I be able to be there for her? These fundamental questions knocked around aimlessly in my brain. I hoped that if I ignored them, they'd go away.

Five weeks after the G-tube surgery and healing, a smaller contraption replaced the offensively large tube. The device, made of plastic, was approximately an inch wide with a slightly longer stem, medically referred to as a Mickey "button." Though it had no obvious resemblance to an actual button, it was plastic and it did open. It didn't open sweaters and close pants; it opened Emma's belly and allowed the plastic tube to deliver formula directly into her stomach.

We were told that if Emma could not eat by mouth, we would have to rely on this form of feeding. Every three to four months, the "button" would need to be replaced.

Not only were these daily feedings disturbing, but the procedure of replacing the "button" felt downright barbaric. In the time between taking the old one out and inserting a new one, we stared at a hole in Emma's belly. Pink and almost throbbing in appearance, it looked raw and violated. "I'm so sorry," I whispered to her. Although she never cried during these replacements, Emma often flinched at the moment of entry, alerting us to her discomfort. Yet this thing that distressed her was not only her lifeline but our inextricable connection to her.

CHAPTER 4

WHEN I WAS FOURTEEN, AND after years of pleading with my parents to change my only-child status to sibling, years after I'd given up my appeals, my sister Holly was born. This, I observed, was a common phenomenon among Soviet immigrants. It seemed to me that the average family in the Soviet Union had one child, occasionally two, never three—usually in their early twenties. Then they arrived, and as if catching a second wind, went on to have another child—an American. I never did any research, but through strictly anecdotal observation, I watched my friends' parents, not unlike mine, procreate—this time, in their mid-thirties. Perhaps they were trying to avoid premature empty-nest onset, like my parents. When I'd asked my mom why they had my sister so late, she replied, "You would have been going off to college soon, and I was going to be left with your father. We would have killed each other."

Perhaps it was something to do with staking your claim in a new country, digging your roots in. And what more audacious way to that end than by starting a new generation?

From the first moment I held my sister, I felt a surge of immense responsibility for her, as if she were my child, immaculately delivered to me to care for and protect. She was a cute little thing with a dimpled cheek, mostly bald but for a long flaxen ponytail. She would grow to be the first "blondie" in the family. "The first blonde, the first American in our family," my mother would gush.

"I don't want to be the first American," Holly would protest when she got older. "I want to be Russian. I want to be like everyone else." She had no interest in being a trailblazer. She wanted to belong, to be part of an established whole, to be connected not just by blood but along cultural lines. It didn't surprise anyone that as a college student, she went on to study Russian literature and history and even learned how to read Russian.

Holly was a quiet, sensitive, and intuitive child who loved deeply. We could not be more different; our energies seemed polarized. Hers was slow and tentative like a calm lake at dawn, at least on the outside. Mine was usually a turbulent sea, after or before a storm. The common denominator we shared for a long while was our insecurities, fears, and anxieties—hers being existential; she lived in the future, in fear of the unknown. Mine were immediate, present—from which I longed to escape.

When she was a little girl of five or six, she developed an irrational fear of being abandoned. At home, while waiting for our parents to return from work, she'd watch the light of the sky turn a silver dark blue, then position herself by the window to watch for them. I don't think she had a sense of time then. Perhaps the long anticipation of looking for them made the wait seem interminable, because by the time they walked in the door, Holly would be in a puddle of tears, overcome by worry.

"What are you afraid of?" I would ask, desperate to assuage her. When she was old enough to explain, she would tell me, "What if something happened to them? What if a car hit them and they died?" My heart hurt to hear this. I wondered what she could have seen or heard to nurture such a deep fear of abandonment and loss. But as she grew and her worries solidified and became more pervasive, I understood if not the source, then its progression.

Holly was a little girl when in the span of five years, we experienced the death of five family members. The hardest hit came when my father's mother, Baba Basya, died. She had been Holly's main caregiver. Until Holly began preschool at four years of age, she spent all day, every day with our grandmother. "Maybe we waited too long to start her in preschool," my mother would later say when she saw how difficult it was for Holly to acclimate to a new social setting.

Though seemingly fragile and often timid, Holly was happy when she wasn't overcome with worry. I assumed accountability for her, unsolicited. Her happiness became my happiness; her tears—my undoing. The more invested I became in her well-being, the more I saw her as a reflection of me. Ironically, as I struggled to find myself during those high school and college years, I worked diligently to mold her little character into how I thought she needed to be. I would ensure that she would never find herself in the position I was in: questioning her self-worth, emotions run amok. It was going to be better with my sister—for myself. She would redeem me, help me reinvent myself. She was my second chance to get it right, because she was an extension of me. I didn't give her life, but I was going to make sure she had a happy one.

I would scour magazines for things to do with Holly on the weekends, then recruit Tolya, then my boyfriend, to join us. We were a little pseudo, surrogate family, playing house. Leaving the cultural desolation of Staten Island, we'd venture into the city, to the free children's art classes at the Met, drop in on readings at children's bookstores, and catch shows in Central Park's Marionette Theater.

Life's winds heralded changes for Holly and me. I got married right after college and relocated back to my beloved Forest Hills. Shortly thereafter, Baba Basya died. With us gone, and my parents working and sometimes returning as late as eight in the evening, after school, Holly was left in the care of a neighboring family. I worried for her. I couldn't imagine how she felt having to eat dinner and do homework in someone else's home, and I saw her orphaned. In my mind, she was Annie.

My mother would sometimes call to ask for advice and gently divulge: "Holly seems sad. I think she misses you." My heart ached to know this.

"I feel so guilty about leaving her," I'd say to Tolya. "I worry about her—she's so fragile."

"Let's bring her to live with us," Tolya said. Just like that.

I paused and looked at him to gauge the seriousness of his words, even though his tone betrayed conviction, and thought, *Who is this man and how awesomely deep is his character?*

"I'm a lucky girl . . . and so is Holly" was all I could manage as I walked into his embrace.

Holly was ten when she came to live with us. Emma was a couple of weeks old and Holly thirteen when she sat on the steps of our duplex apartment crying because I had just told her she'd have to return to live with our parents, who'd be moving back to Forest Hills as well. I reasoned that I could no longer raise her because I was so messed up, because I was depleted emotionally, because I needed to focus all my energy and attention on Emma, who needed me more.

Even so, guilt set in. I let Holly down—for all intents and purposes, rejected her. My aspirations to be the perfect sister and a perfect daughter that my parents could be proud of had failed. What I didn't understand then was that I was rejecting myself.

CHAPTER 5

EMMA'S BIRTH SIGNALED THE highest form of imperfection. To my young mind, my greatest, most original creation was a failure. She was a reflection of me. Her flaws screamed to the universe that I, as her mother, was also flawed. Emma came to embody the physical manifestation of my insecurities, my emotional landscape—the years of feeling unworthy, imperfect. It was as if I was turned inside out for the world to see my beating heart, the blood coursing through my veins, the stress hormones wreaking havoc on my cells and emotions.

The wind was carrying away my straw world from under my feet, a world that I had previously believed was constructed of solid brick, and I found myself grieving a loss, the death of a dream of a healthy child.

Perhaps my dismal presentation alerted the hospital social worker who'd been visiting us that I was in bad shape. She offered to meet with us and gently broached the subject.

"I see you're having a very difficult time dealing with this," she began.

"We are." There was no point in posturing.

"This may surprise you, but you have options outside of choosing to bring Emma home," she continued. Her words hung in the air. I took a moment to register them.

"What kind of options?" I may have sounded overly hopeful.

"Well, there are families looking to adopt special-needs kids."

I did not expect to hear this. Something stopped me from storming out of the room, outraged and offended. I knew I should get up—it was the right, maternal thing to do—but I didn't know what the right thing was anymore, so I stayed and listened.

". . . Some people have a calling in life, you might say," the social worker continued. "It's the only way I can explain it." I looked at Tolya for a reaction—a betrayal of *his* thoughts. I could only assume that he was in shock, like I was. This new information landed like a boulder in our laps.

"I don't know what to say," I managed. "I'm just really surprised. I know there are people who adopt healthy children, but who would want . . . a sick child?" And as I said this, a wave of self-disgust swept over me: that I could think this, and even worse say it out loud. Was I so morally deficient that I would consider giving my baby away because she would never fit the perfect mold that I had created in my head? Was I selfish enough to do the unthinkable in exchange for an unburdened life?

"Give it some thought. I know it's a lot to digest."

As with most important decisions, I resorted to researching, to ensure that I wasn't alone in my experience. Perhaps I was looking for permission to make a less-than-desirable choice and needed not to be the first one to do so. Someone else had to have set a precedent. This search was how I came across *Shattered Dreams, Lonely Choices: Birth Parents of Babies with Disabilities Talk About Adoption* by Joanne Finnegan, tucked away in the corner of a Barnes & Noble shelf. I devoured it in one sitting, and I walked away feeling less of a monster, knowing that I wasn't a lone wolf rejecting her cub.

Later that night, as I lay in the comfort of my bed, starkly aware that my two-month-old baby was in a hospital, I realized that at that moment I was deciding her fate. I voiced my darkest, ugliest thoughts to Tolya. Thoughts that pain me to remember, thoughts that if I could go back in time and reason with my scared, young self, I would shake from her head.

"I can only see myself housebound, not being able to work, giving up my life to raise a sick child." I imagined an insular world, with Emma existing on the margins, isolated—in an "other" world, in which I would have to exist alongside her in the otherness. This thought catapulted me back in time, to all those lonely adolescent years in Staten Island, when I didn't belong. Where I was the outsider.

I could not see Emma fitting neatly into life, where I could only imagine her suffering. To bring her home and raise her, I was convinced, would be a constant reminder of how acutely I felt my displacement in high school and beyond, when I felt like a misshapen puzzle piece that did not fit either. I imagined her displacement would be immeasurably worse.

It didn't help matters that I did not know anyone in my immediate circle of family or friends whose lives had been remotely touched by the possibility of such an existence. No one to ask for guidance of. No one to compare myself to. No one to empathize with me. I was not being forced like Sophie, in *Sophie's Choice*, into the devastating act of having to choose to save her son or her daughter from certain and immediate demise in a death camp. I was voluntarily and consciously considering the possibility of rejecting my own flesh and blood. A child who had been born into this world, without asking—only to be given away.

I felt utterly alone, stranded in a vast ocean without a raft, guzzling the salty water of tears—going under. The hospital social worker had unwittingly thrown us a life vest, and I latched on to it. But then I would think of Emma.

"What kind of monster am I?" I looked pleadingly at Tolya.

"You're not a monster," he said. "I'm scared too."

They say that children choose their parents, that God or the universe doesn't give us more than we can handle. Yet I did not want to be this child's choice. It was more than I thought I could handle. Surely Emma had made a mistake by choosing us. Here I found myself, a social worker having decided to devote a life to children in need, feeling completely inept and unaccepting of raising my own less-than-abled child.

Emma deserved better. *I deserved better.*

"I can't do it." The instant I said it, I felt the truth of my words. "I can't raise her."

We were in bed, my head resting on Tolya's chest, in that space below his dimpled chin, above his heart. I imagined I heard it skip a beat but quickly realized it was my heart knocking on my rib cage, asking to be let out, or in.

I feared Emma would be my albatross. That the grief of raising a disabled child would level me, that I would be decimated by the blow and not be able to rise from the ashes. But more than anything, I understood that I had taken on too much. The well-intentioned act of taking in my sister, combined with the prospect of raising a child with extraordinary needs, led me to throw my arms up and, in an act of naked rebellion, reject both. In a blind rage, in resentment, I emancipated myself from the shackles of responsibility. I cut off my nose to spite my face and gave it away.

"I'm behind you whatever you decide," Tolya said, lifting my chin so that my eyes could meet his truth. Tears blurred my vision but not his words: "Because I know that you'd be the one making the biggest sacrifice in caring for her."

I looked at this boy, barely a man, my husband, my best friend, the father of our child, and I didn't know whether to feel gratitude for his support or fear for being given free rein to make the most important decision of our lives. Was he giving up his right or his responsibility? Would the burden of this irreversible potential mistake rest squarely on my shoulders, for me to carry for the rest of my life?

"We'll only do it if we find a good adoptive home for her," I said. He nodded in agreement, or in capitulation.

On a subconscious level, the precedent had already been set by my parents in giving Holly up to be raised by me. I'm certain, more than anything, that they believed she would be in good hands, perhaps better hands than they were able to offer. I used similar reasoning: Emma would be raised by a better equipped, more competent family than I could promise her.

I have no recollection of the phone call that we made to the hospital social worker, relaying our decision and ultimately giving her permission to start looking for a suitable adoptive family for Emma. I reached a point of no longer being able to look at myself in the mirror. My reflection disgusted me. It revealed my dark heart.

In sharing our decision for adoption, we received varied responses from family members. My mother-in-law wanted to know if it would be better to place Emma in a long-term facility near us instead, so that we could see her often. I knew she was well intentioned and didn't want to part with her granddaughter, perhaps feeling that it was a less rejecting gesture. For me, this was not a viable option.

I felt strongly that I owed my daughter the love one can only get from family, either her own or another's. We never considered visiting her in a facility. I imagined a human zoo with bars. If my parents disagreed with our decision, they didn't let on, understanding that the burden was ours to carry. I didn't know at the time that there were vast resources to help families raise children with special needs at home. This was uncharted territory for us, and the mountain was blocking out the sun.

"I think we found you a prospective family." The social worker from the adoption agency was on the other line. I held the receiver with too tight a grip, causing my arm to shake—feeling my nerves, like taut rubber bands ready to snap.

This was what I had secretly longed to hear, so why did it land so heavily in my chest? How many people have heard those words in their lifetime? "I've found you the perfect house" or "I saw the most beautiful wedding dress for you" or "I have just the lipstick color for your complexion." But shopping for an adoptive family for your disabled child is not in the life plans of most families. I certainly had not anticipated that it would happen so quickly. Just days prior, we began the process, never considering there may have already been people, good people, waiting.

It's like waiting nine months to carry a baby to term. The day arrives, you finally go into labor, and you realize you're not ready. You thought you were. You've been imagining the day, replaying it in its various possibilities. But here you are, no longer certain that you can do this—that you've got the right stuff to see it through. Holding the receiver, I listened to my shallow heavy breathing, unable to respond.

I handed the phone to Tolya. "It's for you."

"Who is it?"

"It's the adoption agency." Tolya gave me a quizzical look as if to say, *Have you completely lost it, saying it's for me as if this has nothing to do with you?* But he said nothing and took the receiver. I lowered myself into the chair behind me, relieving my buckling knees.

"Hello. Yes, this is Mr. Ditinsky. It's fine. My wife asked me to get the information from you . . ."

Minutes later, returning the receiver to its place, he turned slowly to face me.

"There's a family in Pennsylvania that has three adopted Down syndrome kids. Two boys and a girl. They would like another little girl. They're Orthodox Jews." He paused to give me a chance to react.

"Wow. That's a lot of information," I said finally. "Not only do they already have adopted kids, but they're raising special-needs kids *and* they're Jewish? Could we have asked for a better profile?"

"I know," Tolya said. "It's almost unbelievable."

"I guess let's set up a visit."

If the universe was trying to send us a sign, it was being deafeningly clear. What better way to bring two atheist Jews back into the fold than by forcing them, head and heart first, toward their abandoned roots? Our families had escaped persecution so that their children and their children's children would have the freedom of choice: to practice religion or not, to raise their children Jewish or not—heck, even to give their children away, to be raised by a Jewish family or not.

We were the proverbial "three-day-a-year Jews"—going to synagogue only on the high holidays, Rosh Hashanah and Yom Kippur, except that we didn't even go to synagogue. I would describe us as "traditional Jews," sitting down with family to acknowledge and pass on our history and traditions to our children and grandchildren. It was also the "thing to do" as Soviet immigrants, just as it was a thing "not to do" as Soviet Jews in Ukraine. We did it because now we could, because there were people who previously told us we couldn't. It was not an act of rebellion; rather, it was a gesture of assimilation into a new country—a country where pine trees were put up only on Christmas and not on New Year's, as was the norm in the secular Soviet Union, to celebrate the winter solstice.

I remembered my first New Year's in the States. I had asked my mother why we couldn't get a tree to decorate, as we did every year when I was a child in the Ukraine. "Because we are Jewish," my mother answered, seemingly outraged at the question. *Since when are we Jewish, and what the heck does that even mean?*

As far as belief was concerned, Tolya was, for as long as I knew him, a devout scientist. He could often be heard to say,

"If you can't prove it, it doesn't exist." This was his response to all things religious, mystical, or, as he would say, "magical" in nature. "If you believe in God, you may as well believe Santa Claus and the Tooth Fairy are real." I would argue that this was not a fair comparison, but my objections fell on deaf ears.

If Tolya was an atheist, then I was an agnostic. I wasn't certain of anything. I recognized on a very superficial level that I didn't know what I didn't know, and so I refused to commit to anything. Perhaps I was too lazy to spend time on religious pursuits. More likely, I lacked the foundation for religious practice, other than the occasional praying to God to help me get a good grade on a test, compliments of Judy Blume's book *Are You There, God? It's Me, Margaret*—the extent of my religious education.

Tolya and I had gotten this far without practice or belief, but this was different. In my continued search for answers, I came across a talk being given by Harold S. Kushner, author of the best-selling book *When Bad Things Happen to Good People*. Rabbi Kushner wrote the book after his three-year-old son was diagnosed with a degenerative disease that would end his life in his early teens. I'd heard of the book. Its title sounded intriguing and promising. My desperate state led me to look for anything that might quiet my questioning, devastated mind and soul. Emma was less than two months old at the time, and the conversation about adoption had not yet taken place.

I asked Tolya if he had heard of Kushner's book. He hadn't—not surprisingly, given that at the time I was the self-help book fanatic, while he found truth and wisdom on the pages of *The New York Times* and *The Wall Street Journal*, with the occasional classic novel sprinkled in between.

"Rabbi Kushner is giving a talk," I said to Tolya. "Will you come with me?"

"Fine." Practical person that he was, I was usually the one that fought to harness out-of-control situations. Tolya was not the "let's talk our problems through" type, as my personality and my profession dictated that I be.

Decades later I would struggle to recall the talk we attended. A vague image of the lecture hall in its atmospheric heaviness was all that I remembered, but no recollection of the Rabbi, how he addressed the audience, or what, specifically, he had said. Tolya, to my great surprise, would recall that we approached Rabbi Kushner afterward and even spoke to him privately about Emma. "What did he say?" I asked.

"He gave us a sort of spiritual answer, not so much a religious one, know what I mean?" Tolya replied.

"Not really." I was normally the one with the better memory. Tolya's brain often acted as a sieve when it came to committing to memory things that were not important to him: the names of relatives and loved ones' birthdays. He wrote things down because he didn't have time to try and remember and chose not to occupy his mental real estate with inconsequential details. The events following Emma's birth, however, somehow failed to get documented, and not surprisingly, the usual rules of life no longer applied. Order was abandoned. The future was unpredictable.

The most I could muster was to reconnect with the feelings and thoughts that the talk left me with. The takeaway was an even deeper regret that we didn't blindly or consciously have faith in God—a God who had a reason and a purpose for putting us through this ordeal. I was envious of those people who didn't question their circumstances. They seemed to accept things, even to embrace them. It would have been infinitely easier to believe that everything was *beshert*, a Yiddish word meaning "meant to be." *Who says it was meant to be and why?* I wanted to scream.

CHAPTER 6

THE DAY WAS OVERCAST, with ominous, steely low-hanging clouds that promised rain. My mother's words reverberated in my head, in her distinctive Russian accent: "Rain is for good luck in our family," she would often say. Then she would rattle off testimonials to her theory: The day she and my father married. The day we arrived in the US from Soviet Ukraine. The day I took first place in my piano recital competition when I was twelve. I used to laugh thinking how ridiculous meteorological superstitions were. But that day, as we made the almost three-hour drive to Pennsylvania to meet the prospective adoptive family that would potentially be instrumental in changing the trajectory of our lives forever, I silently hoped my mother was right—that the universe was again confirming its cosmic favor.

In the car, I voiced what I imagined we were both thinking: "What if we like them?"

"I know what you mean," Tolya answered.

"Are we doing the right thing?" I asked.

"I don't know."

I see us then, how impossibly young we were. How scared. How foolish to think that others had the answers. How little we trusted ourselves to know what was right for us, for Emma.

We pulled up to Pine Lane and saw the house—a white-painted brick ranch that looked well maintained with a grassy front yard and a modest flower garden leading up to the front door. This was suburbia: quaint, sleepy. It stood in glaring contrast to the concrete parking lots of my childhood in Queens.

As we walked up to the front door and rang the bell, I felt my heart begin its little dance of runaway palpitations, the ones I had been living with for nearly a decade—the familiar but still unwelcome anxiety that rose like bile in my chest. Only this time they were for Emma.

The man who opened the door towered at least a foot over us. His eyes were kind and his voice jolly, something we hadn't anticipated.

"Hello, I'm Moshe. Come in, come in." He extended his hand to Tolya, speaking in a rapid-fire way. I held my hands to my sides to not make the same embarrassing mistake that I made six years ago while entering an Orthodox family's home. Tolya and I had spent one summer during college exploring Israel as part of the Volunteers for Israel program. The program had arranged for us to experience a true Shabbat dinner, and in my complete youthful naiveté, I had entered the family's home offering the host my hand to shake. He merely looked at it and continued to usher us in. My sense of outrage quickly dissipated once Tolya explained to me the impropriety of a religious man touching a woman who was not his wife. *Oy.*

Atop the half a dozen steps that led to the main floor and living area stood a largish woman, similar in stature to her husband. She wore a long-sleeved top, a skirt that extended below her knees, and a long brown wig. Smiling amiably, she invited us in. "I'm Leah," she said, but kept her hands at her sides.

I stepped into the living room. Two little boys were playing with Legos, and a younger girl was marking paper with a crayon on the living room floor. Though preoccupied, they looked up and smiled when they saw us and heard their names rattled off by Leah.

"The boys are six and eight and the little girl, Chana, just turned three," Leah offered. All three children were adopted, and all three had Down syndrome, with the identifying features of roundish angelic faces, tiny noses, and slanted eyes. I recalled that Down syndrome people were notorious for their generally happy dispositions, easy smiles, and affectionate natures. They looked happy. The tension in my chest lifted.

"We've prepared a little lunch. Won't you join us?" Leah gestured toward the open dining room extending from the living area. A clear plastic tablecloth covered a dark mahogany table, which held a platter of bagels and scattered containers of different spreads and cartons of apple and orange juice.

Moshe took the children's hands and guided them to their seats. Once seated, he proceeded to say a quick prayer over the food. *Baruch ata adonai . . .* Memories of the Star Jewish Day Camp from my first two summers in the US flooded me in waves of warm nostalgia. This felt comfortable, familiar—familial. Emma would do well in this home. Love unquestionably resided here and occupied this little space. I relaxed, sinking deeper into my chair.

We sat in awkward silence and watched Leah pour the orange juice and Moshe butter bagels. They were working as a team.

"You have such a beautiful, full family," I said, "and I'm sure you have your hands full with the children's special needs . . ." I paused. "I guess we're wondering why you're looking to adopt another child, especially one like our Emma?"

"That's a fair question," Moshe said. "You see, the boys have each other, and we'd like Chana to have a sister so she doesn't feel left out or alone." I met Tolya's eyes, wondering if he was thinking what I was thinking. This was family life. It was as if their adopted children, with their various levels of developmental limitations, were expected to experience the completely typical dynamics of a family in which siblings fought, connected, had a kinship, and experienced the same multitude of social layers that traditional families did. There was no sense of anything being out of the ordinary in this household. If anything, the vastness of love that circulated under this roof and bounced from each exceptional individual to another was more than ordinary.

We observed in silence one of the older boys trying to spread cream cheese on his bagel. It was obvious that he was struggling mightily with the task. After a minute or so of effort, he made a gesture by placing a fist into the open upturned palm of his other hand and lifted his head to make eye contact with Leah.

"You need help, honey?" Leah immediately responded.

I looked at Moshe for an explanation.

"David just used sign language to ask for help," he said. "Because people with Down syndrome often struggle with verbal language, they're taught sign language to help them communicate their needs. The children all understand English, Hebrew, and sign—three languages. Most people barely know one—and they say *they're retarded.*" He nodded toward the children and let out a hearty laugh that reverberated through the space. I could have fallen where I was sitting. Tolya squeezed my hand under the table. This was love—pure, unadulterated love. I looked at this remarkable couple. I could see Emma in their arms. I could see them do for her what I could not.

As we said our goodbyes, Leah gently echoed her hopes. "We would really love to have Emma with us. I can imagine this must not be easy for you."

"Thank you," I said. "I can't tell you how much I appreciate you saying that."

"You know, Chana was the tenth child of an Orthodox family. The mother couldn't deal with the child's diagnosis."

I froze, stunned.

Was she judging the other mother? Was she judging me or giving me permission to take a similar action by acknowledging that I was not alone in feeling this way? Guilt crept into my throat once again.

I got into the car, trying to focus on all the good that I witnessed and not on Leah's last comment. I spent the bulk of the drive home analyzing myself into a frenzy, staring at the road unfolding in front of me, wary about feeling optimistic, cautious at showing the beginnings of an exhalation. A suspension of reality would have been welcome, but the truth seemed apparent. "They're God-fearing people," I said. "At least we know that they won't hurt her."

Tolya nodded.

I think we both believed that God-fearing people did not make mistakes. At the very minimum, religious people lived by the rule of a higher power that told them how to behave. But then again, didn't wars and genocides exist in the name of a God and religion? If an Orthodox woman with all her beliefs in the *bashert* and God's will can give her less-than-perfect child away, then what can be expected from a heathen like myself? That's what I told myself then. I didn't have to do "the right thing." All I had to do was what was right for me.

I turned to look at Tolya as he drove, facing the road. His profile betrayed gentleness and strength. It spoke of character and warmth all at once. I looked down at those hands I loved, the way they rested gently on his lap with just his fingertips touching the wheel—beautiful hands, strong from years of hitting a tennis ball but gentle enough to hold his fragile daughter with just the right amount of tenderness. A pang went through me as I imagined those hands empty—empty of Emma. I wondered if our marriage would survive this blow, having heard of too many marriages crumbling in the face of lesser insults. I feared that this was a hurdle we couldn't clear. A lump settled in my throat as I realized we were driving to an empty home—a childless home.

"I feel barren," I said, looking at my husband.

"What do you mean?"

I couldn't describe it.

I delivered a child, but I felt I had nothing to show for it. That was what I meant. Because Emma was not healthy, it was like it didn't count. It was like *she* didn't count.

"I just want to be a mother, but I want healthy children. Am I so disgustingly selfish to expect that?"

"No, of course not." Tolya's voice was somber but gentle. "Everyone wants that. I want that."

"Do you think we could try to get pregnant again." *Did I just say that?* "Is that crazy?"

"It's not crazy. Let's try." My husband was a good man, with such a good heart—much better than mine, I thought. I felt awash in my love for him.

Still my anxiety welled up again, and what I couldn't tell him was that I felt like the basest of human beings—that even thinking about wanting to get pregnant again made me feel like I was looking to replace Emma.

Emma, who was still here, still fighting for her life.

And yet, a part of me wanted a do-over.

CHAPTER 7

ST. LUKE'S SPECIAL-NEEDS NURSERY building resided in the Chelsea neighborhood of Manhattan. It was a relatively new construction with a pink-toned brick façade and large windows. If you stood in front of it and looked up, you could glimpse colorful paper cutouts, the kind you found decorating preschool windows where healthy children dwelled. Under different circumstances, it may have even appeared welcoming. As it was, we were there to tour Emma's temporary placement.

The hospital had informed us Emma was medically stable enough to go home, and they could no longer keep her. But the adoption paperwork had yet to process. I reasoned to Tolya and with myself that bringing her home was not a viable option for several reasons: we were not equipped with any of the things that she needed, as we had no feeding pump, no pulse oximeter, none of the necessities that monitored and sustained her. But the larger, truer reason was our reservations about bringing her home just long enough to give her up again.

I was fearful of getting more attached than I already was; it also felt like bringing her home was making a false promise to her. Keeping Emma at a distance ensured that I wouldn't change my mind about giving her up. I couldn't allow my heart to open and embrace her. I was afraid to love her, afraid that my love for her would overwhelm my rational mind, which was dictating my impulse to relinquish. I told myself that to let her go was our only chance at future happiness. In the interim, while waiting for the adoption to be finalized, we followed recommendations to place her, short-term, in a long-term medical facility.

Aside from the many other services they offered, St. Luke's nursery proved to be a place for children who couldn't survive at home without medical support. There was a second group of children, I learned from the social worker, whose parents essentially abandoned them so that the facility served as their permanent home until they aged out. Then there was us.

We were a special case. We were rejecting Emma, but we weren't abandoning her to the institution permanently, and we were showing up. I told myself that what we had decided to do was better. The hospital staff believed Emma was a temporary patient and thought she would be staying long enough for the doctors to develop and implement a plan so we could take her home with us.

On our first walk-through, while still at the research stage, St. Luke's social worker met us in the lobby, and we took the elevator to the eighth floor together. No one spoke. I kept my head lowered, staring at the floor. The elevator doors opened, and we stepped out into the wide hallway. Linoleum tiles typical of a hospital setting led us farther onto the floor. And then I saw them: beautifully framed photographs of special-needs kids with a range of disabilities. There were the smiling kids with Down syndrome. There were also images of children with other syndromes, the names of which I did not know. Many were black-and-white photos; some were in color. The black-and-whites appeared to stand out against the taupe-colored walls.

In my own photography, I was always drawn to black-and-white film. The stark contrast, the drama, the tension created served well to remind me that oftentimes the world was not the happy Technicolor rainbow that we see, but a struggle between good and evil, lightness and darkness, conformity and deviance. These beautifully rendered images depicted children with exaggerated features and "funny-looking" faces not unlike our Emma's. I felt my knees buckle.

Shameful irrepressible tears burned my face as I walked past the beautifully innocent portraits. Tolya took my hand. I covered my mouth. The social worker saw and stopped walking. She placed her hand on my arm and looked somberly at me, then at Tolya.

"I'm fine. I'm sorry," I said, shaking my head.

"It's understandable," she said. "This is a difficult place to be in. But we'll take good care of your daughter. You needn't worry." I wondered if she had knowledge of our clandestine plan for adoption. My twins—guilt and shame—emerged from their hiding place as a voice in my head whispered, *This is my child.*

Within a week of our visit we transferred Emma to St. Luke's, where she remained "under observation" for the next three months. St. Luke's proved to be my daily residence as well. Having taken maternity leave, with no intention of returning to my job as a family therapist, life was on pause. Each day was the same as the one before it. I woke up early feeling numb and took the train into the city and did not leave until dark. I would kiss her goodbye in her crib—or cell, as it appeared to me. Metal bars, intended to keep her safe—to keep the outside world from harming her—separated us from her.

I tried to keep my emotional distance from Emma. Her eye contact was fleeting, but when we connected, I saw into her soul, and it was pure and beautiful, and I needed to turn away. I scanned the room to focus on anything else: the large and always bright light filtering through the almost floor-to-ceiling windows that ran the entire length of the wall, the view of Seventh Avenue, or her roommates.

Emma shared a room with two boys. The first boy, whose name escapes me, shared the room with Emma for a few days.

He was the size of a one-year-old, though his face suggested a child of two or three. His head was disproportionately small and almost conical in shape, ending in a tip like the slope of a mountain. His ears were large, too large for his head. He had a button nose that turned up and the widest of smiles with the fullest of lips. He greeted me with an electric smile each time I came.

The first time I saw him his appearance unsettled me. But over time, I became more comfortable with his uniqueness. Each day I looked forward to his magnanimous smile and the way his face brightened when I walked over to his bedside and talked to him in a sing-song voice. "Hey, little guy. How are you?" He moved his arms and legs in excitement, and I wanted to ask, "What are you so happy about?" *And why shouldn't he be?* I thought, answering my own question. Life's burdens didn't weigh on him. He neither knew nor cared how the world perceived him. He lived in the moment, free of judgment, which was more than I could say of myself.

I recalled a *Twilight Zone* episode titled "The Eye of the Beholder." It depicted a woman, beautiful by our society's standards, whose fellow citizens all looked hideous with pig-like snouts, sunken eyes, and large, twisted mouths. The doctors worked hard to correct her appearance so that she could look like everyone else. That episode left an imprint on my psyche.

Because to say that I did not consider how Emma's dysmorphic features would present themselves as she matured and they became more pronounced would be to lie. Yes, her eyes were "beady" like mine and, worse, unfocused and spaced far apart, her lips two slim lines of shiny redness. Her hair was so sparse and unruly that she looked like she was losing hair instead of growing it. But she wasn't a monster. She was by all measures not glaringly different in appearance from most infants. Still, in the time that I imagined raising her, I feared that I would be put off by her physical appearance and love her less, because she wasn't conventional looking—because she was funny looking. I worried that my vanity would take my feelings hostage and strip me of the acceptance and love that Emma deserved.

Then there was three-year-old Angel. Angel, we learned, was deprived of oxygen during delivery, leaving him with brain and respiratory damage. He had the most beautiful, true-to-his- name angelic face, porcelain skin, and a halo of thick black curls. He also had a tracheal tube—an offensive hose connected to an opening in his throat to help him breathe. No one ever came to visit Angel aside from the occasional volunteer. Though he couldn't move, Angel was always felt and heard, with his devastatingly loud, raspy breathing that filled the large hospital room with every gurgled inhale. Sometimes I'd walk over to his bed to see him lying on his side, his eyes open, always open. He didn't seem to see me but only stared blankly into space—the space that was his entire world.

Then one morning Angel was gone, his bed empty.

What forces deemed it okay for a child to be born only to suffer? I cried for little Angel. I cried for my Emma and for myself. I cried for all the sadness in the world and for the unfairness of Emma's diagnosis. I cried for all the hopes of motherhood dashed.

By the second month, I was losing ground keeping my emotional distance.

Holding Emma in my arms, I sat in a chair and pretended I had achieved the immigrant dream of living in the city, in a luxury apartment in the sky, with my new perfect baby. Yet my reality spoke a different truth. Even so, those fleeting moments felt perfect, until I would look down at Emma's little face, her absent gaze, and lean deeper into the ache of the charade I was enacting.

"She's a good baby," the nurses would say, "quiet." She never cried nor made a sound. Not at all—not for food, not to be changed, not to be held. She demanded nothing. I realized that her seemingly content way of being was not the way of healthy babies. Healthy babies cried out with primal need at the first pang of hunger. They insisted on being picked up and soothed with soft murmurs as they molded their body into yours. They rebelled against the indignity of a soggy diaper. Healthy babies jarred you out of your sleep at all hours of the night, often. They demanded acknowledgment. They commanded love. Perhaps this was where I stumbled. Maybe because Emma never asked anything of me, I felt that I was replaceable.

Maybe because her physical needs could be met by anyone, and I failed in my selfish ignorance to see her more vital, less visible emotional needs, I told myself that she didn't need me—her mother.

My family visited Emma. My parents and Holly, my in-laws, and my friends came regularly. Marianna, my sister-in-law, who worked down the block from the hospital, came almost daily. Everyone took turns holding Emma. Everyone fell in love with her. It was such an easy act—her innocence and dependence engendered love.

One night, when no one was looking, I allowed myself to feel it too, but only briefly. I kissed her and set her down before the temptation became too great to keep her in my arms.

MELISSA, THE FEEDING SPECIALIST, was assigned to try and teach Emma to eat by mouth, as a means of moving toward the possibility of removing the G-tube or, at the very least, being less reliant on it. I looked forward to her sessions with us, anxious to learn and teach Emma steps toward "normalcy" and away from the G-tube.

Melissa had the practiced patience of a Zen master. Holding Emma, she would place the small baby bottle that held an ounce of water—and later, formula—to Emma's lips and stand up. "You want to gently bring the nipple to her tongue and brush it, moving slowly from the back to the front, as you rock her in rhythm with the strokes. This will encourage her to latch on and suck," she gently instructed.

I watched her with reverent awe as she danced with my baby, envious of the connection she was making with my child, the connection I was fighting. I told myself she had chosen her profession—made a conscious decision to devote herself to sick children. I, on the other hand, did not choose to have a sick child. Was it easier to accept things that you had a say in? I believed so.

I marveled at how this young woman imparted survival tactics to my baby. Skills that normally didn't need to be taught because they were innately present—except when they were not. "The goal is to get her to coordinate breathing, sucking, and swallowing so she doesn't aspirate," she continued. Emma labored diligently to learn this dance but tired easily.

The adoption wheels continued to turn, bringing everyone closer to the day we'd have to say goodbye.

While at St. Luke's, Emma suffered from frequent urinary tract infections, which led to the vesicostomy surgery—an egregious word that aptly described the wreckage it left in its wake. Caring for this new hole in her body added another obstacle to the medical mountain. I worried about the pain Emma underwent, but I also wondered if this would lead the adoptive family to have a change of heart—to reconsider the adoption in light of a more complicated medical future. I reminded myself that their adopted kids with Down syndrome appeared healthy. They certainly lacked Emma's fragility. "Are you sure you know what you're getting into?" I wanted to ask them. I couldn't fathom handing her over only to have them reject her when they decided she was too difficult to maintain.

Shortly after her vesicostomy surgery at the local hospital, Emma returned to St. Luke's for recovery. Dr. S, the resident MD, had come to check on her. We were still in search of any answers we could gather. "Can you give us a sense of Emma's prognosis for the future?" we asked.

He furrowed his brow and answered with gravity and apology in his voice, "From my experience, babies with her type of diagnosis don't live more than a year."

His words sent a cold shiver through me. What took me back more than the death sentence that he had just handed us was the conviction in his tone. How could he know this, especially since Emma's diagnosis was so rare and there were no comparisons?

I would realize years later that he was speaking his truth, but at the time his truth was drawn from comparing Emma to the group of children he had the most experience with, namely hospitalized, abandoned ones. The Angels of the world, who likely died young not because medical science failed them but because the adults who were charged with holding and loving them were missing. So I held Emma all day.

I dedicated myself to building Emma up emotionally, so that she would feel my love—until she no longer could.

CHAPTER 8

DON'T WORRY. SHE'S IN GOOD HANDS, Leah and Moshe told us the day they came to pick up Emma. She was already five months old.

They met us in her room, and it occurred to me that they were meeting her for the first time—committing to our child, sight unseen. How much faith must they have had, I thought. They received important information from us on how to feed her via the G-tube and with a bottle. We showed them her vesicostomy opening and how we placed a sanitary napkin across it to keep the urine from leaking outside her diaper and onto her clothes. I proudly told them that she now took two ounces of formula from a bottle topped with a very small nipple opening to help her control the flow and avoid aspiration.

Years later, I would turn to Tolya to confirm this memory, only to find out that he had a completely different recollection of the events. He did not remember ever seeing them on the hospital floor in Emma's room, ever.

"How could this be?" I would ask him. "We would never have given her up without instructions. We would never be that irresponsible." Besides, I thought, that would have been heartless. I was prepared to accept the title of coward, but I was not without a heart.

Memory is a funny thing. It's amorphous and cunning. It leaves you floundering, fighting to stay afloat. It wears disguises, camouflages itself to blend into the landscape of the season. It can be as white and clean as virgin snow. Too often, though, it's as dark and murky as muddy soil, pockmarked with rotting leaves after a November rain.

When I attempted to excavate the long-buried details of that time, I found that the raw emotion was still there. I would also realize that the mind has a wise way of self-preservation. What you cannot remember cannot haunt you.

One thing was certain: we relinquished Emma to the adoptive family outside of the hospital because we were too ashamed to have the nurses and therapists who had cared for her and grown to love her know our dirty, cowardly secret. So we dressed Emma, packed the bags with her things, and secured her into the car seat she would be traveling in. We agreed to meet Moshe and Leah in the outdoor parking lot across the street, where they had left their car.

In a parking lot.

The day was sunny, the sky a baby-blue hue. The forecast was unlucky, with zero percent chance of showers. We didn't idle outside long. We took turns kissing our baby goodbye and handed her over.

"Thank you for everything. Please take good care of her," I whispered through the burning in my throat. Blinking back tears, my eyes met Tolya's, which were brimming with sadness, threatening to spill over. Something about seeing a man—my husband—cry is so frightening. I did not want to be witness to it—to be brought to that brink, to look down and over the vastness of the cliff on whose edge we were both teetering.

"We will," Moshe responded in his too-jolly voice. "Please don't worry. She's in good hands."

And then they were gone.

CHAPTER 9

I WAS PREGNANT AGAIN. To say that I was excited would be dishonest. Neither the process nor the fact of the pregnancy was eventful. My expected elation was tainted by the awareness that an act of substitution was about to take place, an act of bait and switch that looked like it might be successful. I was replacing one baby with another. I was getting my do-over.

Jobless and spiritless, I spent my days reclining in a bean-bag chair, staring at the television as I watched my belly get bigger. I worried that all the crying I was doing would harm the new baby growing inside of me, as would the guilt I was feeling. I tried not to focus on this, and not to stress, but I could not stop.

Still, for this, my second pregnancy, I was determined to do things differently. I found a practice that specialized in high-risk pregnancies—not because we were considered high-risk but because we'd already been burned once, by ignorance or negligence or faith—or fate. The practice was considered high-risk because it specialized in multiple pregnancies and births. But that day of the first appointment, we were pressing for answers, and for an amniocentesis test.

"To be perfectly honest, if you didn't have a history with your first child being born with a genetic abnormality, I would try and talk you out of the test," Dr. N stated matter-of-factly, "because you're under thirty-five, healthy, and because the risk of miscarriage caused by an amnio is a possibility that we'd want to avoid. But, seeing your concern, I'm fine with ordering the test . . ." He paused. "As long as you understand the risk."

I had always understood that knowledge was power. Wasn't it a fact that we got tested for Tay-Sachs because we were Eastern European Jews (who fell in the high-risk category) so that we could decide whether to continue with the pregnancy? The elephant was in the room; the prospect of a chosen termination, an abortion, loomed large. But Tolya and I had already had that private conversation about whether we would abort a sick child.

"I couldn't go through what we did with Emma again," I had said categorically.

"I couldn't either," Tolya agreed.

We fully understood that this was a moral hot button for many people in this country. Still, we were the products of a more liberal Europe, where terminating an unwanted pregnancy was a question of practicality—not a taboo—and where abortions often functioned as birth control.

That is not to say we knew what we'd do if we found out there was something wrong with the baby, but we needed to have the information so that this time we could make an informed decision and go in with our eyes open.

The prospect of a healthy baby brought with it hope and guilt in equal measure. I became convinced that I had made an irrevocable, regrettable mistake. I felt Emma's absence in my core. And even though I was nurturing a new life inside me, I felt dead.

We had insisted on an open adoption that would allow us to visit Emma and stay in touch with the family. Soon after we placed Emma, Leah began to update me regularly on her progress. She proudly reported that Emma was now taking six ounces of formula by mouth. I marveled at this transformation, but it also intensified my guilt. Though I was happy about Emma's progress, I couldn't help but be surprised, even if I shouldn't have been. After all, I knew that babies naturally thrived in caring families. This was why we chose the path that we did. Still, I missed her terribly and felt the ache of exclusion that I had imposed on myself.

Then the phone calls took a disturbing turn. "Emma is in the hospital with RSV and pneumonia," Leah phoned to report.

RSV, we learned, is a respiratory virus that can be single-handedly fatal to healthy babies. I could not imagine what the combination of the two, pneumonia and RSV, was doing to Emma's already compromised immune system. Why couldn't she understand that I was powerless to help my baby? I was sitting on my hands, miles away, worried, hopeless, and useless.

"I think that she's preparing me for the worst," I said to Tolya that night when he returned from work. "Why else would she be calling me with such upsetting news?"

Months had passed since we separated from Emma, and I felt paralysis set into my bones as each day seemed to bleed into the next, indistinguishable.

When I was a little girl in Ukraine, a neighbor taught me how to knit—just the basic knit and purl stitch. I would knit long wool scarves, but because I never learned how to end a piece, my scarves would remain unfinished and I would proceed to unravel them, only to begin again later. This is how this open adoption felt, like my unfinished scarves, like unfinished business.

Alone in the apartment after the adoption, I took up knitting once again. I needed my hands busy and my mind blank. My favorite pastime, reading, no longer relieved me. My brain no longer retained information. I would make a Herculean effort to understand the words but immediately find the meaning had evaporated. Knitting was a kind of meditation. It cleansed my mind and allowed me to focus on the simple task of making one stitch after another, one stitch after another. It required no effort on my part and minimal brain activity. I needed to check out and tune in to the simple, repetitive, and purposeful motion of one needle caressing another, over and over again.

It was easy for me to get lost in just being and creating. Knitting had a rhythmic dance, with its own simple melody, its own cadence, its own beat. I'd hoped it could be the balm my soul needed, but ultimately found it ephemeral, as melancholy knocked on the door of my heart.

My mother saw my sadness. "Honey, I'm worried about you," she said. "Maybe it would help to be busy." I shrugged, not knowing anything anymore, devoid of opinion. "I can see if you can do something part time at my job, just to get your mind off things," she continued.

"I guess," I replied to the job offer. "We need a second income again if we're going to be able to afford this baby." I knew that my mother was right, but it was not about the money. The truth was that I'd always needed to move, to do. Keeping busy had saved me in the past and had kept me sane. *Keep pressing forward, or sideways, even backward. As long as you keep moving, you'll be okay.* I needed to drain the reservoir of dark thoughts that had collected in the sea of my mind. The still water had turned fetid and was making me sick.

I looked at my mother's face and saw my pain reflected in her eyes. I knew she was suffering in her own way. In all this time, we hadn't bothered to ask my parents how they were dealing with having their grandchild given away. Still, they knew to tread lightly. "We know this is a difficult decision you have to make with Tolya," they said to us. "We are behind you, whatever you do." They stood by me. I watched them get attached to Emma. I watched them fall in love. I saw the sadness in their eyes and the regret that they couldn't take away our pain or heal their grandchild.

Like many mothers, my mother would say, "If I could take this pain from you and onto myself, I would." I knew she meant it, and I believed her. I believed her because I was now a mother myself, and I knew the helplessness of not being able to relieve my child's pain.

My mother arranged for me to do collections at the Ivy League university club where she worked as a bookkeeper. It was a good gig, but the gray cloud over my head remained.

At this new job, my responsibilities included calling delinquent club members and asking for payment. I put on my most intimidating twenty-seven-year-old voice so as to be taken seriously and, with the greatest of gravitas, requested that they pay their bill. It was ludicrous, really. I fancied myself a wise guy, threatening, "Pay up or you'll be sleeping with the fishes." I'd hoped that the everyday act of engaging with others would help reinstate a sense of normalcy to my life, a much-needed distraction from fixating on my apocalyptic, maudlin thoughts.

But then the next wave hit.

"I have to tell you something," Tolya said after we sat down to dinner one night, another exhausting day of marathon collection calling behind me. I had always dreaded this kind of opening statement and told him many frustrated times, "If you're going to tell me something, please don't preface it with these words. Just say what you have to say." From my experience, this kind of statement was not typically followed by "Honey, I bought us a house" or "I love you and I want to marry you" or "I played the lotto and won the million-dollar jackpot." No. A statement like that typically preceded bad news. The blindfold before a magazine is emptied into your chest. The words meant to soften the blow before the guillotine dropped.

"Just speak, for God's sake, but make sure I absolutely need to know this. Remember, I'm carrying your baby, and you don't want to send me into premature labor," I joked. But Tolya did not smile.

"Okay, so what I haven't told you is that I've been visiting Emma in Pennsylvania," he said. I felt the air leave my lungs.

"I was there today. I found Emma in the hospital again, and Moshe was with her." He paused in an attempt to collect himself before he delivered the second bullet. "Moshe is there with her because apparently . . . Leah left."

"Left the hospital?"

"No. Left the family."

In mute disbelief I listened and heard only my pounding heart. He paused again to give me a chance to absorb the information. My initial instinct was to feel betrayed, to feel that I was the worse parent, to be boldly reminded that it was my idea to give her up. Tolya had been visiting Emma behind my back because he missed her and wanted to see her; his actions signaled his true paternal feelings, sentiments that blatantly deviated from the pact we had made. And just as quickly as the internal earthquake settled and my ego recovered from the trauma of the news delivered, a geyser of emotions spilled to the surface.

"Tell me everything," I said, in that moment realizing I was glad he had been visiting her.

"This is what I understand." He told me that he called Moshe to see if he could visit that day, and Moshe told him that Emma was again in CHOP, the Children's Hospital of Philadelphia, with pneumonia. Moshe offered to meet Tolya in the hospital. Tolya had gotten lost driving there through the dark, unfamiliar streets, only to finally get there and find Emma in a frightening state—tubes extending out from all parts of her body, sedated. Moshe divulged to Tolya that Leah had abandoned the entire family, leaving Moshe with four special-needs kids. Moshe had taken medical family leave from his job to care for the kids.

When he finished talking, he appeared deflated. I, on the other hand, felt energized—the recipient of the wind that had just escaped my husband, with ideas that circled my head.

"You know what this means, right?" I said, trying to contain my excitement. I went on to remind him that we gave Emma to a family under certain conditions—a two-parent household—and since those conditions no longer existed, maybe we could have our rights restored. I didn't think Moshe would mind because I was sure he felt over-whelmed with all his responsibilities and with Emma being so sick. I said that we should call the adoption agency tomorrow, give them the news, and find out if we could get Emma back. I had forgotten to inhale. The next breath I took filled my lungs with hope, excitement, promise.

My maternal heart, which I believed had withered and flatlined, sprang back to life, more resilient than ever. It was akin to feeling famished—a gnawing inner emptiness—and not knowing what would feed your hunger until someone offered you sustenance, and you said, *Yes!* In the same way, I didn't know to wish for the universe to smile on me in this way. But when it did, I understood my course.

"We have to try to get her back," I said.

"You're smiling," Tolya said. "I was afraid you'd have a different reaction, but you said exactly what I was hoping to hear." With that he put his arms around me, and we cried quietly—each of us in an overlapping bubble of disorganized emotions, too many and too unknowable to name or understand.

The next morning I was on the E train to work, holding on to the overhead railing, facing my mother with my seven-month belly competing for space, watching her eyes widen and her brows elevate with surprise at the news I was sharing with her about Emma.

"Bring Emmachka home," she said. "We'll help you."

CHAPTER 10

IF YOU DIG DEEP ENOUGH in the sand, you will eventually hit water. I knew this from the countless hours I spent at the beach as a little girl. As soon as I reached a certain depth, the water seemed to effortlessly fill the basin of sand I had created by diving my little hands into the grains.

Once I had unearthed my own feelings for Emma after Toyla's confession, new information about Emma trickled in like underground water.

"We visited her too," my mother said. "We missed her. Your father and I didn't want to upset you."

I pretended to feel injured and excluded, but secretly I was proud of both my parents and my husband. They acted on their instincts and love for Emma.

"It was your father's idea. You know your father. You know how he feels about Emmachka," my mother said. Yes, I knew my father. Everyone knew my father. My father is one of those rare people you feel lucky to know. Despite a difficult childhood, raised by a single mother after World War II, with no education beyond the eighth grade, my father is one of those remarkable people who wake up happy in the morning and end their day the same way they began it. In the hours in between, he touches people with his words, humor, generosity, and love of life. "We visited her twice," she continued. "Both times she was in the hospital. We got her *Get Well* balloons and stood over her bed, crying. She looked so sick."

We learned new information about Leah and Moshe as well. When we returned to the adoption agency to see if we had our parental rights back, in light of the changes in conditions under which we gave Emma up, we found out a different backstory. We learned that theirs had been a second marriage and that they had not long ago converted to Judaism. That fact alone was a great deal to process, knowing, as Tolya and I did, the enormous commitment and responsibility life as a practicing Orthodox Jew demands. So demanding, in fact, that neither of us, born into the Jewish faith, could conceive mustering the necessary commitment. It was an impressive life choice—to live devoted to and believing in a higher power and its teachings, regardless of what one may have previously followed—but one that must have stressed their marriage.

I was furious with the adoption agency for withholding pertinent information that could have influenced our decision, and with Leah for abandoning her husband, the children, and Emma. At the same time, I understood that to judge her would be too easy and too harsh—and only a finger point back at myself. Because my betrayal was less forgivable.

Yet when the storm passed and I pondered life's vagaries, I realized with sober clarity that if not for the way all the events unfolded, we would not have had the gift of knowing—unlike most biological parents who give up their children to forever wonder if they made a mistake—what life was like both with and without our child. We had been given a rare chance to correct a grave mistake. We knew what life was like with and without Emma, and we preferred the former. I gave a mental thanks to the adoption agency and to Moshe and Leah, as I realized that this was the real do-over I had asked for.

AS IF ON A RESCUE mission, we moved quickly. We arranged to meet with Moshe to collect our baby and bring her home.

It did not surprise me that he did not fight us. Rather, I sensed relief in his voice when we called him to tell him our plans. "I understand, absolutely," he said.

We got into the car and drove. We made no arrangements, took nothing with us—not food nor clothing for Emma. We expected to have everything ready for us, as we sent her with bags full of clothes. We also knew that they would have all her feeding equipment to return to us.

I wondered if Emma would recognize me. I wondered how she'd changed and how much of the five-month-old we relinquished I would now recognize in her. To quiet my mind, I told myself that we were leaving empty-handed but would be returning with the greatest gift—a second chance. I remembered reading someone's observation that life can be fair: it can give you second chances.

We walked up the three steps to the door that Moshe held open for us, and came in. Tolya was close behind me. I fought the impulse to push past Moshe, run in, find Emma, and scoop her up in my arms. Competing with this impulse was the loud rapping of my heart in my head. Was it fear, anticipation of what was about to happen, or both that took me hostage?

After we briefly exchanged niceties, Moshe led us to the playpen, where we found Emma lying on her back. I peered in. It had been almost six months since we last saw her, on the day that we gave her away. As I lowered my gaze upon her, I was startled.

She was unrecognizable to me. So much so, I doubted that I would have been able to pick her out of a lineup of babies. The tiny fifteen pounder I remembered had grown three times her size. Her wispy, sparse hair had transformed itself into a golden, thick halo of ringlets. Her once gaunt and longish face had filled out into round, pinchable cheeks. Her fat little thighs were *pulkes*, I already imagined myself play-biting. (I would later learn that the pudginess was the result of bloating caused by the steroids she was on to treat the combination of RSV and pneumonia.)

Time slowed down.

"Hi, my love. I missed you." I bent down over my pregnant belly, careful not to tip over and keenly aware, as I placed my hands under Emma's arms to lift her, I was taking her exactly where she needed to be—into my embrace.

She blinked, her eyes widening, and then bestowed upon me what would be the first of her many gifts—a smile.

There was so much I wanted to say to her, beginning with my vow to her that, as long as I lived, I would work toward earning her forgiveness for my foolishness. But there was plenty of time for that. I leaned in and whispered quietly in her ear, so the others could not hear. "I will make it up to you."

CHAPTER 11

"EMMA IS NOW ON OXYGEN when she sleeps," Moshe stated nonchalantly, as if announcing that she now wears size-twelve-month-old clothing or that she can point to her nose or imitate clapping.

"What does that mean, she's on oxygen?" I glanced at Tolya, as if directing the desperate question toward him, or maybe to confirm that he heard the same words.

"So, with all the hospitalizations for pneumonia and RSV, the doctors say her lungs have been compromised—damaged, you might say—and now, when she sleeps, she desaturates."

"Desaturates?" I repeated, like a child learning a new word.

"Meaning her oxygen levels drop," Moshe replied with patience and a tinge of sadness in his voice. He pulled out what I recognized to be a nasal cannula. I recalled the clear plastic tube with two little prongs that were placed just at the entry to Emma's nostrils when she was still in the NICU. "She uses this at night. It's attached to this oxygen tank." Moshe pointed to a sea-green metal cylinder towering ominously near Emma's playpen. It was almost as tall as me, about a foot in diameter, and looked like an artillery shell.

I felt the floor disintegrate under me. We had handed them a medically stable child. Then I recalled Leah telling me that she had made the hole of the bottle nipple larger. Without realizing, Leah was probably, inadvertently allowing the milk to enter Emma's lungs, resulting in aspiration, pneumonia, RSV. We would have to do better.

"Thank you for taking care of her," I finally found the words to say to Moshe. "It must not have been easy for you."

"It's no problem. I was happy to do it. She's a sweetheart," he replied. "Here's the pulse oximeter that gauges her oxygen levels when she sleeps." He picked up a machine the size of a jewelry box to illustrate. "When her oxygen levels drop, the machine alerts you to it by beeping," he continued.

"How do we travel with her?" Tolya finally said. "What if her levels drop when she falls asleep in the stroller when we're out?" I was grateful he thought to ask the practical questions; at the same time, I could see his worry.

"Oh. Well, the company that supplies her oxygen will also deliver a portable tank like this one," he pointed to a smaller unit on the floor. "You can just put this in the basket of the stroller and take it with you. In fact, you can have it on your drive home in case she falls asleep in the car."

Fear gripped me, but I needed to stay strong. Besides, I told myself, this man had been caring for all of these children alone. Moshe's three other children had remained scattered in the outer corners of the living room, somehow occupied. "Are you going to be okay with the kids on your own?" I asked, lifting my chin in their direction.

"I'll be fine. Don't worry about me. Take care of your daughter. She's a good girl," he said, with sympathy and knowledge in his voice.

We packed Emma's bags and tucked her into the car seat in which she had made her trip here. We thanked Moshe again for everything and descended the few steps toward the door. Just then, the door opened and in walked Leah, as if she lived there and was just returning from the grocery store.

"Oh, hi," she said almost cheerily, as though nothing happened, as if she weren't instrumental in our world turning upside down and now, perhaps, right side up.

"What are you doing here?" I blurted, without considering the inappropriateness of my inquisition, as I felt myself vibrating with anger.

"Oh, I forgot something," she responded nonchalantly. I felt the Richter scale in my brain spike. *Forgot something?! Did you forget your kids, your husband, maybe? Or is this all a ruse?* I looked to Moshe for a clue, an explanation, but he was poker-faced.

"I'm sorry things didn't work out," she offered. *Which part are you sorry about?* I wanted to scream. But, just as quickly, a barely audible voice in my head reminded me that, if not for her actions, I wouldn't be holding Emma.

We exited, closing the door on a crazy chapter in our young lives.

When we pulled out, butterflies took flight in my stomach as a new kind of excitement took over. We were making our getaway.

Tolya had secured Emma's car seat to the back, facing the rear window, and sitting beside her, I leaned over.

"Hi, lovey! We're going home. Everyone's missed you and can't wait to see you." She turned her head slightly in my direction, and her eyes darted back and forth as if she were searching for the source of the high-pitched, sing-song, excited sounds. I noticed that her amblyopia—or lazy eye, in which one of the eyes wanders inward or outward—was still there, and I made a mental note to ask the ophthalmologist if anything could be done to correct it.

The soothing motion of the car gradually put Emma to sleep. We drove in silence, and it amplified the unspoken words to an intolerable volume. I had to break the trance, as it was slicing open my heart like a dull serrated knife run back and forth on an imaginary seam.

The old me would have asked, "Are you scared?" but I felt myself shifting. "We're going to be okay," I said, even though I had no sense of what okay meant.

"We will do our best," Toyla said. We didn't know if any of it was true, but we were changed. There was no turning back—literally, physically, metaphorically. We had no choice but to move forward in the car, in our lives, without a map or directions other than what the eyes could see.

We had survived bad odds and a change of circumstances whose path we consciously chose to follow. My heart palpitations sped up in the familiar way, and the almost comfort of these normally unwelcome, unannounced feelings gave me peace in recognizing that I'd been here before, with this fear, this anxiety, this urge to flee. I had lived through this and come out on the other side—not unscathed but a little stronger, with an extra layer of protection, and the knowledge that there would be scar tissue, but that the scab would form and the skin would close and that there would be healing.

CHAPTER 12

TWO CRIBS NOW FLANKED OUR BED. Joshua had arrived a month after Emma's return to us. She was already thirteen months old, but because her presence at home was still so fresh and new, with Joshua's birth it felt as though I had delivered twins—instant children, instant family.

This little boy was healthy, and I felt boundless gratitude. I marveled at his light-gray eyes, which would later turn a subtle shade of hazel. With his dad's and my eyes both being brown, this was a display of genetics at its best, with the recessive genes of my grandparents and Tolya's father having their say. "He's so funny looking," my mother would joke. Commenting on the hint of a future Jewish nose and making fun of an anti-Semitic Soviet joke, my father would say, "So little, and already a Jew."

"He's gorgeous," I would insist, feigning outrage at their taunts. I recognized their words as the superstitious tactics often used by Jews to keep the evil eye at bay. It was the reason a red string often adorned an infant's wrist or ankle and why a compliment from a stranger would unfailingly be met with a "pooh, pooh, pooh"—the magical, mystical triple-spit defense. I recalled a favorite joke that perfectly illustrated this practice: A little boy was found wandering the streets of the Russian-Jewish community of Brighton Beach, Brooklyn. He was crying, because he got separated from his mother. When a concerned stranger asked his name, he answered, "*Shayna punim*, pooh pooh pooh," which translates from Yiddish as "pretty face, spit, spit, spit."

But if I were to compare the two pregnancies and their outcomes, I would be stricken by the sheer randomness of life, by how little to no control we have of circumstances. In theory, all the exercise and self-care during Emma's pregnancy should have led to a healthy baby. In turn, the mostly sitting and weeping I was doing during Josh's should have wreaked emotional havoc on my nerves and, by extension, on Joshua. It's unsettling to realize how roll-of-the-dice life really is—that biology is a temperamental beast and that learning to let go of control could save one's life.

Joshua was as textbook a baby as Emma was not. But that very difference made parenting him a breeze. It was as if we had lived through a war and returned home to the safety and normalcy of regular civilian life, almost boring in its simplicity. Emma's needs demanded so much attention—the theoretically simple acts of her feeding and sleeping (with oxygen) so overshadowed her brother's care that we almost took it for granted. Josh seemed to raise himself.

Of course, if an outsider were to catch a glimpse of me on the red leather sofa bed that had survived Tolya's adolescence, his being single, and our dating phase, he might have found the scene overwhelming: Joshua at my breast, nursing, while my other hand held a bottle to Emma's mouth as she reclined in her baby bouncer, next to me, with the simultaneous drip of her formula that extended from the stand holding her bag of liquid nourishment. Multitasking *par excellence*. Careful of preventing Emma losing her hard-earned skills of eating by mouth, we paired her G-tube feedings with her oral ones so that she would make the connection between eating and satiety. She made her enjoyment of pureed fruits especially apparent by raising and lowering her arms in a jerking motion while her eyes danced, shifting uncontrollably left and right.

Equipment dominated our apartment. Joshua's side table held the requisite collection of diapers, wipes, creams, and pacifiers. Emma's contrasted starkly with an arsenal of the same, plus an oxygen tank; feeding bags; a stand called the Kangaroo Pump, from which the feeding bags were suspended like an IV drip; various syringes; replacement G-tube buttons; nasal cannulas; sanitary napkins; and a pulse oximeter, which resembled a cable box but instead of delivering entertainment, announced, via lights and offensive beeps, Emma's oxygen-saturation levels.

"Thank god for Pampers," my mother would say. (Russians used Pampers to refer generically to all disposable diapers, just like Bounty stood for all paper towels.) "In the Soviet Union, I would spend all day washing your dirty cloth diapers."

Yes. Thank God for the modern conveniences of life in America, I thought. "Thank God we had Emma here, in this country," I would respond. "Can you imagine if she was born there?" I paused. "She wouldn't make it." Diapers would have been the least of our problems. Eating and breathing would have trumped all that.

In bed the first night of my return from the hospital with Joshua, curled up with my head on Tolya's chest and my hand resting on his heart, I listened to his steady pulse, not unlike the beat of the metronome that sat atop my piano throughout the years of obligatory lessons. Joshua slept swaddled safely in his crib, while Emma, in a crib adjacent to his, flailed her arms as if she were falling or drowning. She did not like to be constrained. Maybe because of her limited mobility (she couldn't even roll to her side yet), the things she could control—her limbs—she wanted free, to slice the air with and occasionally to examine her hands, the appearance of which always seemed to surprise her. Moving about, she would invariably loosen the toe sensor attached to the pulse oximeter, sending the machine into alarm mode. Too often, and to our great annoyance, Emma would take the opportunity to pull off the nasal cannula attached to her cheeks with two pieces of medical tape, place the thin plastic in her mouth, and chew on it absentmindedly.

"Here we are," I mumbled into Tolya's chest. The digital clock on the side table read two o'clock in the morning. "Do you remember where we were two years ago at this hour?"

He shook his head. "I don't remember anything anymore."

I allowed myself to get lost in indulgent nostalgia, reminding him how two years ago we were probably seen traipsing all over Manhattan—maybe catching a midnight screening at Angelika, then driving to the famed H&H Bagels on Broadway and Eightieth, because by that time we'd be starving. The bakery was open twenty-four hours, and it churned out carby yummies that we would inhale plain and steaming, because there'd be no need for toppings. They were stand-alone amazing. Now, at two in the morning we were listening for sounds coming from a machine that monitored our daughter's vital signs.

I got up to check on Joshua. Instinctively, I leaned in closer to his face to make sure he was breathing, turning my ear toward his mouth. When I didn't pick up any sounds, I turned my attention to his chest to watch it rise and fall. His sleep was deceptively quiet, while Emma's was imposingly loud.

These became the two worlds I straddled. This, the balancing act: I danced between the healthy child and the medically challenged one. But the dance for Emma was much more extravagant and had many more steps.

Emma's collection of equipment and medical needs heralded a parade of specialists. Doctors, to attend to her eyes, ears, lungs, stomach, bladder. An assembly line of workers on whose conveyer belt Emma would be stopped long enough to have something attached or removed. I recalled my childhood doll whose flimsy limbs kept coming loose, and I'd have to return them to their sockets. Piece by piece, part by part,

Emma was assembled and reassembled. The only way to find our way to these specialists dispensing courage, hearts, and brains was to be referred by the head doctor, the Wizard of Oz of this enterprise—her pediatrician.

Shortly after Emma was born, while still at Long Island Jewish Hospital undergoing genetic testing, we had a visit from a doctor. Pediatricians typically made their rounds to the parents of newborns—peddling their wares.

"Hello. I'm Dr. L." He extended one hand to shake mine and, with the other, handed me his card. "I'm a developmental pediatrician. I specialize in treating children with developmental delays and disabilities." I might have appeared dumbfounded at this information, because it took me a minute to register what he was saying—that Emma would need a special pediatrician, not just an ordinary one. Because she wasn't ordinary.

So when the time came to make an appointment with Dr. L a year after our first meeting, I dug deep into my wallet to find his business card nestled among other cards from a former life. Why did I hold on to it for so long, even after we relinquished her? *Beshert.* The word again settled into the folds of my brain. Did the universe know that she was going to return to us because it was meant to be? Did I know it, subconsciously, while fighting against it consciously, deliberately?

Dr. L's office was a ten-minute ride from us, located in a private house—a ten-step walk up. I didn't think much of it at the time, because *non-ambulatory*, *foot orthotics*, and *wheelchairs* were not yet part of our everyday vocabulary. That would be the future and the reason we'd have to change pediatricians to ones that offered disabled-friendly access. But at the time, and for the next seven years or so, it would work. I lifted Emma up in her stroller or pulled it up the stairs on its hind wheels, slowly—careful to avoid the inevitable bump that accompanied each step—like I'd seen other moms of healthy babies do.

Our first visit with Dr. L proved to be a comfortable one, even though on the way there I worried about how I'd explain the last thirteen months. But when the time came to give Emma's history, our history—the information surfaced organically.

"First time here?" Dr. L asked while looking over her chart.

"Yes. Well, actually, you first saw us at LIJ, when she was born. You gave me your card." I paused, hoping he wouldn't ask the next question.

"So, you're changing pediatricians? Who did Emma see before?" Of course, that would be the next logical inquiry. I could feel my cheeks turn crimson and my heart pick up pace from a trot to a gallop. *Here we go*, I thought. And in one excruciatingly long exhalation, I chronicled my ugly past, starting with "It's kind of a unique story . . ." and ending with "And now we're lucky to have her back." I don't know what kind of reaction I expected to the shameful facts I detailed. Dr. L seemed unimpressed. I didn't see so much as a raised eyebrow, though I looked for it. To his credit, he gave nothing away. If he was appalled or he disapproved, he didn't let on and acted as if he'd heard this story often. *He's good*, I thought. *We're going to be okay here.*

"All right then. Let's have a look." He proceeded to undress Emma, removing her diaper to reveal the vesicostomy, the G-tube. Running his finger over the vertical scar on her chest, he turned to look at me, as if asking for an explanation. "That was the Nissen fundoplication surgery to treat her gastroesophageal reflux, the vesicostomy was to treat her grade four urine reflux, and the G-tube to prevent aspiration. She's also on oxygen when she sleeps, because she desaturates."

Who just said that? I thought, surprised that I had retained these foreign words until it was the right time to unearth them—as though in hibernation until the thaw uncovered their slumber. I recalled the psychology class about what

information got relegated to the archives of memory: things
of importance or interest, emotionally charged things, things
that ensured survival.

"Are you in the medical field?" Dr. L asked.

"No," I laughed, "but I feel like I'm in medical school."
He smiled and nodded to indicate that he understood. Turning his attention back to Emma, he rolled her over to examine
her backside. This time he ran his finger over her sacral
dimple—an indentation in the skin on the lower back—and
glanced at me. "Yes, they checked her for spina bifida. She's
fine," I replied on cue.

"Are you okay with her equipment? Do you know where
to order her oxygen and other supplies?" Dr. L asked.

"We are. We got that information from the adoptive family,
but we need recommendations for specialists." Without a word,
Dr. L took out his prescription pad from his jacket pocket and
began scribbling. When he finished, he handed the paper to me.
There was a pulmonologist, a neurologist, a urologist, and a
gastroenterologist listed. At the very bottom, there was an 800
number. Dr. L went on to explain that Emma's diagnosis and
delay entitled her to receive therapies—like speech, physical,
occupational, and more—to address her delays and help her
reach her potential. Only years later would I realize that he was
referring us to the Early Intervention Program, a government-
run program for children from birth to three years of age who
have developmental delays and disabilities.

The next several crazed months would bring an army of
people into our lives, each one helping us navigate our new
and bumpy terrain of life with Emma. There would be evaluators, service coordinators, nurses, and doctors. My wallet
expanded in size—stretched by the bulk of the business cards:
the pulmonologist with Columbia-Presbyterian, urologist
with NYU, gastroenterologist at North Shore, neurologist
at LIJ. Organizational skills were never my strong suit, but

necessity made it so that appointment making and keeping came to define our lives.

At the center of this was Emma. Somewhere on the periphery of the maelstrom was Joshua, patiently awaiting his turn.

CHAPTER 13

WE RENTED A SUMMER HOUSE for the month of July, in a bucolic community of the Pocono Mountains, at my mother's suggestion that time away from the bustle, stifling heat, and humidity of New York would do everyone good. We would spend the next five summers this way. Outwardly a stylish and metropolitan city girl, born and raised in the capital city of Kiev, my mother was really a country girl at heart. She loved telling and retelling stories of how she spent every summer since she was a little girl at her grandfather Chaim's house, in a quaint village in Boguslav, just outside the city—a poor man's version of a *dacha*. After our immigration, she often reminisced fondly about the large river rocks where she whiled away endless hours, watching the neighbors' goats roam the grassy hills that led into a river bank. In the evenings, she would make her way home, where a steaming plate of homemade pierogis, made with sour cherries picked from the tree in the backyard, would be waiting for her. I spent many summers there myself, so I understood her nostalgia and the temptation to escape the city. The Poconos was as close as we could get to Boguslav.

Pines and oaks hugged a split-level four-bedroom structure. A wooden patio overhung the backyard, extending into the woods. Deer sightings were not uncommon—some even coming close enough for us to make out their spotted flanks and twitching ears. Eventually one fawn became the scapegoat for Joshua's forced separation from his pacifier. "Sorry, Joshie, the deer mommy took it to give to her baby," we said to him. He must have believed that the baby deer needed it more than he did, because he did not make a fuss.

This little community, with its pool and clubhouse in one direction and a lake in the other, was a lush oasis painted a lazy green. The neighboring houses were spaced well apart to allow for privacy so that the only time you might really become aware of them was while driving at night in pitch darkness, with just your high beams on and the warm glow emanating from the houses marking the way.

Josh was only two months old, so he could get away with sleeping in a bassinet next to us. A playpen served as Emma's bed. The days were comfortably languid—no deadlines to meet, other than the scheduled feedings of the kids, which between Joshua's nursing and Emma's drip, felt like I was running a ludicrous catering service. I was never alone, though. My grandmother, Baba Manya, as we called her; her oldest daughter, my aunt Alla; and Holly spent the entire month with us, while my parents and Tolya took turns staying a week at a time. Boring it was not, especially when my father was around.

I always marveled at my father's exuberance and lust for life, at his humorous way of seeing the world, no matter how chaotic or catastrophic. He always managed to find a joke, remembered or made up, to leaven any situation. A week around his energy was exactly what my sanity needed. I could imagine the grandfather he would evolve into once the kids were old enough to appreciate his antics and largesse. They would adore him, look for him to clown around with, be fed by him (he is a creative cook), share a joke with him. If experience was any indication, he would morph into the greatest grandfather (Deda Fedya—Grandpa Fedya), as he was the greatest father to me.

When I was a child, my father was my best playmate, maybe because he was young, maybe because he was young at heart, maybe because he grew up without a father. My earliest, fondest memories had him in them. Here are some of them: I'm playing bingo or checkers or cards with him on the floor of my bedroom. Here is me on a homemade swing fashioned by him—a wooden plank for the seat and ropes suspended from the ceiling of our fifth-floor balcony—being pushed from behind and swung from one end to the other. "Hold on tight," he would say with his serious voice as I'd laugh and squeal in excitement and trepidation. Anything for a laugh. It was as if the admiration and love he sought trumped sometimes even the notion of safety and reason. Still, I always felt safe, protected, and entertained in his company.

My most endearing memory is of us burning pictures and words into our balcony's wooden railing. My father would pull out the magnifying glass on a sunny day and, by positioning it just so, catch the right angle of the bright midday sun, then stand statue-still until we'd see the smoke rise miraculously from the wooden surface—revealing underneath the brown mark of what would eventually prove to be the first letter of my name or a drawing of a star. As an adult, I would trace this very memory to my obsession with the smell of a wood-burning fireplace, scouting vacation rentals for just such an amenity, even asking Tolya to burn wood chips that he'd purchase at Home Depot so that the scent of a quaint chalet in the mountains of Switzerland's town of Zermatt would waft through the apartment in winter.

Weekends were especially crazy, in that good way, when everyone would descend on the house. Most meals would be served and eaten outside on the deck, at the ragged wooden table, weather permitting. It was beautiful in its simplicity— sharing of meals, stories, laughter. "Four generations here, you realize?" my father would announce ceremoniously over the dinner table. As the kids got older, his toasts would evolve into "If wouldn't be me, wouldn't be you." Everyone would laugh—less at his braggarts and more at his broken English.

"This is what I love—family," my mother would gush. "Everyone together, just like in the Soviet Union with Baba Manya's sisters; her mother, Baba Emma; Deda Chaim. We always got together this way. We had so much fun then." Everyone would nod in agreement. "Did I ever tell you about how Baba Manya took care of the family during the war?" she would continue.

"Yes, Mama, you told us, but I want to hear it again," I responded, knowing full well that she was looking for permission to retell the tale; we were a storytelling family, after all. And so, my mother, with pride in her voice and tears in her eyes would relive her mother's heroic exploits.

When the Second World War broke out in Eastern Europe, my grandmother Manya, with her two younger sisters and her mother, were evacuated from Boguslav and relocated in Kazakhstan until the war's end. Her father, my great grandfather Chaim, was called to fight. During this, perhaps in response to the stress, her mother, Baba Emma, fell mysteriously ill and was bedridden, unable to walk. Baba Manya, who was only thirteen at the time, went to work at a construction site carrying bricks. She used the meager pay from this labor to put food on the table and pull everyone through the war. Shortly after the war ended, at eighteen years of age, Baba Manya was married off to my grandfather Yefim, a man fourteen years her senior, whose wife and two young sons were killed by the Nazis. I would wait patiently for my favorite part, the big finale: at forty-four years of age, Baba Emma gave birth to her fourth daughter, Raya, just a few months after her daughter Manya delivered her first child, Alla. "Baba Emma didn't have breast milk to feed Rayachka, so Baba Manya nursed her sister Raya while nursing her own child." My mother exhaled triumphantly as she finished.

This was the family thread I was learning that connected us: a web of love, enriched by Emma's and Joshua's appearance.

Holly was there as well, helping change Emma's diaper. She even learned how to G-tube feed her (which no one except her and my father were brave enough to do). "I used to change your diapers not long ago," I'd tell her while changing Emma's.

"I know," she would say, smiling. "You did a lot for me, and you don't let me forget it," she would say, half joking. I recalled the toast eight-year-old Holly made at our wedding, eagerly talking into the camera: "I want to wish Tolya and Diana lots of happiness and lots of babies so I can be their aunt." Her wish came true.

The Poconos were good for everyone, as we anticipated. Emma was thriving. She seemed happy—her smiles easily elicited.

My father, who lived to make people laugh, took full advantage of his mustache to tickle Emma's belly with it. She wriggled—as much as her low muscle tone and the extra weight, caused by the steroids administered to her while in the hospital, would allow—and laughed her silent laugh. For as long as I could remember, my father had sported his signature mustache to hide his fabled almost nonexistent upper lip. Even after mustaches went out of style with the Village People, in the seventies, his loyalty to hiding his lip remained. I had to admit, it was aesthetically a smart move. The one time he surprised us by shaving it off, we immediately encouraged him to grow it back out.

The Poconos heralded many firsts; the most lasting and wondrous was Emma's laugh. The first time we witnessed it, she was sitting on the patio in her high chair when my father decided to play with her by vigorously shaking an orange toy maraca in front of her face. "Look, Emma." *Shake, shake, shake*. The next thing I saw astounded me. Emma's face broke into an enormous smile; her full cotton cheeks completely swallowed her eyes as drool danced on her lips. If you didn't know any better, her expression could easily be mistaken for pain or crying. Her body shook with such force that when she was done, she fell slack, like a marionette whose strings were unexpectedly released. "Oh my god," I exclaimed, directing everyone's attention on her. "Look at her face. Have you ever seen anything like this?" Emma's laugh was an exhibition of pure, unmitigated joy. It was lung emptying, tremendous—and utterly silent. *This girl*, I thought to myself, *is something else*. From that day forward, I would steal every opportunity to make her laugh.

The last week in the Poconos brought with it a harbinger of what we could expect from life with Emma. One morning just as we were about to get her up for her feeding, I reached for the button to find it very loose and partially dislodged; one slight tug, and it came completely out. We'd never seen it outside her body, nor did we have with us a spare replacement. This was the button Emma returned to us from Pennsylvania with. It must have been left there too long, because the balloon that anchored the button was deflated, and the 5 ccs of water inside was swampy brown. The water must have slowly seeped out over time, making it easy for Emma's exploring hands to extract it almost fully.

"Tolya, oh my god, come look!" I yelled into the other room, hearing the panic in my voice. He ran in and looked down at her belly and then at me holding the button in the palm of my hand like a peace offering.

"Oh shit. What the hell?"

"It came loose. She must have pulled at it," I said.

"What do we do?"

"We have to go to the hospital. Maybe they can replace it." I didn't really believe it, even as I was saying it, but had no other answers.

The Scranton hospital emergency room was virtually empty. It looked like a ghost town, and when they took us in, they treated Emma as if she was their first special-needs patient, which I suspected she was. "I'm afraid we don't have a replacement device like that," the emergency room doctor said, pointing to the button. Let me consult about this and see what we can do," he continued somewhat dejectedly. "Is she able to eat by mouth at all?"

"No," I said.

The doctor returned after what seemed like eons, informing us that the only thing they could do was insert a temporary tube until the button was available. Emma was taken away and returned with an egregious-looking foot-long rubber tube that may have been a catheter. It slightly resembled the original tube that was first inserted after her G-tube surgery, but this one looked larger, more offensive. Seeing it again felt like we were moving backward. "Ugh, this thing again," Tolya said. "I thought we were done with it."

"Two steps forward, one step back," I said. This would become our mantra that we'd fall back on many times over.

Country life was nurturing and had its benefits, but it was not medically sustainable. Though we welcomed the suspension of reality, the city was where Emma would best thrive.

CHAPTER 14

THE LESSONS I WAS LEARNING about control and letting go continued as Emma's care became more layered.

By the time her replacement button arrived, the area of the skin around the rubber "feeding" tube began to get red and irritated looking. Dr. L concluded that Emma developed a latex allergy, which we learned was not uncommon for people who had undergone numerous medical procedures or surgeries like Emma had. Hence, all future medical questionnaires prior to surgeries or seeing new specialists would have two words written in under the allergy category: latex and Tobramycin.

We became regulars at North Shore Hospital's Gastroenterology Clinic. Our first order of business was to return the button to its proper place—Emma's belly. It would be our one and only lesson, given to us by the physician's assistant, and we would repeat the procedure every three to four months. But the first time left me shaken. "Go ahead and insert it," the PA instructed me in a casual voice, as if asking me to perform a benign task, routine in nature. With a trembling hand, I placed the stem of the button to the opening in Emma's belly and gently pushed.

"It's not going in," I said, looking up at the PA. I heard Tolya's didactic words in my head, "Never force anything," whenever I'd fumble with something I was trying to fix or make work. *Words to live by*, I thought, *in more ways than one.*

"You can try dabbing a little Vaseline around the opening or wetting the stem with water," the PA continued patiently. I did as I was told and returned once more to the gaping, raw orifice that now seemed to be screaming at me, like an angry mouth being force fed. Emma was vacantly staring at the ceiling above her, oblivious to the goings on.

"I'm sorry, baby," I said as I pushed the stem in with greater force—too much force for my liking. It felt like I was stabbing her, and she registered discomfort by wriggling and letting out a little moan. "Is it going to be this difficult every time?" I asked. The PA assured me that it wouldn't, that Emma was probably more sensitive this time because of the redness and irritation of the area. I got a flash memory of a hot needle piercing the softness of my earlobe, imagining the PA saying that it will be like changing an earring. New normal.

Back home with a brand-new button and new knowledge, we breathed a sigh of relief and carried on—until the next wave hit. One night, I was startled awake by what sounded like a loud snore thundering through the darkness. Preparing to rib Tolya awake—assuming him the culprit—I heard it again, but this time I realized the frightening sound was coming from the direction of Emma's crib: a guttural, throaty, choking sound that reminded me of my Jewish relatives trying to pronounce Chanukah—in that phlegmy, throat-clearing way. "Tolya, wake up," I said, shaking him out of his dead-man's sleep.

"What?" he mumbled.

"Listen."

The sound came again as if on cue: "Kheeegh." I leapt out of bed and took the three strides that delivered me to Emma's cribside. Tolya was beside me as we peered down, forcing our eyes to adjust to the dark with only the aid of the moonlight caressing the room. I turned on the small lamp on Emma's dresser to find her wide awake, the nasal cannula pulled off her face and in her mouth as she chewed on it happily. Again, the disturbing sound came from her throat.

"What the hell?" Tolya said, sounding alarmed.

"I don't know, but we have to go to the emergency room. This sounds serious." Though to look at Emma, you wouldn't really think anything wrong, by her demeanor. I remembered what the pediatrician said about deciding when to intervene with medication—for instance, in the case of a fever or pain. The child's temperament should dictate whether to take action or allow the body to try to fight it. I looked for any indication of pain or discomfort in Emma's demeanor, but she was her happy, silly self, especially now that she had our middle-of-the-night attention. I dialed my parents, quickly relayed the information, and asked them to come over to be with Joshua while we flew to the emergency room.

Once in LIJ's emergency room, things happened quickly. Emma's diagnosis got her seen immediately. It also helped things along to have the doctor hear her make these sporadic, disturbing sounds: "Kheeegh." She was wheeled away and brought back some twenty minutes later. They discovered the cause for her bizarre behavior, and our angst.

The doctor invited us to sit down. He extended his hand. In it was a piece of gauze, on which lay what we immediately recognized as one of the two pieces of medical tape that we used to secure Emma's nasal cannula to her cheeks. "Does this look familiar?" the doctor asked. "We found this in the back of her throat. The sound she was making was probably her trying to cough it up." I didn't know whether to laugh or cry. I mean, how do people usually react in these situations? The problem was that I didn't know any other people that faced these types of situations. Relief washed over me as I realized that we'd circumvented something with a decidedly worse outcome. I exhaled, tuning in to my instincts that were telling me all was okay.

We explained to the doctor what we understood to have happened—that she removed the cannula and began chewing on it, which is how the tape got into her mouth. I think he chuckled with us and didn't call Child Protective Services, as I feared for an instant he might. We collected our baby and went home.

"Well, that was interesting," Tolya said once we were in our bed again. The sky was just starting to lighten, inviting in the day.

"It's not going to be boring with this girl, that's for sure," I said. "What is that called, trial by fire?"

"Whatever it is, we're in the middle of it."

Emma was an enigma—a puzzle to be put together. Some days when we found ourselves in the vortex of a new medical crisis, it felt like we were peeling away her onion-like layers to reveal another layer, and crying.

Then there was the issue with her eyes. Aside from the "lazy eye," for which the ophthalmologist prescribed an eye patch that made her look like an adorable pirate, there was the business of the blocked tear ducts. Every morning before getting Emma out of bed, we would find her eyes glued shut by thick, yellow, hardened crusty discharge that buried her lashes and sealed the world out. *See no evil*, I thought, just like one of the three wise monkeys that made up the stone statue sitting on my living room shelf. Hands covering ears, eyes, and mouth—they represented the maxim "Hear no evil, see no evil, speak no evil." I told myself I would make sure Emma never saw or heard evil toward her as I methodically wiped the warm water-soaked cotton balls from the outer to the inner corner of her eyes. It would take many swipes—to Emma's annoyance—and though the gunk would be gone, it would leave her eyes red and irritated.

"Usually, blocked tear ducts resolve on their own by the child's first birthday." We were sitting in the ophthalmologist office, Emma on my lap, after he'd examined her. "But in this case, with the chronic infections caused by the blockage and because the antibiotic drops have proven to be only a Band-Aid, I would recommend surgical correction." *Ugh, again*, I thought. *This poor girl.* "The procedure is called "probing," and it would permanently open up the ducts so that tears can properly drain through the nose." *Probing*, I thought. *What an apropos description of this little girl's life thus far.* "Has Emma been under anesthesia before?" was the next ludicrous question. I paused and brought my arms tighter around her.

"Yes. Many times."

Winthrop University Hospital—where Emma underwent the probing procedure—was a small medical facility when compared to behemoths like LIJ and North Shore, with which we were more familiar. Pre-surgical testing, which took place two weeks prior to the procedure, would require Emma's now even pudgier, pillowy arms to be poked for veins, which were buried so deep under flesh and fat that a second nurse would have to be called in to mine for blood when the first one failed. I refused their request to hold Emma's arm down, instead choosing to sing to her, as a distraction, while she squirmed and moaned under the invasive, blind searching pain of the needle. I never wanted Emma to connect my presence with pain but the opposite—comfort and safety. But also, I couldn't stand by and witness her suffering.

Medical professionals, upon seeing Emma's limitations, would address me with excessive gentleness, as if I had to be fragile and sensitive to be raising a special-needs child. I knew they were being sympathetic, and I appreciated it. Sometimes I'd see something bordering on admiration, and I'd appreciate that even more. Often, just like Dr. L, they'd ask if I was in the medical field.

Emma was wheeled out of the operating room after the probing, with the inner corners of her eyes red and bloody.

Dried blood marked the site of the intrusion. "I'm so sorry, baby," I said, leaning in to touch my lips to her forehead—an apologetic gesture for the necessary evil we were putting her through. She let out a groggy moan. I would be apologizing to her often in future years, and even though her tear ducts were opened so that her tears would flow freely, they never did. We never once witnessed that trace of liquid sadness, and that was fine by me.

Thus began the juggling act of our family life.

In one of my readings I serendipitously came across writing by Emily Perl Kingsley, author and parent of a child with a disability. "Welcome to Holland" gorgeously detailed the experience of raising a special-needs child.

In the poem, Kingsley uses a metaphor of excitement for a vacation to Italy, which she equates to the typical giving birth and raising a child experience. This first becomes a disappointment when the plane lands instead in Holland. But as she looks around, she notes that:

> *The important thing is that they haven't taken you to a horrible, disgusting, filthy place, full of pestilence, famine and disease. It's just a different place.*
>
> *So, you must go out and buy new guide books. And you must learn a whole new language. And you will meet a whole new group of people you would never have met.*

Unlike flashy and fast-paced Italy, Holland (which is supposed to represent life with a special-needs child) has its own beauty of windmills and tulips and Rembrandts.

> *But everyone you know is busy coming and going from Italy . . . and they're all bragging about what a wonderful time they had there. And for the rest of*

your life, you will say "Yes, that's where I was sup-
posed to go. That's what I had planned."

She concludes by saying that the pain from the loss of
that dream will never go away:

But . . . if you spend your life mourning the fact
that you didn't get to Italy, you may never be free
to enjoy the very special, the very lovely things . . .
about Holland.

I read this piece to Tolya through tear-blurred eyes. "It's
a great analogy," he said when I was finished.

"I guess we could consider ourselves one of the lucky
ones," I said. "We get to have a foot in each country." Sometimes I meant it, felt lucky. Other times I didn't. We were
always straddling the reality of both.

CHAPTER 15

I HELD THE PHONE PRESSED tightly to my ear as I tried to process what Emma's new day nurse was telling me through panicked breaths. I should have known better than to leave the nurse on her first day on the job, but I couldn't imagine anything going wrong. My blind trust would soon turn to vigilant hovering with each new caregiver allowed into our home. This nurse proceeded to tell me that in the process of laying Emma back into her crib, belly down, she must have gotten too close to the railing, causing the G-tube to be pulled clean out of her stomach. I flew home to find Emma in her crib, on her back, with a gaping hole where the button would normally be and digested curdled yellow formula spilling from the opening. I sent the nurse home and called the nursing agency to find us a new one.

People began showing up in our home. Someone who identified herself as a service coordinator from an agency called SKIP of NY [Sick Kids (Need) Involved People] walked us through the process of getting Emma evaluated for services—physical therapy, occupational therapy, speech/feeding therapy, special instruction. Evaluators with these specialties examined Emma—handled her this way and that, asked me questions, tested her abilities, wrote their reports with recommendations. This was the world of Early Intervention that offered itself to us, to Emma, because she needed the help, was entitled to it.

At the time, I didn't process this—didn't have a name for the program—but merely felt immensely grateful that good people, strangers, were coming to work with Emma and with us as her caregivers, sometimes as often as three times a week for half-hour sessions, so that Emma could reach her maximum potential, whatever that would mean.

In a meeting in a conference room in a building in Jamaica, Queens—convened to determine the appropriate services for Emma—a "city official" first asked us open-ended questions, such as "What are your concerns and priorities for Emma?" which returned blank stares from us, unlike the ones from Emma, who reclined contentedly in her stroller chewing on her sleeve. Then the official asked more specific questions: "Is she rolling, reaching, eating anything by mouth, making eye contact?" To most of these, the answer was no, which made me feel increasingly sad and scared at the same time. But we pushed forward, accepting of our situation, accepting of the help, and "thank you," "thank you," "thank you" was all we could say in return.

This was a country, I realized, (unlike my "mother country," which treated everyone the same regardless of special need) that lived up to its promise to take in "the tired, the poor, the huddled masses . . . ," and once you were safely under her wings, she protected her weak, disenfranchised, less-than-abled citizens, like a mother goose shelters her young. This was a country that had government agencies like the Office for Persons with Developmental Disabilities, that understood the importance of caring for its disabled people. This was a country that passed laws like the Individuals with Disabilities Education Act (IDEA), ensuring that every child, regardless of disability or delay, had access to an education. This was a country that qualified Emma for the Medicaid Waiver program, which provided services to people who would otherwise be in an institution, nursing home, or hospital so that they could receive long-term care in the home.

"Can you believe this?" I kept asking Tolya. "Can you believe how lucky we are? How lucky Emma is?" It was ironic to think of Emma as lucky, I realized, but I understood deeply that if life kicked you sideways and someone stopped to pick you up where you fell, you were lucky.

Not really knowing what to expect but ready and anxious to learn, I opened the door to the therapists. The first occupational therapist, who was charged with working on Emma's fine motor skills—the way she used her hands—came three times a week for thirty-minute sessions. Each visit she'd sit on the carpeted floor, placing Emma on her back in front of her, and open her fisted hands with two-handed strokes, the entire time carrying on an animated conversation with me about what I suspected was her real passion—furniture refurbishment. I sat on the beanbag chair next to them and feigned interest, nodding and making the polite obligatory sounds of active listening, the whole time wondering when she would direct her full attention on Emma.

Never did she explain what she was doing, and I did not know enough at the time to ask the appropriate questions. As much as I enjoyed interior design and could get lost in conversations about furniture styles and arrangement, I understood that her enthusiasm in this case was misplaced and that the time was not being used wisely and for the right purpose. I agonized over the decision to have her replaced, always overly sensitive about not hurting people's feelings, but in the end, I concluded that I needed to do what was best for Emma. I was her voice, and this woman had to go.

On the other hand, Lisa, the physical therapist, was entirely different. She came in carrying a round orange therapy ball about two feet in diameter, on which she would place Emma. Sometimes Emma would find herself on her back on it, being encouraged to engage her abdominal muscles so that she could sit up. Other times she'd be on her belly being gently rolled back and forth while Lisa's hands rested safely on her back and legs, holding her in place. This movement would force Emma to elevate her head and chest. On a good strong day, Emma would smile through the exercise; on a difficult one, she would moan in protest. Always, there was accompanying drool that escaped her parted lips and protruding tongue and, when she was on her belly, trickled down to the floor below. Lisa would end up dedicating ten years of her professional life to Emma. She would see Emma through orthotics (foot braces), surgeries, post-surgical care and healing, standing and walking equipment. Though she didn't object much when Lisa handled her, Emma was not excited to see her. Lisa made her work.

Then there was the first speech/feeding therapist. As great as she was, her name escapes me. I'll call her Sunny because that's the impression she left each time she came. Young and energetic—probably fresh out of school—Sunny brought music and exuberance to every session. Emma adored her. Seated in her adaptive wooden Rifton chair with a padded back and a removable tray, Emma would smile a welcoming Chicklets-for-teeth grin and prepare to be sung to. Because part of the goal was to get Emma to accept more food by mouth, Sunny would use something called a Nuk brush, a plastic stick with bristles on the end, to stimulate her oral motor area—lips, tongue, cheeks—for chewing purposes. That, Emma was not having. She hated having anything in her mouth unless it was cloth, like her sleeves or her bib. Over time, an aversion to anything resembling food settled in, and our disappointment grew. We noticed that in the process of bottle and spoon feedings, Emma developed a disturbing rattling sound in her chest each time she inhaled. That worried me.

"Why does she chew so aggressively on her bib and shirt but refuses food?" I asked Sunny one day.

"Well, probably because she's so deprived by not eating by mouth that she craves the oral stimulation and satisfaction of chewing. A bib is safe." She explained that the rattling was also worrisome to her and suggested we have Emma undergo a barium swallow study, which would show us what was happening to the food that Emma ingested, to rule out aspiration. I made a mental note to ask Dr. L for a referral for the test. In the meantime, Sunny sang the "Open Shut Them" song: "Open shut them, open shut them," she would belt out with accompanying gestures—both of her palms facing Emma as she opened and closed her hands to the words.

"Give a little clap, clap, clap . . .

"Open shut them, open shut them, put them in your lap, lap, lap," she sang as she placed her hands on her lap.

"Creep them, creep them, slowly creep them, right up to your chin, chin, chin." Sunny walked her fingers up Emma's arm, to her shoulders.

"Open up your little mouth, but . . . do not let them in, in, in." The finale had Emma folded in half, laughing silently at Sunny's pretend effort to put something in her mouth. It was wondrous to see Emma's reaction to the music and her seeming understanding of the nuanced humor.

The barium swallow study took place at North Shore Hospital and involved Emma accepting food with barium sulfate, a metallic compound that shows up on X-rays, mixed in. I warned the test administrator that it would be difficult to get food into Emma's mouth, that she would not readily open, and sure enough, she didn't make a liar of me. I held her in my lap, but every time I brought the nipple of the baby bottle to her mouth, she would immediately purse her lips and bring them tighter together. Finally, the administrator suggested that we try to sneak a small medicine syringe filled with formula into the side of her mouth. This worked, but not effortlessly. "She's a determined little girl," the woman pronounced with an admiring smile.

"That she is," I agreed.

The X-ray revealed that Emma was "pooling" liquids in the back of her throat, meaning that she wasn't actively swallowing but letting liquid food accumulate at the opening to her esophagus and airways. Without the ability to direct the liquid in the right direction—the esophagus—she ran the risk of having the formula passively enter her lungs, thereby aspirating. This may have been the reason her lungs sounded the way they did. There was a likelihood she was silently aspirating the whole time we were giving her formula by mouth.

"Does this mean we can't try and feed her by mouth anymore?" I asked.

"You may, but I would advise you eliminate liquids and stick with solids, like purees," the GI doctor said. "The thickness of the purees will give her time to process the food and give her more control of where it goes. Liquids move too quickly—are less safe." *Another setback*, I thought as I left the hospital.

It was hard to hide my disappointment from Sunny as I relayed to her the results of the test and the new feeding protocol. But she wasn't discouraged. She continued to sing her songs and show me how to sneak in little spoonfuls of purees while Emma laughed and was distracted. Still, even if the first half of the plastic spoon made it past her lips, it would be stopped dead in its tracks by her deadly clamp of a bite. With a dollop of food inside, and her obvious victory, Emma would laugh in response to my feigned-frustrated, playful outbursts of "Hooliganistaya, devochka paganistaya," which loosely translated into "naughty hooligan of a girl." She loved it, because she recognized it and because it rhymed.

"Don't call her a naughty girl," Tolya would protest in the beginning. But I would shut him down with my defense:

"It's not like I'm calling her an insulting name that she would understand. As far as she's concerned, we're playing, and as far as I'm concerned, it's a term of endearment, and she loves it because she laughs, and it makes her happy so it makes me happy, so it can't be bad."

"All right, all right. Point taken."

She was teaching. I was learning her particular brand of genius.

Lisa taught us how to do "chest PT" on Emma, to loosen the phlegm in her chest and help her bring it up—in theory. This never seemed to work though. No matter how much we cupped our hands and vigorously tapped her back with alternating motions, nothing ever emerged from her lungs. Her cough was deemed "unproductive." Daily use of the nebulizer treatments, to treat "asthma-like" symptoms, didn't seem to make a difference. This "breathing therapy," which sent a misty vapor of medicine for her to inhale through a tube that we held in front of her face, just made her smile, laugh a congested laugh, and continue about her business.

Sometimes, I wondered what she thought of everyone always milling around her like worker bees while she "chilled" doing whatever she was doing, or not doing. She must have found the scene hilarious; so many things made her laugh. Years later I would find a picture of her next to two-month-old Joshua, both lying on their backs in the crib. In the photo, Joshua is crying hysterically, his face red with the exertion, while Emma lies alongside him, hysterical as well, but with laughter. Even this she found funny. Happiness came so easily to her.

The truth was that if nothing was bothering her physically, Emma was the most content, delightful little girl. If you devoted the slightest bit of attention to her, she was your best friend. I think she learned to believe that people were her playthings and were there solely for her entertainment and pleasure. No one could expect to be allowed to sit idly by and not sing, clap, do hand games, or roll around on the floor in rough play with her. If you sat close and opposite her, she would place her hands around yours and force them together—instructing you to clap for her and yell, "Hurray, hurray for Emma"—because there was never a bad time to receive praise through applause. And if you were going to sit there, you might as well make yourself useful.

Because Emma was nonverbal, Sunny taught her some basic signs like "give me," "more," and "all done." If she wanted you to repeat whatever song you'd just finished singing, she would sign "more" by tapping her fists together. Activities or songs that she loved could expect to be repeated dozens of times, until one of us, usually the adult, got tired and excused themselves away.

The "all done" sign was sometimes used correctly when something was being done to her that she wasn't keen on, like a new person in her space trying to carefully maneuver the button so that she could be fed. Before she learned to sign, however, in the very beginning, Emma would scratch the interloper's hand or arm or leg with such intensity that she would shake with the intended effort of delivering pain—sinking her nails into exposed skin. I marveled at the notion that she knew to scratch only bare skin—never where clothing covered the extremities. Once I even noticed her reach up a nurse's pant leg so that she could have direct nail-on-skin contact. It was like she knew instinctively the most effective way of communicating her needs, and she was not to be misunderstood. The signs were all well and good, I could imagine her thinking, but a swift draw of blood from an untrimmed fingernail—now that delivered the message much more expediently and clearly.

My mother liked to tell the story of when I was two and a precociously early talker in Soviet Ukraine; the daycare teacher once remarked that "If not for Diana, I'd have no one to talk to all day." I learned early on that words carried heft and power. I worried about Emma not being able to speak, to tell me if someone was hurting her. Signs could only take you so far.

Still, she was teaching us her language. Eschewing conventional verbal communication because it was not at her disposal, Emma went for the subtle or not so subtle nonverbal exchange. A scratch, a bite, a push, though not socially acceptable in most circles, was forgiven Emma. How could we be mad at her? She didn't know any better—resorting to elemental means.

There was a freedom to this. She didn't have to bother with editing herself before she responded to words or actions, like I did—forever censoring myself, sensitive to the propriety and diplomacy of the spoken word; *don't offend, don't alienate*. I edited myself greatly and frequently. Typically, the expletives imploded in my head so that only I heard them. And the emotions that followed the triggering situation, and my immediate suppression of speech, left me feeling frustrated and cowardly. Worrying about how my words would be received—and in turn, how I'd be perceived—was exhausting.

Emma's arsenal of defenses, however, was limited; we knew that. And so by extension, my authority was limited as well. I couldn't punish her. She was already punished by life, I believed. When I'd scold, saying, "No, Emma! No biting (or scratching)," she would crack up at the apparent absurdity of the statement, as if she recognized our pathetic efforts at limit setting for what they were—unenforceable and therefore laughable.

CABIN FEVER BEGAN TO CREEP IN. Joshua was five months old and Emma had only been back six months, but I felt the walls closing in on me. My breast milk was slowly drying up, even though I was still pumping and nursing, and I conveniently took this as a timely green light to extricate myself from "full-immersion motherhood." The need to "move" was playing its old familiar song, and I craved a change of scenery.

"I can't be home like this much longer," I told Tolya one night after putting the kids to bed. "I need to go back to work, if even part time. I need to talk to grown-ups." As soon as those words occupied the room, I sensed the familiar cloak of guilt settling on my shoulders. I mean, hadn't I wanted this, fought for it in life's most unlikely of circumstances? I recalled my mother's words: "Your grandfather Yefim used to say to me 'of course it's easier to go to work than to stay at home and raise a child' when he saw me running out the door." I told myself I wasn't abandoning them—merely needed to feel a bit more fulfilled, which the outside world promised to deliver better than the day-to-day of wiping baby butts, nursing, singing the same repertoire of songs on repeat, and speaking in a newly exaggerated, high-pitched voice as if the kids were hard of hearing.

"Okay," Tolya said. "Let's talk about it. Would you go back to social work, do counseling again?"

"Ha! Me? Counsel people now? I'm so messed up *I* need counseling. I'm in no position to be helpful. I may do more damage than good, and my clients are suffering enough," I said with a chuckle.

"All right, I get it." He paused, then continued, "Actually, I've been thinking about it, and I think you should try real estate."

"What? What are you talking about?" I did not anticipate this answer. "Why would I do that? I'm a social worker. What do I know about real estate other than that we own our one-bedroom apartment and it's a co-op with volunteer board members who like to play God?"

Tolya explained that it was a good time to take advantage of a rising real-estate market and reminded me that I could have access to clients' décor styles, which he knew I loved.

He was right. Interior design had been a stealth passion of mine since we married. On our honeymoon to Spain, I fell in love with a Kandinsky-looking wool rug that I'd glimpsed in a window display of a furniture store in Madrid. I pleaded with Tolya to buy it for me. He thought I was crazy.

"We have the same rugs in New York for half the price," he insisted. "Not only can we not afford it, but do you realize how difficult it'll be to travel back with it?"

A few well-measured newlywed tears later, I had my rug. Though practical and level-headed, Tolya was sensitive to my hurt and would surrender to my sometimes-irrational whims to keep my sadness at bay. Which is why he arranged to have the store send the rug to Barcelona, where our return flight was from. Years later he would revel in retelling the ludicrous story of how the airline initially lost our rug. "What did it look like?" the person at the baggage claim office wanted to know. "Like a missile!" Tolya exclaimed, frustrated. "How do you lose a massive rug?"

I considered my husband. Just when I thought I knew everything about this man, whom I'd known for more than a decade, he managed to often surprise me with his expansive heart and quiet intelligence. He listened actively and offered up answers I wanted to hear: Miss Holly? Bring her to live with us. Need to get out of the house? Go out and sell apartments. Underneath the enviable outer equanimity of character was a kind, deeply sensitive man who worked hard to meet my emotional needs but also managed to nurture his own. In supporting me in the decision to give Emma away, he was giving me what I needed, while visiting her behind my back because he missed her was giving himself what he needed.

It's why I fell in love with him the first night we took a walk around the block together and he reached for my hand. *He's a good guy*, I thought. My mother would echo these sentiments throughout the years—often a recipient of his kindness and almost reverent respect. "He is such a good man, Diana. You are very lucky."

"What about him?" I'd joke in protest. "Isn't he lucky to have me?"

"You're both lucky," she'd say, "but he's nice. You—not always."

I couldn't disagree with that. She was right. I could be critical, argumentative, and judgmental more times than I'd like to admit. It was a character flaw. Tolya, on the other hand, never had a bad word to say about anybody, nor did he care what others thought of him. How I wished I could live like that. He was a "good boychik."

In a matter of months, I'd completed the real-estate course and went to work at a local agency that specialized in co-op sales. This proved to be the perfect gig for me. Most showings were walking distance from where we lived. I would make sure to schedule appointments in the evenings after Tolya's return from work or ask my parents to stay with the kids if he couldn't replace me, and run out. Though easy for me, it wasn't sustainable for long. My parents still had day jobs, and Tolya's work often kept him overtime, troubleshooting or meeting deadlines.

"We need more help," Tolya said. This prompted us to look for a babysitter for Joshua.

Josh and Emma were, for all intents and purposes, like twins, with parallel needs, developmentally still equal. Josh at six months was getting the hang of sitting independently, as was Emma at nineteen months with pillow support. They were physically the same size and weight, but that's where the similarities ended and Josh began to surpass his sister in important motor milestones. He was rolling; Emma was not. He was propping up on extended arms when on his belly and finding his crawling legs. Emma hated belly time—didn't have the strength to elevate and turn her head even to clear her airways. Josh was starting to hold his bottle; Emma no longer had a bottle to hold.

The first several months were arguably the most trying. With both kids still one-hundred-percent dependent on us and Emma's care more layered and complicated, the mere thought of traveling outside with them for a simple walk in the neighborhood brought on planning anxiety and could not be undertaken by one; it required recruitment and support of at least one other able-bodied individual. One of us would fill the basket of the tandem double stroller, which occupied almost the entire foyer area, with diapers, wipes, sanitary napkins for Emma's vesicostomy opening, a bottle for Josh, and a feeding bag for Emma with all its accessories: Mickey button, syringe, and cans of Pediasure. The portable oxygen tank with attached nasal cannula also found its way into the oversized basket. We found ourselves spending great pockets of time on the floor, dressing and undressing the little people left in our charge. Regardless of indoor temperature, these acts left us sweating and out of breath.

On outings, Emma occupied the back of the stroller to be closer to the oxygen tank. We also kept her strategically out of the view of curious strangers, who would invariably stop to gush at "the twins." When she'd fall asleep, we'd lower her seat and put her nasal cannula on, and I would make every effort to not stop for passerby admiration. I wasn't ashamed—I was avoiding the questions cloaked in concern and the explanations that would invariably ensue. I didn't want *that* kind of attention and feared pitying glances. Quiet guilt resided in the shadows of my brain as I felt Emma's back-of-the-stroller placement, weirdly echoing banishment to the "back of the bus." I had issues to reconcile; there was no denying it.

But when Emma was awake and upright, my heart swelled with pride at the words "Such a pretty girl. Look at that hair."

Do they not see it? I would think. *Do they not see her difference, her unfocused gaze, her tongue protruding ever so slightly past her lips?* I would laser focus on their expressions, trying to gauge the moment of recognition. But it never came. Why did I care so much? Why did I ascribe so much power to others' opinions? These were the questions that gnawed at my heart and chiseled away my own weak foundation.

MEANWHILE EMMA WAS GOING THROUGH nurses like diapers. Each one worse than the last. They left a memorable trail of incompetence. Then, one day, Oksana—Emma's fifth nurse—came in like a gust of summer wind, then moved around our apartment like a benevolent hurricane that put things together rather than tearing them apart. An immigrant from Uzbekistan, a country in Central Asia, she spoke Russian and brought with her vibrant energy that was often exhausting to watch. "Kakaya kookla," what a doll, she said upon first meeting Emma. My heart was awash with gratitude at such endearing words. *She's a keeper*, I thought.

Oksana was all grandiose laughter and levity, and she managed to get things done. We only had to show her once, and she took to the task of caring for Emma as if she were her own. Sharp and confident, Oksana's competence and tenderness took over, and we could breathe a sigh of relief seeing that Emma was in good hands.

With a crew of helpers assembled to allow us to return to a modicum of normalcy in life—therapists, nurses, and babysitters—I joked with Tolya, "We're going to have to install a revolving door." My parents, in-laws, and Holly added to the usual suspects of caregivers, and just like that, we had our little village, in which we had to learn to live.

I was grateful for it but also looked forward to Emma entering school.

CHAPTER 16

THE PSYCHOLOGIST'S OFFICE OCCUPIED the second story of an attached private townhouse. Years later, I would find myself moonlighting for this very agency, conducting bilingual psychosocial evaluations for Russian-speaking students. I would schedule home visits, interview the family, and submit a report—additional income. But on this day, I was a hopeful mom to a special little girl who would soon be starting school. We were here for evaluations that would place Emma in a special-education preschool.

The psychologist was an older woman in her sixties with dry hair and an even drier personality. She sat behind her desk while Emma and I occupied the chair opposite her, and rattled off questions pertaining to what Emma was capable of. "No, she doesn't consistently respond to her name. No, she doesn't usually make eye contact. No, she doesn't understand simple routine commands. No, she's not able to imitate actions." She scribbled my answers on a notepad, barely raising her head to meet my tear-rimmed eyes. Why was this so upsetting to me? I knew all this before—lived with and understood Emma's limitations—so why were this woman's questions tearing at my heart now? Perhaps it was the residual shame of having an imperfect child, or the sadness of having Emma fail a basic test, or the notion of being yanked from my typical autopilot mode and being asked to acknowledge out loud to another Emma's and, by extension, our world.

My maudlin ruminations were abruptly halted when I felt Emma's body go lax in my arms. I looked down in time to see her throw her body back, her eyes roll back into her head, and white foam appear on her lips. She was shaking and writhing in a way I had never seen anyone do.

"Oh my god, oh my god!" I heard my voice pierce the charged air around me. "What's happening?" My head jerked in the direction of the psychologist. "Is she dying?" I was shaking with almost equal force and struggling to keep Emma's tense body from escaping my grip. *I'm losing her*, I thought as my tears spilled over and trailed down my face.

"She's having a seizure," the psychologist said in a flat, non-emotive tone, as if she were stating the obvious. She rose from her desk and came around to where Emma and I were quivering.

"Is this the first time she's had a seizure?" she continued. I nodded, trying to process what she was telling me. *Seizures. Isn't that for people with epilepsy? What is this? Where is this coming from?* my brain screamed.

"I'm going to call the ambulance. She needs to go to the hospital," the psychologist announced in her business-as-usual tone. In the meantime, Emma continued to seize. "What do I do? How do I help her?" I was desperately pleading with this icy stranger who appeared on the opposite emotional spectrum from me.

"There's not much you can do. Just turn her to her side so she doesn't swallow her tongue. She has to ride it out."

Ride it out?

How is a mother supposed to stand by and watch her child being gripped in the jaws of an electric storm that was doing god-knows-what to her already punished body. What is this going to do to the few hard-earned skills that she'd acquired? Will it strip her of what little she already had? These thoughts flashed like lightning bolts in my head. *Ride it out?* Like an ocean wave that was threatening to swallow her up while she flailed and struggled to stay above its surface? I watched as the seizure, true to its meaning, took Emma by force and threw her against the inner walls of herself like an animal in the wild trapping its prey between clenched teeth and thrashing it left and right. And I was expected to watch her "ride it out."

It felt like eternity, but Emma was finally still. She opened her eyes briefly just as I felt her body release and mold into my embrace. As she surrendered to sleep, my body collapsed over hers and I wept.

The EMS arrived and I heard, in the fog of emotion, the psychologist answering the barrage of questions that I had no answers for: "What happened? What did it look like? How long did it last?" I thought I heard "less than a minute" and someone else say "petit mal." This was a familiar term. My beloved high school French lessons immediately returned to me. *Petit is small, mal is bad*, I thought. *However bad this thing is, at least it's small.* Where there's an up, there's a down. Where there's a small, there's a big. Where there's a petit, there's a grand. I'll take the former, the lesser of two evils. I grasped this notion tightly and held on to it for many, many years, until I would learn that, in fact, it was a grand mal.

Tolya arrived at Schneider's Children's Hospital shortly after we got there by ambulance but not before Emma was taken away for testing.

"What happened?" he said, walking tentatively toward me.

"She had a seizure. Out of the blue. I don't know," I said, shaking my head and squeezing my eyes to keep the tears from escaping.

"Where is she now?"

"They're doing a spinal tap," I answered. I didn't elaborate, knowing full well that Tolya wouldn't know what it was, but I needed the gravity of the situation to be firmly dispersed into the ethos between us. Like me, his only familiarity with the term until now would be in relation to the parody band spoofing the style of rock heavy metal, the movie that I was sure he had seen. I had the dubious benefit of learning of the test's real medical use first, and I was dispensing the information slowly and with the gravity it warranted.

"What the hell is that?" Here it comes. He sounded alarmed, and I immediately regretted my decision to prolong the delivery.

"It's a test they do where they take fluid from the spinal cord to test for meningitis as a possible cause for the seizures."

"Meningitis? What is that? Isn't that bad?" Here we were again, volleying new medical words, scrambling for meanings, playing a sick version of Scrabble, like small children learning a new and foreign language.

They kept Emma overnight to run an EEG to track her seizure activity. The next day we received a brand-new diagnosis: "Seizure Disorder." It felt like we were in the business of collecting diagnoses, disorders. Little kids, little problems; big kids, big problems. I was starting to understand this refrain but, in our case, on a whole different fucked-up level. *Poor Emma* was all I could think. I wanted to change places with her.

The only consolation to the new diagnosis was that it replaced an old one; Emma no longer desaturated when she slept, so we could dispense with the oxygen tank, which was a huge win—one less piece of equipment to have to send her to school with. One step forward, one step back.

The following day we met with the hospital's pediatric neurologist to discuss treatment options for the seizures. The neurologist was a "seasoned" doctor but a little too seasoned for my taste. She spoke slowly and with a slight tremor and looked like she was long ready for retirement.

"I'm going to prescribe Phenobarbital, which has been proven successful for younger children, and we'll see how it controls her seizures," she stated.

"Are there side effects we should be aware of?" I asked.

"The only side effect may be lethargy or a processing delay, but it shouldn't make a significant difference for Emma." Was she implying what I thought she was—that because Emma was "slow," it wouldn't matter anyway? Anger rose in my chest, but I couldn't say anything; after all, her medical health trumped everything else, right? That's what I told myself. Keep her healthy and worry about the rest later. I hated having those lesser-of-two-evils choices again, but then beggars can't be choosers. Take what you can get. Set your greed aside, prioritize. These were our options.

SCHOOL: ANOTHER FOOTHOLD IN THE world of normalcy. Emma was turning three and on the cusp of aging out of Early Intervention, graduating from one program and entering another. Early Intervention was housed under the Department of Health and Mental Hygiene, and this new program was the Department of Education, Committee of Preschool Special Education (CPSE). A whole new brigade of evaluators came to our home again, to write their reports.

These were exciting developments. "She'll be in school and get picked up by bus, and she'll be in a group with other kids." I gushed with anticipation of new possibilities for Emma, for us.

We had arranged a visit to Stepping Stones, a CPSE preschool not far from our home and reputed as one of the best programs in Queens. Because of her profound delay, Emma would qualify for a classroom with a high teacher-to-student ratio, to allow for individual attention, and be under the twelve-month program, meaning she could attend school even through the summer.

The tour of the school presented to us a new frontier of special education that we would become intimately familiar with over the years. Though it looked like a small structure on the outside, the interior housed two other levels, below and above the main, and many classrooms filled with students with a wide range of disabilities. There were walkers and talkers; a little girl in a wheelchair offered me, a stranger, her toothy grin and a spectacled glance while we shared the elevator ride. Ramps appeared to dominate the space for the non-ambulatory like our Emma. Everywhere we turned there were teachers and therapists accompanying students traversing this maze from classroom to gym to speech room. Here was a child being helped up the stairs by the physical therapist as she held one hand to the railing and the other in the adult's while the therapist bellowed loud encouragement and praise. "Good job, Katie," we heard her say. "One, two, buckle my shoe, three four, shut the door . . . ," she sang. And everyone was talking, and the air buzzed around my head, the energy dizzying and exhilarating.

Emma became a preschooler. She loved it: the attention, the break in the day from the daily rolling on the floor of our apartment, chewing on her sleeve. There, people talked to her, played with her, sang to her. All. Day. Long. We loved knowing that she had the opportunity to socialize with her peers, like typical preschoolers.

Our very first parent-teacher conference found us meeting with Christine, the head teacher. Christine seemed to get a kick out of Emma.

"Every morning, I come in early to the classroom to set up and prepare for the kids' arrival," she said. "I set out supplies, arts and crafts. Emma comes into class, and as soon as she's positioned by her table, the first thing she does is lift her arms and, with a grand sweep, wipes all the items off the table and onto the floor," she concluded with a chuckle. Tolya and I looked at each other, not exactly sure how to respond. Should we apologize for Emma's rambunctiousness or laugh it off with her teacher, who seemed to be more amused than upset.

"I say 'no, Emma, we don't do that,'" she continued, "but she just laughs." We nod, because we recognize our daughter in her teacher's description.

"Yes, she does that at home as well," I said. "We say 'no' and she just finds it hysterical." I wondered if on some level, she knew that we couldn't do anything to enforce it. Our authority was limited. The same rules almost didn't apply to her. A consequence is not a concept she understood, so we could not put her in a time out for the duration of time equivalent to her age, like the British Supernanny recommended on the television show. When Emma bit, out of frustration, I would try to introduce the idea of compassion and pretend to cry. "Ouch, you hurt Mama," I'd say. Well, this, she was categorically not having, and instead of a compassionate response, I'd get a slap in the face for my troubles. It was as if tears were not acceptable; sadness had no home here. You laugh or get out, or endure Emma's wrath.

"She's a very friendly little girl." Christine continued to describe how Emma loved to swat at the person sitting next to her at circle time and group activities, as a way of getting their attention. "Sometimes she ends up scratching her classmates, intentionally or not."

"Oh no. That's not good," I said, worrying that Emma would earn a reputation as the "problem" child and be separated from her classmates or worse.

"Don't worry, we're handling it." Christine was reassuring. "We just make sure to sit Emma next to little David." She paused. "David wears a helmet."

Now it was my turn to laugh.

MY LAUGHTER WOULD SOON TURN to worry as I turned my attentions to Joshua. He had turned two and started his own little preschool at our local YWHA, the same building that Tolya and I watched get built some twenty years earlier, where he competed on the swim team. Life was coming full circle, with us and our childhood friends raising our kids on our old stomping ground.

Attendance at the Y required that Josh get a physical. I took him to our local Forest Hills pediatric group (different from Emma's group), where he was weighed and measured, and found out to my dismay that he had fallen *off* the growth chart. He was in the fifth percentile in height and below zero in weight. This worried me, so I shared with the pediatrician my concerns.

"We can do a growth hormone test, but seeing as he was a little guy to begin with," he said, referring to his birth weight of six pounds, eight ounces, and eighteen inches long, "he's probably fine." I let him continue. "You and your husband are low average in height." He paused. "He may just not be very tall when he grows up, and there are worse things he could be than short," he concluded, smiling up at me from his five-foot stature. *He's right, of course*, I thought. *There are worse things Josh could be than a short Jewish pediatrician like Dr. Stein. I could live with that.*

It was important for me that Josh be "normal," average—at least as far as growth charts were concerned. My healthy boy had to be average. At the time, the irony escaped me—that in the midst of dealing with Emma's life-threatening seizures, I was worried about Joshua's height.

Once enrolled in daycare, Joshua's verbal skills exploded. For someone who had only eight words at eighteen months, now at two and a half, he was stringing words together first in Russian and then in English as he heard his teachers and classmates do. He'd come home and I'd ask him: "Joshie, what did you do in school today?" and he'd say, "We had pizza for lunch today," then pause, cock his head to the side, and ask, "You know that story?" I'd try to keep from laughing. "Yes, love, I've heard that story before." Everything was a story to this little guy.

I took comfort in Joshua's being able to relay to me his daily experiences. But it pained me equally that Emma needed witnesses to testify on her behalf. And it was up to me to gauge from the reporting whether she was happy and if she was treated well. I was always left worrying that she was ignored, or that the staff neglected to change her diaper in time, or that her moans for attention went unheard.

Still, she was in school, cared for by dedicated teachers and therapists. She was participating in the world, and that was normal.

CHAPTER 17

"PICK UP JOSHIE, HE'S CRYING," I yelled to Tolya.

"I'm in the middle of changing Emma's diaper," he shot back.

I walked past my husband with Hanna, our newborn, hanging off my boob and purposefully bumped his shoulder before making my way to pick up Josh.

I had worried my marriage wouldn't survive raising a special-needs child. We were surviving, but we were struggling. A third child added extra tension—we were outnumbered.

We had discussed having another child, reasoning that Josh shouldn't have to solely shoulder the responsibility of caring for Emma after we were gone. Two children could divide and share the work. Also, we secretly hoped that when the time came, one of the two would be a good, kind soul and put us into a nice nursing home—and not on a boat, out to sea.

The daily responsibilities of juggling childcare, house work, and our jobs began to exert its weight. Tolya and I seemed to be sleepwalking around each other. We barely spoke, and when we did, it was about the children, the logistics of caring for them, the frequency of bowel movements and their consistencies, doctors' appointments, nurse schedules, preschool agendas, reminders to order formula and other supplies for Emma. We were going through the necessary motions, but we were on cruise control. The tedium of the care stripped away at us.

That summer—after Hanna's arrival—like the previous three, we rented a house in the Poconos community. With three children in tow, all under the age of four, we piled into our eight-seater Chevy minivan complete with playpen, which served as Emma's bed; a bassinet that still comfortably fit two-month-old Hanna; strollers; a myriad of toys and a month's supply of diapers for two; formula for both Hanna and Emma; bottles; wipes; and clothing. To our neighbors, I'm sure it looked like we were moving permanently.

During the almost three-hour drive there, gloom descended on me like a dark veil. A veil that reminded me of the twenty-four-seven responsibility waiting for me, of being tethered to three demanding, each in their own way, kids. Dread of the month that lay ahead seemed to empty my lungs of oxygen, and I felt the old familiar inability to take a deep breath. Where the country house had once served as a respite, it now loomed like a destination of work. When we arrived, I remained in my seat, unable to move.

Tolya emptied the minivan of all the children one by one. He went about it in the most focused way. "Hi, Emma, did you have a nice ride?" he said gently as he lifted her out and into her stroller. He unbuckled Joshua and lifted him out with an exaggerated jump, pulling him up by his hands as his little feet left the edge of the van floor. Hanna continued sleeping in her car seat, which he was now holding.

"Come on," Tolya said. "What are you waiting for?"

I didn't know what I was waiting for. Maybe I was waiting for the burden of three kids to lift. Maybe I was waiting for guilt to leave me.

We bear children for selfish reasons, and to believe otherwise is to deceive oneself. We bear children so that we can have walking outside of our bodies the best possible versions of ourselves. Children serve our need to continue our bloodlines, a sad effort at immortality. We bear children so we can be proud, so we can brag, so we can have someone to love and be loved, so we can be cared for in our old age. If we're not careful, we bear children to have the upper hand, to be able to control someone because we have no control of ourselves. If we've failed to do the emotional work prior, our children may end up being repositories for all our insecurities, anxieties, sadness. But at the end of the day, no matter the reasons, we ultimately want our children to be happy and healthy.

Watching my three children and thinking of the inequities they might all suffer paralyzed me. My girls especially. When I tried to imagine my girls' futures, I wanted to see boyfriends, prom dress shopping, menstruation conversations. I could see that for Hanna, but Emma would have none of that with me. These stark differences between my two girls tore at my heart.

But there was something else I was waiting for too, and I was reluctant to admit it. I was waiting for a moment for me. I was waiting for my husband's love. Maybe I was waiting for the leaden weight pinning me to lift, or for Tolya to direct his attention to me, if even briefly, the way he had done with the kids. Maybe I was waiting to be handled gently the way he did his daughters, to be taken and held.

I mobilized myself and helped get the kids inside and situated. Then I walked out the door of the house, got into the van and behind the wheel, and turned the key that was still in the ignition. The urge to drive—away, anywhere from here—rivaled the storm of tears that was brewing inside me, crashing against the walls of my chest, threatening to break the gates. The storm won. I released the death grip I had on the steering wheel and wailed. I came undone. Tolya must have noticed that I was missing and went looking for me. He found me locked inside, hysterical.

"Open the door." He pulled at the handles, looking alarmed. "What's going on? Why are you crying?" I shook my head, refusing his demands. I didn't know how to tell him what was going on in my brain because I hardly understood it myself, but he looked so worried, and I began to feel embarrassed at my childish display. This was no way for a mother of three to be acting, I thought. I unlocked the door, and he yanked it open.

"What's going on," he said again. "You're scaring me." He didn't reach for me, but his tone was gentle, like talking to someone on a ledge, threatening to jump.

"I've been feeling ignored, overlooked by you," I began. I'd always been good at naming my feelings, and all it took was Tolya's directed concern, and the answer to his question materialized easily. "I watch you with the kids, and I'm envious, which is so ridiculous because I read that fathers usually get jealous of the attention and the bonding that happens between a new mom and her baby. How is it that I feel excluded instead?" I rambled through guzzling tears while Tolya stood there and listened.

"I had no idea," he finally said when he saw me spent and silent.

"You haven't touched me in months." I didn't see that coming and was surprised by my own words.

"That's not fair. The doctor said no sex for six weeks after delivery," he said, remembering well, the third time around. He was right, but it wasn't the sex I was missing; it was the intimacy—the honesty of touch, the affection behind it, the forging of connectedness.

"You don't get it." I gave up. "It's fine. You're right." I was depleted and had nothing in me with which to expound on my sense of victimhood. By then, the cathartic effect of the tears gave way to clarity, and I felt simply . . . silly.

"I'm sorry," Tolya said as he folded me into his embrace.

Later in bed that night, I thought back on the day, on the last half hour spent entangled in the familiar grasping for love, like quenching a thirst that you didn't know you had until you brought the cup to your lips and realized how parched you really were. In the dark, listening to Tolya's sleeping breath fill the empty pockets of air next to me, I tried to unpack my thoughts, my fears.

Stories of marriages dissolving under the strain of raising a sick child came flooding back. "A sick child can make or break a family," I remembered hearing. "The husband left the wife to raise the very sick child by herself," a friend told me of someone's sad situation. Was that my buried fear? Did I worry that Tolya would leave me, leave the kids? Never. I knew my husband's heart, at least where the kids were concerned. And I believed he loved me, even though he didn't often say it, as he was never the demonstrative type—unless he had a glass of wine in him and his inhibitions dissolved in the liquor.

A memory flashed back to me: us dancing to our wedding song. I am serenading my newly minted husband. Three hundred guests have surrounded us within a circle of love. As the last note of "You're My Everything" lingers in the air, Tolya dips me back, brings me up, and proceeds to French kiss me in a most aggressive way—his tongue, as if a separate entity, ravaging my mouth for all to see.

Lying in bed that night, I knew Tolya would never abandon us, but I worried that our once free and innocent love for one another could abandon us if we didn't tend to it carefully, if we allowed the daily hardships to build into resentment, blame, and worse. I didn't want a loveless marriage. I knew of them, having witnessed the dance my grandmother Manya and grandfather Yefim had enacted. I'd listened to my mother's childhood stories of her parents' bitter fighting and her sadness at not being able to invite friends over for fear of embarrassment.

And in the end, after forty-five years of marriage, at age sixty-five, did my grandmother not pick up her things and move across the street with her boyfriend so that "she could finally be happy"? That she did. But her loyalty to the father of her children was steadfast as she continued to cross the street each day with bags of produce and homemade meals, ensuring that my grandfather was well fed and his clothes freshly laundered until his last days.

"Why did you wait so long to leave him? Why now that he's old and sick?" I questioned her, outraged and defensive on my beloved grandfather's behalf.

"It wasn't something you did—break up a family. I had your mother and her sister to think about. I chose to sacrifice my happiness for the sake of the family," she explained, without apology or shame. While I respected that, her story reminded me of a joke I'd once heard: An old Jewish couple in their nineties go to a lawyer to get a divorce. The lawyer, surprised, asks them why now? Why did they wait so long into old age? "We were waiting for the kids to die," they replied.

I did not want to be that couple.

CHAPTER 18

WE IGNORED OUR ISSUES AND fell back on old coping mechanisms: Tolya on planning and organizing, and me executing the plan.

Our teamwork began to save us.

Emma's graduation from Stepping Stones preschool arrived. This was a monumental step for her, for us as a family. A great accomplishment, considering her prognosis or lack thereof in her first year of life. She was moving up the educational ladder. Another check toward our unified efforts at "normalcy."

We realized, having immersed ourselves in the world of special education, that it wasn't the scary place of sad parents and disregarded children that we had feared it would be. On the contrary, the special-needs community that consisted of teachers and their assistants, therapists and social workers, was a bright and technicolored universe full of selfless, tireless individuals, most of whom seemed to love their work and perpetually sang our daughter's praises. Every progress report from every teacher and therapist, regardless of developmental goals achieved or not, always ended with "Emma is a lovely and sweet little girl and a pleasure to work with."

I glowed on the inside with pride for Emma. Her condition saved her from having to agonize over an extra point on a test, as I did. Instead she got an A+ for personality, and that was good enough for me.

Tolya and I took the day off from work and headed for the school. Once there, we were directed to a room different from Emma's classroom and found a seat among a handful of parents. There weren't many of us occupying the seats, but then it was a small class, eight kids maximum, perhaps as few as six. But the sense of pride that filled the spaces between us "special" parents was palpable. And then we saw them, walking in independently or being walked in by adults on wobbly legs or wheeled in their adaptive strollers like our Emma, dressed in white caps and gowns. This was the real deal. They may have played the graduation song in the background, I don't recall. But in my head, the music that accompanied my high school, college, and graduate school graduation ceremonies played on. My vision blurred; wetness found its place.

The lights were dimmed, and our attention was directed to a slideshow on a large white screen against the wall. Smiling, squinting, staring-into-space faces appeared briefly and then disappeared to make room for scenes of kids in their classrooms, at their desks, in adaptive bicycles, draped over therapy balls in the gym. Scenes of bubbles being popped or just admired—awed expressions. Spoons delivered hand over hand into drooling mouths, pride stamped on their smiles. Then a farm scene of some kind. Ponies, kids on ponies— Emma on a pony! *When did this even happen?* I wondered. *Why did I not know about it?*

Hippotherapy, they called it—therapeutic horsemanship, for people with disabilities. I had read about it, and here was Emma—exhibit A. Something about seeing her on a horse, where I would never expect or imagine her being, sent a shock of pleasure up my spine, and my heart again expanded against the walls of my chest. Nothing more normal than a child on top of a pony, I thought. There she was, helmet and all, upright and looking right into the camera as if nothing was wrong, as if in just a few minutes she would virtually leap out of the saddle and land with feet squarely on the ground, pat the horse's head, and walk away, thanking her for the lovely ride.

Emma looked more at ease on the horse than I did on my first and only time in the saddle, when the horse I'd been riding, in complete disregard of my efforts to steer it down the beachfront of the Belt Parkway, proceeded to lower itself to the ground with me still on its back. Before I could disengage myself from the stirrups, I was on the ground with my temperamental horse on its side and my legs underneath it.

Diplomas were being given out. "Emma Ditinsky! Congratulations on your graduation!" Emma was helped up from her chair and stood with great effort and the teacher's support, rocking slightly on spindly legs. A broad smile of shining drool graced her face at the realization and pride that she was upright. We've never clapped so loud or so hard as we did in that moment of firsts for Emma.

I SUSPECTED THAT RETURNING TO work and to my career, which I had found so rewarding, would do our marriage good and help me feel more like myself again. So, I answered an ad in the education help wanted section of the New York Times for an Early Intervention Official Designee (EIOD) position, with a title of Senior Health Care Program Planner Analyst, working for the Department of Health and Mental Hygiene. None of these acronyms made sense to me, but the salary that it promised got my immediate attention. At the time of the ad, I had been working part time as a social worker, providing play therapy and parenting skills training to families in the Early Intervention Program, which was the same government program that sent therapists to the house to work with Emma until she aged out of it at three years old. It didn't dawn on me until months later, after I was offered and accepted the position, that I was in the role of that same person who, five years ago, met with us and Emma and generously approved all the physical, occupational, and speech therapists, the Lisas and the Sunnys, to come to our home and work with Emma.

I had started as a parent, then was a provider, and now I had the privilege of facilitating these meetings with families and offering their children with various delays, like our Emma, help. Life had come full circle, and I found myself holding in my hands the opportunity to give back, pay it forward. What a gift this was.

That September, Emma started kindergarten in a new special-needs school that taught elementary through middle school students. 811Q, or Marathon, as it was known, was a large two-story building with hundreds of students, not unlike Stepping Stones but on a much bigger scale. Emma was placed in a classroom according to ability (or disability) and as close as possible in age, with a main teacher and two or three assistants. On our first visit of the classroom, my heart tightened to see so many children in wheelchairs with their heads held upright by supports that extended from tall back rests, because they couldn't hold them up on their own. I saw eyes staring up, unfocused into some middle distance, heads tilted back, mouths open, while others without the supports struggled to lift their heads up, only to have them immediately drop onto their chests, drool escaping onto their shirts. Emma by comparison looked like a healthy child, like she didn't belong there. She could hold her head up all by herself and laugh, recognized us, her loved ones, and showed excitement when she saw us. And I thought, *These poor kids*, and then I thought, *Their poor families*.

I was so proud packing her backpack for her first day of school and placing the notebook into which I wrote all the things that she could do, her likes and dislikes. *She loves all music, "The Wheels on the Bus," "Itsy Bitsy Spider," "If You're*

Happy and You Know It," I wrote. *She can sign "give me" and "more" and "all done." She pushes away if she doesn't want something or she doesn't like what someone is doing to her, and sometimes she'll scratch out of frustration. She laughs and smiles when something pleases her, and she's basically a happy, low-maintenance little girl.*

It was important for me to have others know that. I feared that her needs and the attention she demanded would cause people to reject her, dismiss her, neglect her. I also knew that her "resting face" was expressionless often, when not engaged. Her eyes were typically unfocused, lids at half mast, the low muscle tone in her cheeks forcing a downward almost scowl. To a stranger, I assumed, she appeared "checked out," not present, unaware and not understanding. I wanted people who cared for her to know that she had a lot going on in her head, that she deeply understood love and kindness and sought it everywhere and from everyone.

I had been at my new job a few months, and though stressful and busy (my week consisted of conducting five IFSP meetings a day, four days a week), I was managing and felt safe, having been promoted from provisional to permanent employee after successfully covering a meeting on September 11 for one of my colleagues whose husband worked in the Twin Towers. A sense of responsibility for the work that I did and the meetings that I chaired weighed heavy on me. For the longest time, I assumed that if I were to call out due to illness or childcare issues on meeting days, that there'd be no one to cover me, and the families who'd waited so long for their services to start would be turned away, their children's services postponed.

The other driving force for me was to never find myself in a position where because I was a parent of a special-needs child, I was given special treatment. I never wanted to use this dubious status as an excuse for any exceptions or allowances that made me stand out from my colleagues. I guarded this information so vigilantly that many of my coworkers, as well as some supervisors, did not even know that I had a disabled child. They knew I had three small children and the responsibilities that went along with being a working mother, but Emma's condition was not the primary or secondary subject of conversations, so when facts about Emma's condition were invariably revealed in exchanges about the kids' personalities or schooling and such, there was always shock, dismay, and pity—which I wanted least of all.

For this reason, calling out too often to take care of Emma because she was sick and there was no nursing coverage was a scenario I avoided at all cost, because I believed it invited criticism. Somehow, taking off to care for my healthy children was acceptable, understandable in my warped logic, but Emma was special, and my worst fear was to face reprimand for being a less-than-exceptional employee because I had a sick child and had to attend to her special needs often. I would not give people reason to resent me, or be deemed falling short of work responsibility because I received special treatment for having a disabled child. Because I myself was not special.

I perpetuated the image of normalcy: normal family, normal life, every step of the way.

I came home and took off my public mask and shared stories from the day with Tolya, the man who once dipped me backward in a dance and French kissed me in public, the man who understood me best and saw the real me.

CHAPTER 19

"PARENTS ARE NOT SUPPOSED TO bury their children," my grandmother Manya said, wiping tears from her eyes. My aunt Alla, my mother's older sister, had just died at age fifty. My grandmother buried her daughter.

I refilled her tea. "I'm so sorry, baboolya." My thoughts drifted back to Emma's prognosis that she would not live past her first birthday. She was now six and thriving.

Baba Manya had outlived her husband, a boyfriend, and now her eldest child. Her physical health was deteriorating, but it took the death of her daughter to bring her emotionally to her knees.

"I'm worried about my grandmother." I was having a familiar conversation with Tolya one day. There seemed to always be a family member that occupied my thoughts, that needed rescuing. "She's depressed. I've never seen her like this. She's always been a pillar of strength."

"Let's bring her to live with us," Tolya said. I'd heard those words before.

The year before, we had purchased the one-bedroom apartment adjacent to our two-bedroom and combined the two, giving us ample space—enough to accommodate a live-in babysitter and now my grandmother.

"With the addition of the new apartment, we have room for her," he said.

"You would do that for me?" I asked, knowing the answer already. He nodded.

"You deserve a medal for familial loyalty," I said, not joking. "We're going to start to look like a halfway house for wayward relatives."

My grandmother moved in.

The first months after moving in found Baba Manya in and out of the hospital. Though there was nothing visibly wrong with her, grief made her ill. After a short three-day "tune-up" under medical supervision, she'd be returned home. This happened each month until antidepressants were added to her menagerie of half a dozen medications.

"It is not the normal order of things, Deeanochka," she said to me one day. "Parents are not supposed to bury their children." Those words were burned into my brain.

Daily love from her three great-grandchildren helped buffer the pain in some measure. By then, independent ambulation was difficult for her, and she'd ask her home attendant to accompany her with her walker to the other parts of the apartment where she knew her favorite people dwelled. We encouraged Joshua to visit her in her room daily and just sit on her bed for even a few minutes while she recited little Russian children's poems. "Meeshka kosolapy"—the little bear with the turned-in paws. "Eedyot bichok kachayetsa"— the little baby bull balancing on a beam. "Zaykoo broseela hazayka"—the little bunny abandoned by his owner. Hanna would be placed in her arms and kissed with such loud, wet intensity that she would not want to return.

"Emmoosya," she would call to Emma in the living room, in a sing-song timbre, "come to Baba." Emma would round the corner with an adult holding her up from behind, wobbling sometimes on bare feet, other times in her foot orthotics and sneakers. There was a method to helping Emma negotiate her environment vertically. I would position her in such a way that her back was against my pelvis and my arms were at a right angle under hers at the same angle, with elbows pressed against my body, to allow little room for movement. My legs pushed her legs forward, one, then the other. We walked together this way, as if on stilts, in a soldier-like march, and I was reminded of the way my father used to play-walk with me, the difference being that my little feet would be positioned on top of his as we speed-ambled in unison, two bodies, one set of legs.

Once Emma was seated in her generous lap, Baba Manya would take Emma's hand, place it in her own with her palm up, and open her little fingers so that she could enact her own special song: "Soroka varona, kashkoo vareela"—the mother crow stirred the pot of porridge and then distributed a portion to each of her children except for one, before flying away. As she recited, her plump finger circled Emma's open palm in a stirring motion and then closed each finger as she counted off the children she fed. It was a bizarre little ditty but one that invariably caused Emma to fold in half, laughing her silent laugh.

It was sobering to see my grandmother, a larger than life presence since I was a little girl, diminished physically and emotionally. The grandmother I carried in my memory wore sparkling brooches pinned to her tailor-made dresses, blood-red lipstick, and Krasnaya Moskva (Red Moscow) perfume, whose scent trailed her like an army of obedient little followers.

"The man must love you more than you love him," I would hear her weigh in on various occasions when the subject was relationships. I think this may have been an Eastern European thing, because I'd heard others make the same proclamation. "A tall man is instantly handsome" was another favorite.

She was a powerhouse of a woman, tall and solid in body and frame with an expansive heart nestled beneath her ample bosom. She commanded respect wherever she went. She did it in the way she carried herself—poised dignity and confidence, exuding an energy that pulled people toward her if you were in her invisible force field. Wise, despite having only completed five grades before having to leave school to help care for her family, she had a keen understanding of human nature. "If you got mad at everyone that offended you with hurtful words or deeds, there would be no one to say hello to," she said of friendships. And when my mother would feel wounded by my sister's or my words or actions and would attempt to commiserate with her mother, Baba Manya's response was always "Na detey ne abeezhayutsa"—we should never be mad at our children; we cannot hold a grudge.

She was a loving woman but not demonstratively affectionate. The mantra of *I love you* that I uttered daily to my kids did not often fall from her lips. We didn't seek her out for hugs or kisses. We found her when we wanted food. Like many survivors of war and famine, food for my grandmother equaled love, and if you were not accepting of her offer of caring for you, she took great offense: "That's it. If you don't finish the soup, I won't love you anymore," I heard her say too many times to forget. Even as a child, I understood it to be an innocuous threat, but it served to crystallize the indelible connection between food and love.

In the Soviet Union, being thin signified sickness, just as being pleasantly plump meant health. Even the language reflected this. When you wished an ailing person a speedy recovery, you wished them to "papravlyatsa," which literally translated to "gain weight" but was meant to say "get well." I was not a good representation of health as a child, in my skin and bones getup, and thus a poor reflection on my grandmother, who was a talented cook with a perennially stocked kitchen. "Poor kindele," she would say of Emma's tube feedings. "Let's put some ice cream on her tongue. Give her some pleasure."

Always self-sufficient, my grandmother least of all wanted to be a burden to us, so upon moving in, she insisted on giving us money out of her monthly social security check, for rent. I refused and balked for as long as I could but ultimately realized that it was important for her continued sense of independence. I understood the burden part, deeply. In raising Emma, it was our mission to leave Hanna and Josh as financially prepared and unburdened as possible for when we were gone. So, we squirreled away extra monthly savings and opened savings accounts, all in anticipation of the day Emma would need a safety net.

I liked the feeling of being able to give back in taking my grandmother in. And even though a large part of her died when she buried her daughter, her regal essence, her largesse, occasionally made its appearance. Like when her monthly doctor's appointments rolled around, she would cast off her flowery house dress and slippers and reach into her savvy fashion past. I helped button her enormous brassiere, with its hundred tiny hooks, while her home attendant, Inessa, maneuvered one of her custom-made dresses over the curlers in her hair that she'd thrown on an hour before. Her signature red lipstick and medium-heeled shoes (she insisted flats were bad for your feet, and sneakers were evil) completed the look, and she transported herself to the young grandmother I remembered growing up.

But then she would rise from her bed and use her walker to take the half a dozen steps to the wheelchair that sat waiting unfolded for her, and lower herself into it. That moment delivered me back to the present, to the acknowledgment that like my daughter, her great-granddaughter, my once power-house of a grandmother could no longer ambulate without assistance and depended on a wheelchair to transport her.

A new obstacle loomed before us; our apartment building was a pre-war structure, built before the Americans with

Disabilities Act, which ensured that people with disabilities had access to civic life, whether leaving or entering their home or a place of business. The problem was that our cooperative had two entrances—the front and the delivery, basement side—both of which had stairs leading to the doors. The solution was a ramp, but the president of our co-op board at the time refused to build one.

When we first moved into the co-op, we seemed to be the youngest family, just as our kids were the only three in the building. We watched senior citizens drag their laden shopping carts up the three steps into the front door and then another three in the lobby to the elevator, or lower them gingerly and with great trepidation down the four steps that led into the basement side door, just as we had been doing with Emma in her adaptive stroller. We told ourselves that when she got older, we would do something about it, but then my grandmother moved in and the game plan changed.

The struggling seniors were difficult enough to see, but most offensive of all was one elderly couple: the wife, wheelchair bound, the husband having to drag a makeshift metal ramp maybe fifty pounds in weight that was kept in the basement office of the superintendent, whose assistance the husband was forced to employ each time he took his wife out.

"Why don't you have the building build a ramp?" we asked one day, having witnessed their labored efforts.

"The president of the board refuses to. We've asked, believe me," the husband replied.

"But it's the law," I insisted. The husband shrugged dejectedly and said something to the effect of fighting City Hall, as in the futility of it. I was livid. This affected us, but more than that, it was an injustice that I needed to right.

One evening not long after, we bumped into the president of the board on Election Day, at the voting center behind our building. She was an older gray-haired woman herself in her seventies, living alone, wielding a heartless power over those less fortunate. Approaching her, we inquired in the nicest, calmest of ways why a ramp had not been built and shared our concerns for our wheelchair-bound child, referencing the law.

"Well, we're actually not bound by the law, because our building was grandfathered in. Also, the side ramp would destroy the garden," she replied.

I was stunned, said "Wow," grabbed Tolya by the arm, and pulled him away, fearing what he might do if allowed to linger.

"We'll see what she sings when she's in a wheelchair," Tolya said through gritted teeth as the violence of the words cut through the darkness. My heart swelled with pride, and a warmth found its way into my belly like molten chocolate. This was hot. My husband was feral, like me.

I found a lawyer to fight our case. It felt empowering to advocate for my child and myself, for a change. Fighting for Emma gave me permission to fight for myself, to claim what belonged to me. Permission to ask for things that I needed without feeling selfish or undeserving, as in the past when my anxiety prevented me from doing so because I felt unworthy. I would continue to fight for my child and continue to prove everyone, including doctors and board presidents, wrong.

The ramp was built months later. The woman in the wheelchair died before she could use it.

CHAPTER 20

CONTRACTURES, THE NEW WORD OF the day. Contractures, we learned, was the shortening or stiffening of muscles, skin, or connective tissues that resulted in decreased movement and range of motion, and it began happening to Emma. The cruel "use it or lose it" adage began playing itself out. Emma's fingers curled into themselves such that she looked like she was perpetually holding something loosely in each hand, and with little opportunity to bear weight, her feet began to point downward as well. The most common treatment for hand contractures was splinting or braces for the hands. Emma's occupational therapist helped us secure these contraptions that went on her hands like fingerless gloves and that she was to wear as much as possible day and night. The splints were designed to keep her fingers extended and her palms open, so that she could manipulate objects better and reverse the contractures that had rendered her hands virtually function-less. No sooner would we put them on her hands and lower her into her crib at night than we'd hear the unmistakable scratching sound of Velcro being pulled apart, emanating from Emma's room.

"You little Houdini," I teased, secretly proud, while also trying to suppress a laugh when I'd find her on her back, Velcro between her teeth and the splint halfway off her hand. She laughed her breathy laugh, pride gracing her face. Eventually, the contractures moved to her feet. Surgery was required, the doctors told us, on one of her legs that was turning in. This would help her stand flat on her feet.

"We need her to be able to at least walk with help, especially when she gets older," I said. We were driving home from the orthopedist appointment at the Hospital for Special Surgery. Surgery was recommended, and I was trying to convince myself of the necessity of sending Emma under the knife again.

"I know," Tolya said. "We won't always be able to lift her and carry her. At some point, she'll get too big." This was a secret language Tolya and I engaged in. The future was imminent, and it loomed large in our subconscious. We didn't know how to put the words to the gnawing possibility that someday, when Emma grew into an adult, we might no longer be able to care for her, either because of our own frailty, her complicated care needs, or both. I envisioned, with a guilty conscience, the days when we wouldn't need to worry about coverage, desperately calling nurses or enlisting my aging parents to babysit so that we could step out to see a movie or even take a vacation. I longed to be untethered.

While she was still little, her care was manageable. She was light enough, still a baby in many ways. In my still young heart, though, I yearned to someday live unburdened, just as I had wanted to do when we gave Emma away. I told myself that our responsibility extended only into her adulthood. Just as Josh and Hanna would leave the nest for college, when Emma turned twenty-one, we would find a good new home for her, where she would be in a community of her peers with round-the-clock care. That's what I told myself and hinted to Tolya, who quietly agreed. We entered a dirty covenant, an agreement that we had years to realize. But for now, Emma needed surgery.

After her foot healed, orthotics—or AFOs, as they were called—were custom made for her to wear day and night. It was a daunting task that I balked against, not because I didn't understand their necessity, but because it hurt me to see Emma constrained by them. Unyielding plastic with their hinges, buckles, straps, and Velcro, they looked like medieval torture devices. They engulfed Emma's tiny feet, extending almost as far as the knees, while their bulk made any mobility outside of walking in them difficult and cumbersome.

In all my fighting for her, I saw her struggling, and so I knew I needed to pull back—at least a touch. I committed to having her wear them during the day, but the night was a different story. I didn't have the heart to do that to her—force her into the limiting hard constraints of the unwieldy plastic encasing her functionless legs even in sleep. As it was, she was a prisoner in her rebellious body during waking hours. I couldn't justify the continued torture of the braces when her body needed to rest–so I freed her. In my mind, comfort trumped function and utilitarianism.

Emma seemed to fight for herself too. I marveled at her adaptability. With her AFOs on during the day, she would roll as her primary means of locomotion from point A to point B. I watched her reach the edge of our sunken living room from the foyer, position herself parallel to the steps, and lunge her body down one step and then the other. It was painful to see and hear the subtle thud of her weight hitting the hardwood floor, but she did it in such slow motion and with such calculated caution that somehow it never caused injury, not even a black and blue. Emma then rolled onto the colorful padded floor mat that we had covered most of the living room with, making it look like a gymnastics studio, propped herself up on her elbow, extended it, and sat up on her diapered bottom, crossing her orthotic-covered feet in front of her like a pretzel. The braces became an extension of her, and she seemed to accept their existence, but oh how I despised those things. No pretty designer Mary Janes for Emma. It was Payless sneakers, two sizes larger than her foot size and extra wide, to accommodate the bulk of the AFOs.

Tolya and I pushed for better transportation for her. Emma traveled to school on a big yellow school bus with a metal ramp that unfolded onto the sidewalk, like a rescue raft from a ship into the ocean. A usually nice bus attendant, with the bus driver's help, wheeled her backward onto the bus, where the attendant secured the adaptive stroller (especially made for bus travel) to the far side, by the window. The stroller was pinned down to allow for no movement while the bus was in motion. I moved back onto the sidewalk and waved from a distance, like the average mom sending off the average child to the average school.

At the beginning of each semester, we held our breath while we opened the envelope from the Pupil Transportation Office, to find an ungodly early pickup time of six forty-five, because Emma was usually the first or second student on the route. The drive itself was normally no more than half an hour, but with morning traffic and the other kids that needed to be picked up after Emma, often she'd spend as much as an hour or more in transit. There were usually no more than three or four other kids besides Emma, but it added up. Later I learned to ask for "a short route" and an air-conditioned bus, for which we had to provide a doctor's note, citing her seizure disorder as a medical reason. Even so, pickup times were never later than seven thirty, as her school day began a little after eight o'clock.

Busing became the bane of our existence. Tolya and I took turns waking at six to get Emma out of bed and downstairs to the bus, which oftentimes came half an hour or more late. There was no rhyme or reason to their arrival times. In the worst case, if we were unlucky to have a particularly disgruntled bus driver, he would arrive ten minutes before the agreed-upon pickup time, wait five minutes, and drive away, deciding that Emma wasn't coming to school that day, or more likely because he was feeling particularly an impatient asshole that day.

"Here's our phone number. Please give us yours," we begged the driver, shamelessly. "We'll call if Emma is not going to school, and you can call us if we're not downstairs when you pull up, but please don't drive away until we've connected." Sometimes it worked; oftentimes it didn't. On the days it didn't and we were left waiting at the curb, Tolya or I would load Emma into the minivan, wheelchair folded in the back, and make the hour-and-a-half drive to her school and back, usually making us late for our jobs.

What made the busing experience miserable were the harrowing nights that preceded those mornings. We had not had a full undisturbed night's sleep since Emma came home. Even after having sleep trained both Joshua and Hanna at three months old, Emma's care demanded that we wake up at least once, sometimes twice, a night and go to her room in response to a rustling sound that indicated she was awake and usually uncomfortable, in her overfilled diaper or, worse, wet sheets that were the result of her flimsy diaper having oversoaked and spilled onto her mattress. It was unavoidable, given that her last feeding of eight ounces of formula and the G-tube flushed with extra water took place right before she went down for the night. A healthy child could wake in the night and use the bathroom to relieve the pressure that woke them, but Emma could not, being captive in her body and imprisoned by her crib. Most nights she lay there squirming in wet discomfort until I, in my half mother's sleep, woke and rose to her.

At least once a week, she would have her four-day constipation break, and we would find Emma lying there moaning, feces covering her hands and face, because it had also found its liquid way out of the diaper.

"Tolya!" I'd yell into the dark room. "Come!" And there he would be, a minute or so later (because he slept like a dead man), turning on the hallway light to avoid turning on the bedroom one, so that we could get to work. Tolya would scoop Emma up gingerly, place her on the floor mat (the same kind that covered our living room) atop a hospital pad, and proceed to change her—clothes and diapers removed, feces wiped down with baby wipes while she moaned in objection to the cold offensive wipes on her body and face. Sometimes, when she was particularly soiled, we'd have to run a bath and wash her off completely. I would remove the sheet and blanket cover, grab Emma's dirty clothes, and wash everything in the bathroom sink so that it could be thrown in the washing machine at week's end before smelling up the entire apartment.

With Emma returned to her crib, we crawled back to our bed—thirty minutes of precious sleep evaporated into the putrid air—only to find the morning come too soon.

The simultaneous timing of Emma starting a new school and a new nurse was not ideal. Our insurance, combined with Medicaid, approved nursing hours that covered from three thirty bus pickup until Emma's bedtime. Susan, the nurse who started with us a few weeks prior, was a quiet woman. Her first day with Emma, we watched from the open kitchen as she sat on the couch for hours while Emma rolled around on the floor. She didn't pick her up or talk to her, other than to change her diaper and feed her, but even then, she was mute.

Communication was not Susan's forte, and neither was her punctuality. The same bus driver that picked Emma up in the morning, who we struggled to ingratiate ourselves to, would often call me at work at three thirty to say that the nurse was not there. More than once, I'd have to leave my job early to get Emma off the bus, the exact scenario that I worked desperately to avoid.

Lack of coverage, spotty coverage, mediocre coverage—this was nursing in a nutshell. Bus driver issues added a layer of worry to the care that Emma received. She was wholly dependent on us for her well-being, and we were equally dependent on, and at the mercy of, others to assist us. At the same time, we were an army of two warriors, fighting to get things done and getting Emma what she needed.

CHAPTER 21

THE SIREN MELODY OF MR. SOFTEE'S ice cream truck, strategically stationed at the entrance to the neighborhood park in Forest Hills, lured children to its window. Yellowstone Park was a convenient two-block walk from our apartment building, serving as the nucleus of socialization for neighborhood kids, not a few bored nannies, and overwhelmed parents, like myself.

The park allowed me to escape the confining walls of the apartment, where I'd begun to feel the need to occupy the kids with activities outside of plopping them down in front of the television and letting the blinking images make zombies out of them.

The pressure to always be "on" to teach and entertain Josh and Hanna was getting to me and creating a resentment within. To escape, I opted for outings to the park, museum, shows, anything to avoid feeling trapped at home. Then I would feel guilt rise in my throat. Shouldn't I be blissfully grateful for these moments with my healthy kids, especially with Emma's challenges? Shouldn't I eat and breathe and want to exist only for my kids' attention? I would make feeble efforts, spurts of activities, puzzles, books, drawings, but in the end I defaulted to others' entertainment of them as I enrolled them in music and gym classes and arranged play dates, the weekends always packed with activities outside the home.

I'm not sure why I was compelled to have them be constantly stimulated, or why I didn't trust myself to be equipped to do that. Maybe I feared a sense of inadequacy in myself—of them being bored by the simple interactions that with Emma were the norm. Maybe it was my need to constantly be moving, doing, and never just being. Only Emma could reach into my well of patience and force me to just be and sing and clap and roll around and laugh.

With her, I was enough.

The park was where I made "mommy friends" that made me feel less on the periphery of parenthood. Most of them worked, like I did, so that most summer, spring, and fall evenings and weekends we would unfailingly make the pilgrimage in anticipation of new gossip, shared grievances, and the feeling of being part of a community.

My kids would do as I had done some twenty years before, in the same park, with the same options, maybe even heading toward the same ice cream truck. I would watch Hanna drop whatever she was holding in her pudgy little two-year-old hands and whip her head in the direction from which the hypnotizing music was emanating, like a cartoon character getting a whiff of a food scent whose cloud would lift it off the ground and carry it to the source. I could almost see her ears perk up as she would break into a wobbly sprint, sometimes falling in the process, all the while yelling, "Ice crim, ice crim," one of her few English words at the time, as Russian was her first language. One time, she fell so hard she dislocated her elbow. After a third such dislocation, the hospital doctor taught us how to snap her arm back into place, on our own, avoiding future trips to the emergency room. With Emma's dossier of medical issues, Hanna's dislocations were shelved as minor inconveniences, like a common cold against the backdrop of a case of pneumonia perhaps. Joshua's scrapes were also relegated to pedestrian events.

I couldn't help but focus on Emma, who sat in her stroller, under the green canopy of the leaves that shielded her eyes from the bright sun, quietly chewing on her soon-to-be-wet bib with the same appetite and zest as if she were biting into a soft cone. She never parted with her bibs. If she wasn't chewing on one, she'd be chewing her shirt sleeve or collar, and we couldn't have that. There was a method to her madness, I was certain, but I couldn't figure it out. Somehow, she knew almost instinctively how to reposition the bib so that a dry piece would land in her mouth. She would turn the pages of the magazine in her lap with one hand, briskly, as if she had no patience to attend to what was depicted, or it didn't contain what she was searching for. With her other hand, she worked the bib. When she'd see me approaching holding a dry one, she would languidly extend the soaked bib in my direction as if she were offering me her hand to kiss while holding a lovely silk handkerchief, then grab the dry one with such an affect of impertinence that she seemed to be saying, "What took you so long?" Even as she sat in one place, she was always in motion, moving. She was her mother's daughter.

Periodically, Emma would lift her head from her magazine in response to squeals or laughter that sometimes passed her like the wail of a speeding fire engine, and she'd smile to herself, like an old soul who derived pleasure from others' joy, or who understood the intricacies of life or the innocence or folly of youth. And I'd wonder, *What are you thinking?* wanting to settle into the folds of her brain and listen and watch the animation, as if on a big screen, so that I could catch a glimpse—understand her better. But I never could.

I imagined her perfecting the art of being in the moment—a meditative ritual that I never could grasp. Did thoughts and images flicker in her mind, which she observed and let go, as the practice of meditation instructed? Was she demonstrating to me the ability to be peaceful within myself, mindful, without the urge to move, run? I wondered about these things, but all I could do was watch.

I'd worry that she was sad, felt excluded from the physical maelstrom around her. Did she understand that she couldn't rise from her stroller and pump her legs in keeping with the multitude of others who were here one minute, gone the next? Did she know her limitations, bemoan or accept them? Instinctively, I drew parallels between my later high school years and Emma's peripheral existence. I needed her to not feel marginalized, apart. I felt her pain in my bones, as if it were my own. Even at the height of my perceived popularity in early middle school, the unpopular kids' seeming sadness and rejection tugged at my heart.

At home, I'd watch Emma sit on the living room floor while Josh and Hanna ran in front of her to and from the foyer, playing. Every so often, she would reach her arm out in their direction as if to try and catch them or say, "Wait for me. Take me with you." My heart squeezed into a tight knot, and I'd say, "Josh, Hanna, go play with Emma, please," and they would immediately stop, descend onto the floor next to her, creating a circle, cross their legs, grab her hands, and sing "Ring Around the Rosie." They'd fall onto their sides or backs, and Emma would fold in half, laughing. Five minutes of this and the kids would be off again. This was as long as they could "entertain" their "baby" sister, being short on attention spans themselves. Emma, too, dictated the degree of her tolerance of her rowdy siblings. When she had enough, she reached for the magazine at her side and resumed the page turning. This signaled for Josh and Hanna to move on and for me to move in. I needed to keep her feeling included in our family life.

"Look at the pretty girl, Emma," I'd say, pointing to the model on the cover of her *Elle* or *Shape* magazine. Sometimes it would be *Women's Fitness* or *Oxygen*, a woman's body building publication, stacks of which our neighbor left in the laundromat and which Tolya brought upstairs for Emma to peruse. I knew it was a ludicrous thing for me to say, as if Emma understood or cared in the slightest about physical aesthetics. She was no slave to the latest fashion trends, could pass a mirror without considering the merits of her reflection, neither indulged in judgment nor considered others' dispensation of it. I envied her disposition, if not her position. "Isn't she pretty?" I'd continue. Without fail, Emma would bring the magazine to her face and touch the waxy cover to her lips, the way I had shown her, simulating a kiss.

BEFORE WE WERE EVEN MARRIED, Tolya and I made travel a priority, starting with our first trip in college with the Volunteers for Israel program, where we lived and worked on an army base in the Golan Heights for a month, then explored the country in our free time. We waited four years to become parents for the sole purpose of quenching our wanderlust before committing to the larger endeavor of childrearing.

We managed to squeeze in a two-week honeymoon in Spain, a later trip to Switzerland with a stop in Germany, Canada, Bermuda, a cruise or two to the Caribbean, and multiple returns to Cancun—Tolya's favorite rest and relaxation default, where we hardly rested or relaxed, busy as we were club hopping, parasailing, motor scootering, and the like. Tolya was, by his own proclamation, not a beach person and a pool hater; having spent years on a swim team had nurtured in him an aversion to all bodies of water.

I had always been the initiator and planner of these trips, answering to my need to be constantly moving, not just on familiar ground on the daily but now, in marriage, pushing the geographic boundaries as far as I could take them. No sooner would we return from travels than I'd be turning to Tolya and asking, "So where do you want to go next?" to which his answer would invariably be "Cancun."

"Promise me that we'll travel a lot with our kids when we have them?" I said to him one day when packing for one of our bi-yearly trips.

"Sure," he said, "if we can afford it."

So, when the kids came along, we set out on fulfilling our promise of showing them the world. But like with all things, it quickly turned bittersweet. Traveling with Hanna and Josh was a joy—seeing their awe to new experiences, people, was a gift. Traveling with Emma was complicated, nearly impossible. There were so many things to contend with, but the heartache I felt for Emma at being confined to only the perimeter of Yellowstone Park made including her in our travels as a family uncontestable. After all, Emma was the ultimate boundary pusher, and we were embroiled in everything with her, so it was only natural that we would push geographic boundaries together as well.

Our first family vacation was a long weekend trip to Sesame Place, with all three kids. We decided to go small in testing the waters of travel. The unambitious short-enough drive to Pennsylvania and the contained three-day commitment ensured that we wouldn't have to pack up the entire house—just half of it. I was cautiously excited about the prospect of the road trip and the real-life family experiences we'd find waiting for us. This was the American family travel practice that I'd seen in so many movies. This was living the American dream. This was passing snacks to the kids in the back, each in their respective car seats, singing along with Raffi songs on the Disney Radio Channel, stopping for hourly bathroom breaks at pit stops and feeding and changing Emma in the trunk space of the eight-seater minivan, wedged between her pack of diapers and formula.

Hanna was two and a half at the time and just picking up on some English from daycare and cartoons. Her Russian accent rivaled her father's so that they both sounded like they just got off the boat at Ellis Island. "I love you, Daddy," she randomly shouted from the back—proudly showcasing her newly acquired bilingual skills.

"I love you, *daughra*," Tolya responded.

"Dora?" Hanna sounded outraged, assuming her father was mistaking her for Dora the Explorer, the cartoon character she sometimes watched on television. "My name is Hanna Banana!" And it was all Tolya could do to keep the car from careening off the road as his body trembled with laughter.

That weekend was exceptionally hot, and temperatures wavered in the low nineties, so Hanna and Josh took advantage of the waterslides and the wave pool. Tolya accompanied Emma on the mini roller coaster, but she rode solo on the swing chairs that spun in a circle, suspended from above. If there's an upside to being in a wheelchair, it's that the ride attendants always let Emma cut the line. I watched as her expression changed from confusion, bordering on shock, to a wide smile as she leaned her head back to look up at the sky and surrender to the dizzying spell of the motion. She was perfection caught in a blissful moment.

But then I saw her eyes roll back into her head just as the ride slowed to a crawl, and the electric storm that rocked her came to collect.

She was having a seizure.

We cut the trip short, giving in to our fear of being stranded away from the familiar if needing medical intervention. Something about Pennsylvania and crossing over into the state's borders seemed to portend trouble: the adoptive family, the summers vacationing in the Poconos, and then Sesame Place. Paranoia settled into my psyche. "Just a coincidence," Tolya remarked when I told him of my observation. Of course, it was.

Though to think about it now, all the potholes we encountered that happened to be in that state forced us to learn new lessons of survival with Emma. The adoption, obviously a biggy, taught us that life with Emma was preferable to life without her. The button coming loose taught us how to change it and maintain her life-sustaining feedings. And finally, we learned that being overstimulated, as can happen with the exhilaration of an amusement park ride, brought on breakthrough seizures.

"How unfair," I complained to Tolya. That she couldn't succumb to unmitigated joy without the threat of punishment by a seizure was more than I could accept.

The next time we took a family vacation, a year later, it was without Emma. It was a trip to Disneyworld, and we were flying. The thought of packing suitcases full of a week's worth of formula, diapers, feeding bags, clothes, bibs, medicines, just for Emma, sent me reeling with anxiety. How would she tolerate plane travel? How and where would she sleep in the hotel room, and how, in turn, would we get rest? What if there was a repeat of the Sesame Place trip, and she was overstimulated and had another seizure?

I hated making that decision, but I saw no alternative.

As the JetBlue flight taxied on the runway and I buckled the kids in, we listened to the pilot's announcement. "We have flight attendant Susan in the front and Mary in the back. And I'm Rich."

"I want to be rich too!" I turned to hear Joshua's squeaky six-year-old voice propelled into the stagnant aircraft air, bouncing off its narrow walls to land on everyone's ears. The plane exploded with laughter, and I thought, *That's my silly boy*, and I laughed alongside everyone else at the innocence that bubbled up in my son's not yet tainted, uninjured heart—an innocence that I had parted with a long time ago.

But as the plane abandoned the solid ground and pushed toward the clouds, a sick, sinking feeling found its way into my belly at the reminder that we were missing one child, because we had intentionally left her behind, again, so that we could move forward somewhere.

I told myself that if normalcy was the goal, then, on occasion, for the sake of the other two children, there would have to be casualties. While I knew this to be true, it did little to ease my guilt.

The following summer, we made another go at a family vacation, this time with all three kids again. A trip to Virginia seemed doable, the drive there manageable. We loaded the minivan with five days' worth of supplies for Emma, which included twenty cans of formula, thirty diapers, five feeding bags, her wheelchair, and a blow-up mattress for one of us to sleep with her on.

July temperatures got the better of us but were particularly difficult to manage for Emma. The walks in Busch Gardens seemed to take their toll. She looked lethargic and was so uncomfortable that only the hotel pool provided some reprieve from the stultifying heat.

Meals out were awkward. As much as we'd try to include Emma by pulling her close to the table so that she could feel somewhat a part of the family dynamic, she would have none of it. She swiped at or tried to grab whatever was on the table in front of her, so everything would have to be cleared, and she'd have no choice but to retreat to her magazine turning and bib chewing, interrupted by moans and attempted scratches at us, indicating that she was done and wanted to be elsewhere.

"I feel bad for her," I said to Tolya the next day as we waded with her in the pool. "She doesn't look like she's enjoying herself." We were both exhausted from being constantly woken up at night by her tossing and turning. Unable to find her place on the unfamiliar blow-up mattress, she'd wake us with a brisk tap on the face or head when she'd realize in the dark of the hotel room that someone was lying next to her.

Evenings were better. When the temperatures dropped slightly, we explored the Virginia Beach Boardwalk. The take-away for me from that trip was twofold: One was the mental snapshot I consciously took of Tolya walking with the kids, pushing Emma in the adaptive stroller, with seven-year-old Josh and four-year-old Hanna each sitting on and straddling his shoulders while holding on to his head—Tolya wearing the T-shirt I got him before the trip that read "Who are these kids, and why are they calling me Dad?" And I thought, *It doesn't get any better than this.* "You are Super-Dad," I said to him, *And we are Super-Family on crack*, I thought to myself.

The second conclusion I reached was the knowledge that family vacations with Emma would continue to be challenging. I didn't want to admit to myself that exclusion with a disabled child would sometimes be necessary.

CHAPTER 22

"DO YOU KNOW WHAT IT'S like to have a child with a delay?" a parent at an Early Intervention meeting asked me.

You have no idea.

We were discussing her daughter's future services. I handed her a tissue from across my desk. She was frustrated. I got her.

I wanted to tell her that I knew too well what it was like to raise a child with delays, not only speech delays, as in this case, but pervasive, life-altering, soul-crushing delays. She could not have known, of course, about Emma. She could not have known that at age nine, Emma remained on a one-year-old level, non-ambulatory, nonverbal, G-tube fed and with a host of medical challenges.

She glossed over the fact that her daughter had made remarkable progress, which this wonderful and generous government program made possible, and she was bullying me in the most personal and hurtful of ways and lashing out like a concerned, protective, feral . . . mother.

She could have been me. I could have been her.

And it was for this precise reason that I did not judge her.

Because the truth is that when we try to compare miseries, heartaches, injustices—there's no comparison. Each person's struggle, no matter how large or small, real or imagined, is the most devastating, the most debilitating, the most grave and insurmountable to that individual. The beholder of such perceived suffering cannot be argued or reasoned with. Theirs is as subjective as one's religious beliefs or political leanings. It is worthy of battling for and defending, ferociously. It is worthy of war. She was a mother who bled for her child, no different from me, and I understood her.

Then there were the other mothers, the ones of whom I could inquire with compassion and knowledge: "Is your son on Keppra or Trileptal for the seizures? Is your daughter on a continuous G-tube feeding at night as well?" They did not know my story, did not know that I had "insider information." But we shared the road less traveled—a narrative—these mothers and me. Our eyes simultaneously glistened with sadness when talking about our children, their struggles, our fears. I felt a kinship with these women, however brief, a shared mission. I also felt gratitude for being part of this community of Early Intervention and being able to give back. I was a veteran; they were only starting out on their journey. I wanted to reassure them that everything would be okay, but I wasn't even sure of it for myself.

When Emma was six years old, my best friend gave birth to her first child. "Please come to the hospital," she called to tell me. "The doctors suspect Down syndrome. I need your opinion. I think she just looks like my father, has his eyes, you know?" she continued. The request unsettled me. What if the doctors were right? Would I have the heart, the gall, to be honest with my friend?

When the moment came and I saw the sweet little girl's face, with all the telltale signs of Down syndrome, all I could say was "She's beautiful. She looks like your father."

Life happens to everyone. It doesn't discriminate.

But finally, I wasn't alone.

Finally, I had someone—a close someone—who would genuinely understand my frustrations, despair, fear. We could lift each other up, compare stories, battle the same enemies and walk parallel lives. I was hopeful, buoyed by a sense of my enclosed little world expanding to make room for another.

But my friend was grieving.

She was standing in the exact spot I stood six years prior. She was in denial, in shock, wading through the same dark waters, grieving a loss. This friend was there for me. Now she was at ground zero, our positions shifted, and I had to be there for her.

The wheels were set in motion. I experienced a strange sense of déjà vu. It was as if I had been meant to be working in Early Intervention at the arrival of my friend's daughter. Preparation was complete and all the necessary steps taken to ensure that everything fell into place. With her baby enrolled in the program, we proceeded to get her all the services she needed. *Yes!* I thought. *This is what the program is for. This is my purpose.*

Before long, my friend's daughter began to take independent steps and string words together, and I felt our worlds diverge. Emma was not doing any of those things and I suspected never would. I berated myself for comparing our two special children, for thinking that if I had been given a choice of disabilities, I would choose Down syndrome, without hesitation. Because there was so much more knowledge about the syndrome and nothing about Emma's chromosomal condition, because Emma was so much more limited and so much more medically involved—just so much more.

It wasn't easy, but I worked to remind myself that while there were so many things Emma did not have agency over, there were critical things she *could* do. Like the way she smiled in acknowledgment each time we walked into a room, and the way she folded in half laughing her silent intelligent laugh when we said or did something funny. The way she blew kisses by putting her lips together and effecting a loud popping sound, and the way she reached for us and put our hands together, instructing us to clap for her. She gave back to us emotionally tenfold, and I was grateful for it.

Still, on a deeper level, I realized I was invoking a ladder of suffering—of incomparable things. I wondered that if there was a choice offered—like in the anecdote told of people hanging their struggles out like laundry on a clothing line and getting permission to swap their worries for another's— whether in the end, you always end up sticking with your own, because you've learned them, embraced them. Owned them. Love them.

Working in Early Intervention, I realized I had front row, center seats to these most special of life's dramas. Tragedies and comedies alike were being enacted in front of me. This was the human condition at its most raw, most vulnerable, most human. Sometimes I felt uncomfortable at being allowed a peek into families' most private of experiences. But I felt infinitely more thankful for the knowledge that ours was not such a singular life as I once thought. Yes, Emma was one of a kind, but so were all the other children: abled, disabled, differently abled. In some circles, we were not so abnormal. Our lives knitted together in similar patterns, had the occasional knots, and sometimes had to be unraveled so that we could begin anew—threads weaving a stronger tapestry.

CHAPTER 23

TOLYA AND I SAT ON the living room floor with our backs against the couch. The news was flickering on the television in front of us. Emma was busying herself with her usual pastime, chewing pensively on her bib while intermittently looking up at the screen, to which she was too close and from which I had called her several times to come.

"Want to have a little friendly competition?" I turned to Tolya, trying to suppress the mischievous smile that accompanied my words.

"What are you talking about?" Tolya answered. Suspicion carved his face. He knew me well but could not have anticipated what I said next.

"I thought it'd be fun to see which one of us Emma loves more," I continued. Suspicion morphed into surprise as Tolya's eyes widened and his brows climbed his forehead. "Let's call her and see who she scoots to." Emma was positioned about five feet in front of us. I estimated an easy win as I casually waited for Tolya to finish his verbal missives questioning my sanity.

"What, you're afraid you'll lose?" I taunted. I also knew my husband well enough to know that he did not suffer from the competitive disease that ailed me. I found this out early on—on our first date.

At sixteen, I was still a cocky teen and Tolya was a year and a half older, though not much more mature. For some delusional reason, I fancied myself a fast runner. I was the opposite of long-legged but believed that the drive to win superseded my height-challenged stature.

"Hey, you know I'm a pretty fast runner," I offered that day as we walked down the tree-lined street past my apartment building.

"Oh yeah?" He gave me a patronizing smile. I must have sounded like some braggadocious five-year-old announcing that she knew all her letters.

"I'll race you," I challenged him.

He looked at me with disbelief and declined, saying that I was being silly.

"You're afraid of losing to a girl?" I goaded then, as well.

"No." He said this in a warning tone, as if dissuading a child from touching the knobs of the stove.

"Then let's do it. On your mark, get set, go!"

Before I finished the sentence, I was off. With my arms pumping, I lunged my ninety-pound body forward with the determination of one being chased by hungry predators. And with no sign of him at my heels, I assumed, in my overinflated arrogance, that Tolya was far behind me. I could taste victory as I glimpsed the end of the block rapidly approaching, then struck the imaginary finish line with the zest of an Olympian sprinter and hit the brakes before I spilled out onto the street and oncoming traffic. Triumphant and out of breath, I turned to gloat, only to find to my horror that my phantom competitor was just that. Tolya had not budged from where I left him at the beginning of the block. I ran alone—raced against myself like a fool against my own ego. My oversized Leo pride could not withstand such an embarrassing assault. I turned my back and continued walking away.

"Emma!" I bellowed in her direction, in my most saccharine voice, "come to Mama."

Tolya glanced at me briefly, shook his head, and sang, projecting, "The wheels on the bus go round and round . . ." And so, a circus ensued.

Emma glanced up—surprise on her open face—considered us both, folded in half as if in a curtsied laugh, and began to push her body forward on her bottom, her legs bending and straightening like a caterpillar. I continue to holler, "Who's my yummy girl?" and sing my rendition of songs I made up with Emma's name in them, gesticulating grandiosely with my arms, beckoning her to me. Tolya continued his steady singing, but his voice had risen in volume and range. For someone to walk in on us at that moment, I imagine, would have been to witness hysterical lunacy on display. It made me kind of happy to find myself in this maelstrom—battling for my daughter's affection. Until I saw Emma's body slowly pivot and head in Tolya's direction.

"Noooooo!" I heard myself yell. "This way big girl. Who's my yummy girl? Mama loves you soooo much . . ." and on and on until Emma, with a drool-covered chin, reached Tolya. He swooped her up onto his lap—both father and daughter triumphant. I sulked a little, pretended to lick my wounds, but secretly I was proud of their bond and not a little delighted at how my priorities had shifted. Emma had helped my competitive nature evolve—a child, who I initially rejected, who devastated me and sent me into a grief spiral, still had me wanting to be the winner, but this time in a competition of love.

My evolution would take more time with my other two children though, and all three would play a role in rearranging my heart. My parents assuredly had a hand in my leanings toward perfection. Early on it was instilled in me by my father, who questioned why I would bring home a 99 and not 100 on a test. And although he was a blue-collar worker with an eighth-grade education, too often I heard the iteration that children must do and be better than their parents. From my stylish mother, who you'd never catch leaving the house without her makeup on, I learned that the impression you made was of paramount importance and, by extension, that others' opinions mattered. And so, perfection and perception became the constants that dictated my life. From my earliest memories, while reaching for my best self, I'd been acutely aware of an audience, real or imagined, with their score cards ready to pop up—gauging my performance. Striving for flawlessness often felt akin to cupping air, but my childhood was built on this and so shaped me.

So, it's not surprising that I would meet the occasional less-than-perfect grade that Joshua or Hanna brought home with an inquiry of how the rest of the class did. It was wrong, I knew it, and Tolya often scolded me on the subject. But I couldn't break the pattern so deeply embedded into my psyche easily, and I continued to struggle.

I fixated on the kids as if they were centerpieces to be showcased, trumped around. When someone asked, I could proudly recite the list of their accomplishments: They were smart and talented and popular and funny. They attended special schools and competed in fencing and played the obligatory instruments. All the things that I was bred for.

It was for us that my parents had sacrificed, by abandoning their roots and shedding the dregs of anti-Semitism, like countless before them. We had a duty to fulfill as immigrant children. A levy was issued, and there was a price to pay for this freedom. And the price was accomplishment and success. Anything short of that would have been perceived as betrayal. This was the promise of America.

So where did that leave Emma? It was why I felt such guilt when Emma was born. My father's words played on repeat in my head. All I could think at the time was *This was not better. This was so not better.*

Was there shame, regret, initially? Inarguably, yes. But as Emma grew and I fell more and more in love with her, I found myself singing her praises, just in different ways from her siblings. Her accomplishments were curated by her. She would not be sculpted like Michelangelo's David. She was already and always the way she needed to be, in the form she needed to take.

In addition to being hard on the kids, I continued to be hard on myself and allow others' judgments to get to me. A therapist once asked if I encouraged Josh and Hanna to play with Emma—if I taught Joshua, who was about nine at the time, how to G-tube feed Emma. After I swallowed my hurt that appeared like a lump in my throat at what I perceived as judgment, I said, "I don't force them. They play with her when they want to, and Josh doesn't need to know how to feed her. That's the nurses' and our job." But the words clung to my psyche. Was this person implying that I wasn't teaching them compassion? Was I being neglectful of their moral education? I didn't think so. As much as I would have loved for them to show more interest in their sister, I recognized that they were kids, doing what interested them. I didn't want them to feel put upon, not yet, perhaps not ever. It was a choice they needed to make for themselves when they were ready.

I already knew them to be compassionate, thoughtful kids. When Josh was about five, he asked me why Emma was the way she was and if she would ever walk or talk. I answered to the best of my ability, and he surprised me with this insightful final thought: "I wonder what she thinks about?" And when we traveled to Paris with the kids one summer, I watched Hanna dissolve into tears upon seeing a little disabled boy of about ten, prone on a cardboard box, outside the posh and extravagant Galeries Lafayette department store— his father seated next to him, begging for money.

The boy was obviously very delayed with little to no mobility. "Why are you crying, love?" I asked her, wrapping my arms around her, even though I knew the answer: "Because I think of Emma and everything she has, the warmth and comfort, and this little boy is on the street." I shed my own tears at her tender and empathic reaction. These and other scenarios told me that by some process of osmosis, or the sheer daily reality of watching us care for Emma, Josh and Hanna were learning by example. And I was fine with that. Besides, normalcy was the modus operandi for me.

Did Tolya and I as parents set different standards for our healthy kids versus Emma? Assuredly, yes. More was always expected of Josh and Hanna, because they had more agency over their thoughts and actions. Emma was instinctively given a free pass. You couldn't be mad at her. She couldn't be asked to try harder, in the way that was demanded of Josh and Hanna. Different strokes for different folks. The same rules did not apply. At the end of the day, we were still refugees whose children had to amount to something, had to achieve, as if to justify our presence in a country that gave us a second chance, to earn our place here. Our healthy children would be the unwitting vehicles for the success of this endeavor.

And so, were Tolya and I not disappointed when after almost a decade of lessons, fencing tournaments, violin recitals, and established skill, they dropped both? Oh, yes, we were. "Where did we go wrong?" he would ask when we were alone or when he'd return from his fencing lessons (because he continued practicing the sport he loved so much), where he would learn of our kids' fencing mates achieving great standing or ranking at tournaments. *Jack got scouted for Columbia, and he's only in ninth grade. Peter got a full scholarship to St. Johns.* It broke his heart a little that his own kids, who he'd put so much time and effort into, were not as passionate about it as he was.

And did my own tendencies toward excellence and perfection miraculously melt away when it came to Josh's and Hanna's academic and social achievements, because I was raising a child with limitations? Sadly, they did not. At least not while in the midst of raising all three. Both Hanna and Josh were expected to achieve their academic and artistic best. Test prep, voice, dance, violin, and acting classes. Our healthy children had to reach their best potential, whatever the height, whatever their ceiling, just like Emma had hers, though there was no comparison.

At times, I was so blinded by the vision I had in my head of how things were supposed to be—because the world was watching, weighing in, seeing if you measure up—that I would make decisions bordering on the obscenely ludicrous. Like the time I subjected Josh to a growth hormone test (because he was so small for his age) and made him undergo a procedure in which he had to drink a substance akin to the gestational diabetes test given to pregnant mothers, then wait an hour to have his blood drawn, only to find out that the lab mistakenly administered the test that checked for gigantism. "It's okay, Mama," my sweet boy, tolerant of his crazy mother, said to me in response to my profuse, mortified apologies. But did I learn my lesson right away? Embarrassingly, no. This test was followed years later, in his adolescence, by a bone age scan in which Joshua's hand would be x-rayed to see if his bones were still growing.

Or when he started kindergarten and a friend unwittingly mimicked Joshua's speech, comparing him to the lisping sloth in the cartoon *Ice Age. Does my son have a speech impediment?* I embarked on a mission to eliminate this obstacle of language development with hours of private speech therapy, which only served to frustrate Josh and make him self-conscious. In all this, I believed I was helping; protecting; curating a future free of misunderstandings, free of taunts by peers; and ensuring that were he to pursue political office as an adult, he wouldn't have to bear the shame of public speaking with a lisp, like our mayor at the time.

Hanna was my star. Among other things, she excelled in the arts. She was the thespian, singer, dancer, orator, feminist, and strong, confident, principled young woman that I would never be. I half joked on Facebook whenever I'd post her many performances that I wanted to be her when I grew up. Even so, she didn't escape my lunacy. I worried about her putting on weight, because my historically brainwashed head and social media told me that girls had to be slim to attract. Appearance mattered, to me anyway. But I had failed to notice this: that it only mattered to me, and that my daughter would take an ignorant statement that I made about an outfit not looking flattering on her and carry a silent resentment toward me for years to come.

I straddled polar universes, one composed of ability and entitlement and the pursuits of happiness through success, and an "other" world in which Emma resided, where achievements were almost invisible to the undiscerning eye, where simple goals were only outlined in her IEP, and where each Lilliput accomplishment was met with a mammoth celebration. The pressure of a successful future for Emma did not cloud my thinking. It was an exercise in survival for us, in getting through the day without hiccups, on repeat.

I felt my best self with Emma. My haughty expectations, like the ones I placed on Hanna and Josh, for academics, values, and intentions did not blemish my attention to her. There was a freedom in our exchange, a lightness of being. I felt my true self with her—no ego interference. No tears at being judged were shed by this little girl. She was perfection and could do no wrong. I watched her fight her hardest battle each day; every day was a hill, a mountain she scaled with nary a complaint.

Was it fair that we were placing conditions on our healthy, abled children when Emma was being loved unconditionally? Was this the lesson she was teaching us? In a world where we were taught to believe that meritocracy ruled, was she quietly teaching us instead the awesome power of undiluted, unconditional love? *That* had merit. We only had to turn off autopilot and pay attention. In hindsight, though, when you're in the eye of the storm and trying to survive, you can be rendered deaf and blind—and dumb—to what's in visible sight. I couldn't yet know that my evolution would not happen in one epiphany, that it would happen organically and slowly, over time, in a subtle and inconspicuous way, visible only to the naked heart. Only years later, when forced to pause, I would ask, *In the end, what was it all for? When your kids are happy and healthy—have a sense of belonging, love and are loved—isn't that what matters?*

CHAPTER 24

MY EYES FLUTTERED OPEN TO the startling and unrecognizable sound that had come from Emma's room.

Thud!

Then her distinct crying. I sprang out of bed and sprinted to her room. It was the middle of the night, and I found Emma splayed on her back on the hardwood floor next to her crib.

"Tolya!" I screamed.

"Oh my god," he said when he saw her. "What happened?" I was already on the floor, having gently scooped her up into my arms.

"Turn on the lights. We need to see if she's hurt," I cried. Emma wailed louder than I'd ever heard her—for longer than I'd ever heard her make any sound. I rocked her and rubbed the back of her head. "Shhh, you're okay, baby. You're okay." She eventually grew calm, but my heart wouldn't stop racing. That night, Tolya slept on the floor of her room next to her crib.

Emma was ten years old at the time of the fall but still sleeping in her baby crib. She had grown but was not the size of an average child her age. As she got taller and learned to pull to stand by holding on to the crib's railing, we continued to lower the mattress until we could no longer do it. That harrowing night, she must have pulled up, leaned over, and fallen out. That was our signal to look for an alternative, safer sleeping solution.

The Sleepsafe bed was finally approved by Medicaid. It was a $5,000 construction we jokingly called the Rolls Royce of beds. Made of light birch wood, it looked like an oversized crib, with a twin-sized mattress that could accommodate Emma into adulthood. Instead of bars, the bed offered two wood-framed panels made of clear plastic, which could be lowered as well as removed so that she could sit up and throw her legs over the edge of it and be helped onto the floor. I'd often climb into bed with her, lying alongside her when she wasn't feeling well—other times just to hang out and play.

For a long time after the fall, even when in the Sleepsafe, Emma stopped pulling up to stand. Her safety awareness was intact. I was impressed that she learned this concept of cause and effect so quickly. *Fool me once*, I could hear her saying.

Since Emma's safety had always been at the forefront of everything, each new nurse that entered our home became integrally connected to that principle. Emma was nonverbal and, as I saw it, defenseless against unscrupulous, negligent, or otherwise indifferent caregivers. Her welfare, her treatment, her very health and well-being occupied my thoughts almost exclusively when I was away from her.

"She can't tell us if someone is mistreating or neglecting her," I would often complain to Tolya. "I want to set up cameras in the apartment."

I was prompted to have this conversation by an incident that had taken place earlier that day. We were "test-driving" a new nurse. She was young and fresh out of nursing school, and her youth and inexperience worried me. The nurse and Emma were in the living room and I was in the kitchen, preparing the kids' lunch. Because we had taken down the partial wall that separated the kitchen from the foyer when we purchased and renovated the apartment, I had easy visual access

to the living room. An internal voice, or mother's instinct—
something—told me to peek in on them. I watched the nurse
with her back to me, whispering on the phone, and Emma
on the floor at the foot of the couch, trying to swat her leg
in an obvious effort to get attention.

Then I saw the nurse push Emma away with her leg.

I pounced—took four giant strides toward the living
room, lowered myself onto the floor, and scooped Emma up
in my arms, hugging her.

"Someday, you may become a mother . . ." I was choking
back tears as I felt myself spit venomous words at the startled
nurse. "And I hope that you have a healthy child . . . one who
can speak and tell you when someone is hurting her. I hope
you never find yourself in the place I'm in right now, having
to be my child's voice."

"I'm sorry," the nurse mumbled. "Please don't cry." I was
so consumed by anger I hadn't noticed it break to the surface.

"Why do this? Why become a nurse?" I said this with
the full intention of delivering a razor cut—to hurt. I was in
defense and attack mode all at once.

I wielded my words like a weapon. Too often my words
had gotten me into trouble. Too often I let petty grievances threaten valued friendships and relationships. Emma
employed language merely to communicate her needs for
love and attention—not to hurt or attack another—that's all
she ever demanded. In her silent way, she collected what she
needed without injuring others' sensibilities or allowing her
inner self to be perturbed. Our different methods yielded different results. But this young nurse needed to hear my voice.

"What are you going to do? Watch hours of footage
when you get home?" Tolya was responding to my insistence
on a Nanny Cam, as they were called.

"Maybe. I don't know. At least I can look back at the
video if I suspect something."

"You can't live like this," he reasoned. "You can't monitor every person that Emma comes in contact with. It'll drive you crazy. You'll hyper-focus on every little thing, because no one will be good enough, nice enough, attentive enough. No one can be you. Then we'll end up going through nurses even faster than before." I knew he was right, so I let the issue rest, until the next time.

Tolya had always been my emotional barometer, molder of character. He reminded me to rise above when someone went low, below the belt. *Don't expect and you won't be disappointed*, he moralized. He was my conservator of energy, reminding me to pick my battles by gauging their significance. I typically resented the ice he threw on my fires, because I wanted to continue to burn. But when my ire diffused and my embers barely singed, I was grateful for his efforts.

Deep down I knew that I couldn't protect Emma all the time. I had no control of situations outside my home, where there were no cameras to show me the truth, where she was at the mercy of another's poor judgment or broken moral compass.

A year before the young nurse incident, a more egregious event shook us to the core. I was working "in the field" at an agency, conducting meetings, when my cell phone rang. I normally didn't answer such calls unless it was the kids' schools or Emma's nurse. The nurse's number flashed on the caller ID, and I excused myself, explaining that it was about my daughter.

"Diana, it's Linda," the nurse said. ". . . Emma fell." Her voice came across shaky and uncertain, as if she herself wasn't sure what she was saying.

"What do you mean she fell?" My voice projected into the four-by-five room and sounded more like a declarative than a question. I could see peripherally that the expression on the face of the mother with whom I was conducting the meeting changed to alarm.

As I grabbed my things and ran for the door, Linda explained. She had taken Emma out to do food shopping for herself. The busy shopping area where the stores began was about a fifteen-minute walk from our building. She went into the fruit and vegetable store but left Emma in her adaptive stroller, parked outside. As soon as she uttered those words, I knew what would come next.

"You left her outside?" I screamed.

Our neighborhood of Forest Hills has its name for a reason. In the warm seasons, it's green and bucolic, and trees line most streets. But it's also very hilly, so much so that walking up such hills, one could expect a decent workout and to be out of breath. Walking down some hills, you almost had to "put on the breaks" in your step. The blocks that contained the shops started at the top of the hill, and this was where Emma was "parked." 108th Street was a busy, wide road that could easily accommodate four traffic lanes but instead used the extra space to park its cars parallel to each other, not one behind the other as is typical of less expansive streets.

No sooner had Linda gone in than she heard someone yell, "The baby, the baby!"

"The breaks must have given out. Emma's stroller went rolling down the street," she continued.

At that moment, I stopped hearing what she was saying— my mind consumed by the image of Emma flying down the steep street and into a parked car or, worse, continuing into the busy traffic. Breath caught in my chest as I uttered the next words.

"Is Emma okay? Just tell me that she's okay!" I yelled.

"I think she's okay. We're at the pediatrician's now. Nothing seems to be broken, but her face is bruised up. . . ." She trailed off.

I'll kill her. I'll fucking kill her, I thought.

After I arrived, the pediatrician confirmed that Emma, miraculously, did not sustain any serious injuries, and that was largely owed to the fact that she was strapped in. The seat belts across her chest served their purpose and added a layer of safety. Her chin was bruised up where her face encountered the parked car that stopped her momentum, but otherwise she was relatively, miraculously, unscathed.

This girl, I thought once again, *is a survivor.*

"How can we justify keeping her after this?" I argued when we got safely home. "Things could have turned out much worse. . . . Emma could have been killed."

"Look," Tolya said, "it's not like she did it intentionally, right?"

"Well, obviously, she didn't do it intentionally, but it was careless—reckless of her to leave Emma outside like that," I argued. "I mean, she did cry in the car on the way home, and I think she said she was sorry, but still . . ."

"I just don't want to go through the whole headache of hiring a new nurse again," Tolya said.

And I understood what he meant: stay with the familiar. We both knew how hard it was to get good nurses and how difficult it was to start from scratch each time. And Emma had demonstrated, more than with any other nurse, an affinity toward this one. So we did.

Regardless of nurses, it became impossible to keep Emma safe all the time. There was the day Emma came off the school bus with a broken arm.

"Diana, come here. I want to show you something." I had returned from work, and Emma's longtime occupational therapist was on the living room floor working with Emma.

"Something strange," she continued as I lowered myself onto the floor next to them and planted a quick kiss on Emma's head. "Emma normally prefers to use her left arm when reaching for something, but today she's refusing to.

And when I try to raise it for her, she seems uncomfortable."
She demonstrated what she was referring to, and Emma produced a notable moan.

"What do you think is going on?" I asked, trying to
disguise the worry in my voice.

"I don't know, but I think you should take her to an
orthopedic doctor for an X-ray."

The X-ray revealed a hairline bone fracture in her upper arm.

"How could this have happened?" I inquired of the
doctor, panicked.

"It's difficult to say, but usually it would take some
amount of impact, perhaps a fall."

Alarms went off in my head. I briefly imagined all kinds
of atrocities in school: Emma falling out of her chair when
being transitioned by an aide, the bus attendant being forceful
with her. But then I quickly realized that that would never
happen. All the adults in her school and on the bus loved her
and would never do anything to intentionally hurt her. The
fall out of her crib took place years prior, and the pediatrician
did not find any injuries at the time. How then?

The school and the bus attendants denied anything having
happened while she was in their care, and I believed them, but
my frustration and disappointment reached its peak.

I had failed to protect her. Again.

After the broken arm incident, Emma's school became
even more vigilant in reporting the minutest of observations.
Prior to the fracture, the letters home included requests to cut
her nails often, because she sometimes used scratching as a
form of communicating her displeasure. Now every black-
and-blue mark, every pimple, was brought to our attention,
made a note of, documented. It was as if they were beating
us to the punch: *We noticed Emma came to school with a
runny nose, a scratch on her forearm, a pimple on her chin,
lethargic, crusty-eyed.* They had to claim it first so that we

couldn't say that this was inflicted in school, that someone was negligent. Annoying as this was, I understood that the school was covering their behinds—ever mindful of potential legal action. I was secretly thankful for it because it meant that someone always had an eye on her. Keeping her safe.

But the truth was, I could wield no more control over Emma's safety than I could over Joshua or Hanna. The moment each of these beating hearts left my body and ventured out into the world, I forfeited the power to protect them from the elements, from physical harm and emotional wounds, from others, and even from themselves. I couldn't be everywhere, always. Which was why I blamed myself the one time I let my guard down and entrusted a nurse with a task not part of her job responsibilities. It was a colossal fail.

On the day of my sister Holly's wedding, I asked the nurse caring for Emma at the time to curl her hair with my curling iron for the special occasion. The nurse was a stylish older woman, and I assumed she was familiar and comfortable with the use of beauty products. She agreed and even seemed excited about the undertaking. But when Emma arrived at the venue, her hair was disheveled, uncurled, and unbrushed. I was furious.

"What happened?" I asked. "Why didn't you curl her hair?"

"She wouldn't let me."

I let it go, not wanting to work myself up on Holly's big day. I borrowed a brush, ran it through Emma's tangled hair, threw some barrettes into it, and forgot about it. Until two days later, when I took Emma from the nurse to get her ready for bed and noticed the palm of her right hand; it was red, and a large white blister covered almost the entire surface area.

"Oh . . . my . . . god," I whispered under my breath as I gently uncurled Emma's fingers and held her open hand palm up for the nurse to see. "What is this? How did this happen?"

"I was going to tell you . . . but . . . this weekend when you asked me to curl Emma's hair for your sister's wedding, well . . . Emma grabbed the curling iron. . . ." At those words, I felt myself step out of my body. Guilt intertwined with rage, rose from my chest, and tangoed in the space around me. I should have known I was courting disaster. *It's my fault. I asked her to do it.*

"Why didn't you tell me this sooner? We sent her to school like this. If they'd seen it, they could have called Child Protective Services on us and taken her away! Don't you get it? THIS IS SERIOUS!" I had unleashed a fury that I had not known I could ever be capable of. Fear stared back at me, and at that moment I knew I could have easily hurt this person. The only thing that stopped me was the voice in my head: *I asked her to do it.*

CHAPTER 25

BECAUSE I LIVED AND WORKED in a world defined by the special-needs community, the question of Emma's future with us loomed large and close. I stormed against our myopic existence. I longed to be able to peek beyond and plan, to imagine and dream a different reality. The program of school and at-home nurses wasn't sustainable long term.

I felt perpetually ambushed by the nurses and therapists at home. It was why many nights I made plans not to be home too early, to avoid sharing the hours with the nurses who were perennial fixtures in my kitchen, my bathroom, my living room couch. I chauffeured Hanna and Josh to their fencing classes in Long Island, carted them to violin lessons, to Hanna's dance and theater classes in the city. Some evenings I returned so late that Emma was already in her bed. Those were the nights I was most torn between the guilt of not having spent time with her and resentment toward the nurses for being there, for our dependence on them, and for their personalities and peculiarities.

One day I came home to a nurse boiling lobster on my stovetop using my large pot. "I'm obviously in the wrong field," I laughed, telling Tolya that night. "I can't afford lobster for lunch." This nurse packed our freezer and refrigerator with her shopping for the week. "Is this ours or the nurse's?" Tolya would ask daily when scouring for a snack. She would take Emma off the school bus and proceed to prepare her elaborate lunches, which invariably involved using the stovetop. The offensively strong odor of fried fish more than once assaulted my nostrils as I walked in the door, and lingered long after the nurse's departure.

Another time I returned home unexpectedly early to find a nurse, Emma's therapist, and the nurse's friend seated comfortably on the living room couch, sipping coffee and eating cake. My breath caught.

"Do you mind taking that into the kitchen, please?" I said in my most saccharine of voices. "You know I don't allow anyone to eat in the living room," I said, directing my words at the nurse.

"I mean, is my house a diner to them?" I railed at Tolya that night. "It's our *home* and their place of *work*."

"I don't think it's a big deal," he countered gently, avoiding eye contact. Arguing about nurses was a constant.

Well, I did. I harbored dreams of coming home to a house without nurses, therapists. I imagined that time wistfully: a reclaimed space filled with space and lovely furnishings, minus all the bodies that perpetually occupied it. "We are living in occupied territories," I bellowed at Tolya, in only half jest. Home only felt like home when it was just Tolya and me and the kids. Otherwise it was like returning to a public place: a market, a cafe, a theater where non-family members enacted their lives.

Working in Early Intervention gave me access to others who had older children with special needs, or knew others who did. Where did those *adult* children go after they *grew up*? These were questions Tolya and I touched on lightly at least once a year. We circled the subject tentatively—danced around it guiltily. I kept my ears tuned to the stories of others and delivered the narratives to him like scraps of gifts, wrapped in flimsy paper to be gingerly uncovered and considered. "One of my coworkers has a niece who's in a group home in Brooklyn," I would say. "It's a Jewish organization called Ohel, I think. She says they take good care of her."

"Mmmhmm." Tolya would nod.

"She can attend her school until she's twenty-one and live with us, but then we can look into placement," I said on other occasions. "There are long waiting lists for these homes, because there's so few of them, so we'd have to start looking years before."

"Okay," Tolya would respond. Only briefly did I allow myself to register his clipped answers.

"I mean, Hanna and Josh will be out of the house by that time too, in college." I bulldozed forward, barely trying to hide my enthusiasm. "We'll visit her on the weekends, maybe even bring her home."

I was faintly aware that I was trying to convince myself that our parental responsibilities only extended until the children, all three, reached adulthood. Twenty-one was a magic number; it represented freedom. *That didn't make us bad parents.* We would have done our time and been rewarded. I knew these were selfish notions, but I couldn't help thinking them.

But of course, on a deeper level, I knew that Emma did not fit neatly into the folds of my plans for Tolya's and my freedom. As with all things pertaining to Emma's care, I worried about how she would be treated by the workers, whether she would understand her surroundings, that we gave her up, rejected her yet again. *Didn't you learn the first time?* I imagined her thinking. What if she was sad, missed us? I couldn't live with that. Still, I needed to test those waters when the time came—because who knew? I thought. We didn't.

There was also the question of our own health and abilities—would we stay healthy and capable of caring for Emma long term?

One winter in 2009, we summoned our resolve, discarded our old reservations, and decided yet again to attempt another family trip with all three kids. Great Wolf Lodge was a close-enough, self-contained little world of waterpark and snow entertainment. The plan was to take Emma snow tubing on the nearby Shawnee Mountain while Hanna, Josh and I skied.

The weather that weekend was not kind to us; it was bitter cold, so after only two hours or so on the slopes, Hanna and I retreated to the car to thaw under the blasting heat. When we'd sufficiently warmed, I went looking for Tolya and Emma, worried that she would be freezing even in her many layers, because of her limited mobility. She couldn't generate heat by simply jumping up and down like the rest of us; she could barely support the weight of her body on her little feet—ensconced in her snowsuit, heavy boots, and bulky jacket.

We found father and daughter at the bottom of the slope, in line behind several other people holding their donut-shaped snow tubes. Emma sat in one of the holes of the double donut, seemingly uncomfortable, or maybe I projected that onto her. But she did not look happy.

"She looks cold," I said to Tolya, and then leaning closer, "Why don't you ask to cut the line? I'm sure people wouldn't object."

"You sure about that?" he countered, not disguising his sarcasm.

"What do you mean?" I spoke through gritted teeth, partly due to the cold but mostly in anger. "You asked and they didn't let you?" I could not wrap my head around such a possibility.

"I'll tell you later," he said. "Let us just go down one more time, and we'll call it a day."

I looked at the literal road that lay ahead of them. It was a moving sidewalk, not dissimilar to the kind they later installed in airports, but this one ascended into the billowy whiteness of the mountain top. Bodies stood motionless with their donut tubes at their feet as the flattened escalator carried them to the promised ten seconds of gleeful pleasure.

"My back started hurting suddenly," Tolya complained that night after everyone went to bed.

"Well, of course." I was vexed about the earlier snow tubing misadventures. "You stood in line, suffering in the cold with Emma—holding her in your arms with all that weight. I'm not surprised. What even happened up there?"

He proceeded to tell me how every time they stepped on the moving escalator and he would try and hold her up, Emma would fold her legs under her and refuse to stand, and every time she did that, he would sit her down inside the tube. "When the girl at the top of the escalator saw me do this," he said, "she stopped the ride and yelled for me to stand Emma up."

"Oh my god. You're joking," I said, outraged.

"I wish I was. So, I would yell back up at her, 'My daughter is disabled. She physically cannot stand.' This happened each time we went up. Emma sat down, the escalator was stopped, and we yelled back and forth until the people on the line in front of me and behind me started telling me to stand her up too."

"Assholes!" I felt my blood percolate and rush into my head, pounding behind my eyes. I realized this was the second time we had been confronted with such insensitivity and inconsideration, the first being with our building ramp. It scorched my sensibilities just the same to know that there were, of course, unkind people in the world, behaving unkindly.

That weekend's physical strain catapulted Tolya into back pain hell. It started with lower back pain that was not subsiding. A visit to the neurologist revealed a herniated disk in the lower lumbar area.

We had been training to run in the New York City Marathon that year. Tolya started the qualifying runs before me, completed them first, and ran that November before the Great Wolf Lodge trip.

"The doctor said that running the marathon and then the strain of lifting and holding Emma on the slopes must have contributed to the herniation," Tolya explained to me.

This was disturbing information. I watched my still young, strong husband hobble gingerly around the house, trying to hide the contortions of pain on his face from me. Tolya listed the options offered him: cortisone shots, physical therapy, surgery. I froze at the mention of the last alternative. "I'd rather not go that route," Tolya continued. "It's dangerous. I could be paralyzed." My mind immediately went to that place, struck by an image of father and daughter side by side in their respective wheelchairs.

His pain got progressively worse. Some mornings I had to get three kids off to school, though until that point, our responsibilities were divided into me taking care of the logistics— therapists, school, nurses—while Tolya picked up the physical burden: the heavy lifting, literally. *This is not sustainable*, I thought. *I can't handle Emma all by myself.* I was scared. Emma was thirteen at the time, and the plan, at least in my head, had been to keep her with us until she graduated from school at twenty-one. My thoughts turned dark. What if I had to take care of two disabled people? Could I do it, or would I give up Emma again? Earlier than planned? I felt vile having these thoughts but couldn't stop them from battering me daily, unyielding in their insistence.

In the end, Tolya's neurologists arranged emergency back surgery with the head of Mount Sinai's neurosurgery department. This was serious. I comforted myself with the knowledge that he was in good hands, but still—surgery was surgery. I drove Tolya to the pre-op appointment with his neurologist in our Chevy minivan. He positioned himself on the floor of the van, tucked in between the second- and first-row seats, because he could no longer be upright.

The surgery went off without a hitch. Tolya was back on his feet but vigilantly careful about the way he moved, lifted, exercised. He yelled at me to bend my knees every time I bent down to pick something up or to lift Emma. "You want to end up like me?" he scolded. I briefly allowed myself the image of lying in bed, incapacitated. But instead of fear or despair, a strange sense of relief presented itself, if only fleetingly, and whispered: *No responsibility, no work, no childcare. Just lay here and read and eat.* Then I gave myself a mental slap for entertaining such thoughts about a horrible fate, recognizing that it was probably frustration and fatigue talking and that I merely longed for a break, a reprieve from the day-to-day.

"We have to be physically okay for Emma," Tolya reminded me.

"Yes, we do," I agreed almost grudgingly. *I want to be okay for me*, I thought egotistically. In this matter, I would realize, Tolya was more evolved. He was in possession of a wisdom I still struggled with. He accepted things, life, Emma. I bucked against things, pushed back, challenged, railed.

Life resumed with Tolya getting Emma up and putting her on the bus in the mornings while I got Joshua and Hanna ready for school. I had my partner again. We were back to normal—our normal. Still, worry of our capabilities remained in the shadows.

Emma's extensive needs required that I work relatively close to her school so that if she was sick and I needed to pick her up, it would be a short enough drive. Which is why I chose to work in Queens and not Manhattan—my preferred location. On one occasion, I received a call from the school nurse: "Emma has a fever and is very lethargic. Please pick her up." The school often called about various things having to do with Emma's health, but she rarely got fevers, so this was on the more serious end.

By the time I'd gotten Emma strapped into the car seat behind me, heavy rain had started to fall. On the expressway, halfway home, the rain began descending in sheets that made it impossible to see more than three feet in front of you. The windshield wipers at their highest speed did little for visibility and only added to the already frantic atmosphere and my nervous state.

Suddenly two tour buses on either side of us began to skid. I understood immediately that I could waste no time and risk being trapped between them, as they seemed to be losing control, so I needed to press on the gas. But as the thought flickered, and before I had a chance to execute my plan, I felt the car gliding smoothly forward—a sensation of being elevated and navigated through the space as if by some divine intervention. The next flash of consciousness was that I wasn't alone—that I had Emma in the car and that I had to keep her safe. As I passed the buses and glanced into the rear-view mirror to see the apocalyptic scene we had narrowly escaped, I exhaled the air I was holding, unaware.

Once safely home, I called Tolya at work. "It was so terrifying. When I looked back, I saw the buses stopped on a diagonal and cars behind them. We got so lucky."

I realized something after that close call: I knew I loved Emma deeply, but until that day, I wasn't sure I loved her enough. Being forced to face the prospect of losing her, and the ensuing grief—I felt my heart rearranged. Someone once said that you can only truly love someone if you accept them.

Maybe now I did.

CHAPTER 26

NIETZSCHE SAID, "WITHOUT MUSIC, life would be a mistake."

We were a family of singers. It was in our family blood, and its pull coursed through my veins, just like "cleaning" was not in my blood, as my mother stated often and pointedly while standing in my teen bedroom, whose carpet color we could no longer detect. Though I don't remember, family members often told the story of how my grandmother Manya took me to perform my little ditties, war ballads, to store shop ladies when I was a mere four-year-old. I left with pockets brimming with reward candy.

My earliest and most vivid memory was of our neighbor Lilly barging into our apartment in Kiev and yelling, "Larissa, turn on the television. Dianochka is singing." And sure enough, there I was, seven years old—my thick shoulder-length hair in two neat ponytails accented by traditional white bows, wearing a blue-and-white sailor dress, belting out a fifteen second solo of a duckling singing about her captain mama. I was the youngest in a chorus of much older girls, and this was a televised music school performance.

Singing was a way of life. Weddings and other large events unfailingly prompted my parents to nonchalantly ask me to take the microphone and go sing one of the few Soviet ballads or songs of unrequited love that I had committed to memory. My parents' house party guests could invariably expect to be treated to dinner and a show, as I'd usually happily oblige. As much as public speaking terrified me, I had faith in my singing voice and looked forward to the applause. Even as an adolescent and young adult, the act of singing in front of hundreds of strangers on a stage—at a Russian restaurant nightclub, as a twentieth birthday gift for Tolya, or in front of three hundred guests at our wedding—did not faze me. It was as natural as breathing.

I inherited my perfect pitch from my father, who told stories of serenading my young mother in their early dating stage. While still living with my grandparents, and before my parents got their own apartment and moved us out, a lullaby by different members of the family often accompanied my bedtime, especially when I ailed from recurrent ear pain. Most family gatherings were dressed in song, as my grandmother and her three sisters belted out Ukrainian tunes at the top of their lungs.

This was the gift we bestowed on one another. I cloaked my children with music's loving message. For Emma especially—because words escaped her, and others' means of communicating did not strike the right chord with her—music was the universal language. It was inclusive and available. It was why upon entering our home, Emma's whereabouts could always be traced to her room, from which soundtracks belonging to musicals like *Hairspray*, *Fiddler on the Roof*, and *The Sound of Music* emanated.

"Do you want *Hairspray*?" I would ask, knowing it was her favorite, as I reached for the DVD player hooked into the twenty-seven-inch flat-screen television. She would look up from the sofa, her bib hanging between clenched teeth, and nod her head so vigorously that the upper half of her torso would move with her. As soon as the music began, she returned to flipping the pages of her magazine, in that self-stimulating way, and only occasionally looked up at the television as if to ensure it was still there. She had little interest in the images flickering on the screen, while the notes seemed to permeate the very fiber of her being, as her smiles intermittently graced her face.

"Emma is the most cultured member of our family," I would joke. "She is a most avid reader and appreciator of the arts."

Everyone in the family had their self-appointed songs when it came to interacting with her. My sister, Holly, sang a Yiddish song that Baba Manya taught her. My mother-in-law, Tamara, sang "Ladooshky," a Russian clapping piece. My mother tried on different songs each time. It was an unspoken rule that Emma got to swat at her and play the game of "not that one, try another." My poor mother never knew what Emma's temperament would dictate on a given day but didn't much mind the mutually understood dance they engaged in. "She's so smart," my mother would state proudly. "She understands everyone has a role." It was true. But if you tried to steal someone else's thunder by singing their assigned song, Emma would reward you with a slap on the hand in admonition.

Anna, the home nurse, sang,

Emma dilemma, pudding pie,
Kissed the boys and made them cry.
When the boys came out to play,
Emma dilemma ran away.

Emma folded in half with laughter at this. Short rhymes set to music were her favorite. Her school nurse sang "Hava-Nagilla," a Hebrew dance song, while delivering her lunch G-tube feedings to distract Emma from pulling at the tube containing formula that hung from the overhead stand. Tolya's most popular single hit was his version of "The Wheels on the Bus," whose passengers consisted of obscure animals like fish, hippos, and giraffes who made no discernible sounds but to which he assigned his own silly renditions. Emma didn't care about correctness—she signed "more" in praise of his creative silliness.

Because she recognized and loved the sound of her name, I incorporated "Emma" into every standard and made-up melody, so "Where Is Thumbkin?" became "Where Is Emma?" The "Ring Around the Rosie" melody was transformed into "Emma is a good girl. Emma is a great girl. Emma is a silly girl, a very funny girl."

We learned early on that Emma was so tuned in to the emotion behind the melodies and felt them so deeply that a sad tune like the one in "I Don't Want to Live on the Moon," played on Sesame Street, sent her wailing as if she were in great physical pain. The "Five Little Ducks" song, in which the last of the ducks wander off and the mother duck can't find them, had a similar effect on her. My singing it in a sad mother duck's voice sent Emma the emotional cues to register a worried expression on her face, until the "five little ducks came back," and she would laugh her silent but tremendous laugh—flailing her arms and nodding her head in celebration of the happy ending.

"Whatever she lacks in IQ, she makes up a hundredfold in emotional intelligence," I would brag to Tolya.

I marveled as she sifted through the sounds of language and picked up the nuances of the spoken tone. One day, the nurse that got her off the school bus forgot our apartment keys and was locked out, until I came home an hour later to see Emma in the building lobby, chewing hungrily on her shirt sleeve. Once inside I proceeded to gently lecture the nurse, whom Emma and I both loved, on the importance of having her cell phone always charged so that we could connect in an emergency like today. As I spoke in a slightly elevated, frustrated voice, Emma reached over, turned the nurse's face toward her, and began to babble "mamamamama" insistently, as if to say, "Don't pay attention to my crazy mother." The nurse picked up on this immediately and hugged and kissed her, saying, "That's my defender." I had to laugh in agreement. Emma seemed to certainly be looking out for the person she perceived was being hurt by the volume and tenor of my voice. I saw that compassion ran through her veins like mother's milk at the sound of her babe's cry.

I saw then that Emma was teaching me how to be in this world, how to navigate through life. She was intrepid, she feared no one. In that sense, she was nothing like me, when at the height of my anxiety in college and grad school, I would avoid raising my hand for fear of the entire class turning their gaze on me in what I was certain was judgment and criticism. She was an audience of one—herself.

She was also my music teacher. Some days, Emma and I would walk over to my piano, and I would help her into my chair. With back rounded, hands bent at the wrists, Emma would slam her fingers on the black and white keys in grandiose gestures, as if she were finishing Mozart's concerto with the flair of brisk movement, readying herself for impending applause. Then she would look at me for the requisite "Hurray, hurray, Emma!" I recalled the years of corrective words from my piano teacher to arch my own hands over the keys, as if creating a tent to harness and protect the notes from escaping into the ethos. Emma's efforts were praiseworthy, her obstacles greater, her control diminished. I had talent but was too lazy to practice, to exert myself in this expected skill of most Soviet children in learning an instrument. Emma did it for the sole purpose of the pleasure and sense of accomplishment it gave her to create loud dissonant sounds—singular to her enthusiasm.

Music also served as a balm when Emma was in physical pain. Some nights I'd be woken by her crying to find her sitting up in her bed, rubbing her head. I knew from previous times that she was in the grips of a headache painful enough to rouse her from her sleep. I also knew that she wasn't intentionally communicating where the pain was coming from but essentially rubbing the pain away, the equivalent of "kissing the boo-boos." I recalled from neuropsychology class that there were medical underpinnings to how this phrase originated—something to do with how touch sent competing messages to the brain that took the focus off the painful area, thereby minimizing the level of perceived pain. She had such a basic and inadvertent way of communicating, and yet it was so effective and self-preserving.

I would crawl into her bed, lower her down next to me, mold my body to hers like two spoons, and sing to ease her pain—just like my mother did with me when debilitating headaches woke me in adolescence. Emma moved her body back and forth ever so slightly, as if rocking herself to sleep, just as I had done as a child. Except I never taught her to rock herself. She was my daughter—we once shared a body. *What else have I passed on to you, besides your love of music?* I wondered, those dark nights, after my singing finally lulled her to sleep and her breathing became slow and noisy. I would have liked to believe that I passed on to her my fighting spirit.

After all, we were strong. We were survivors.

Leonard Cohen sang, "There's a crack in everything. That's how the light gets in." This iteration came from his Zen belief that nothing is perfect—no one is perfect. We are all broken, but it is the entering light that heals and repairs us. For Emma and me, the cracks were where the music seeped in, like salve on a wound—leaving healing in its wake.

CHAPTER 27

JUST LIKE THE BUTTERFLY SURFACES from the chrysalis, Emma's adolescent personality emerged in languid slow motion. If Joshua's and Hanna's evolution resembled a time-lapsed overnight blossoming that one could catch on the National Geographic channel, Emma's metamorphosis was so gradual and subtle that if you didn't know what to look for, you could miss the slight transformations. I didn't know what to look for but recognized it when I saw it.

Physically, both Hanna and Josh surpassed their older sister. By the time Hanna hit her teens, she was already taller than Emma. Joshua and Hanna were both louder and more demanding of notice. Emma's beauty lay quietly inside, in those hidden places whose depth could only be seen by those looking closely and intently.

Because of her physical and intellectual limitations, I could still selfishly enjoy her as my baby. She was maybe sixty or seventy pounds and reached the height of my chest, but I could hold her on my lap, cuddle and wrap my arms around her every day, for as long as I wanted, which I could no longer do with Josh and Hanna because they were always on the go, able to tell me when they were open to a hug or kiss. Not that I ever asked, but they seemed perpetually busy, doing their homework or practicing violin or out with friends.

Emma, on the other hand, was always there, readily available for the taking—to be scooped up in my arms, to tolerate my smooches. She reveled in it. She didn't insist I walk ten steps behind on the way to school, like I was instructed to by Josh and Hanna, nor was she embarrassed to be kissed by me in public, in front of friends. Emma was my perennial baby, and she let me pamper her with uncensored abandon.

As much as I felt that Joshua's and Hanna's love came with reciprocal conditions, Emma carried no conditions for loving me. I realized Emma would never fit into a neat box of typical development, and so to expect something other than what she was able to give would be akin to expecting the sun to rise in the west and set in the east, or for an apple tree to sprout pomegranates. "Don't expect and you'll never be disappointed" was a saying I often peddled to my sister when someone had let her down. But how does a feeling person navigate life without expectations? We expect people to act toward us with kindness if we engage in the same behavior; we expect respect if we bestow it. But ultimately, we have no more jurisdiction over peoples' actions than we have control over who we love or who loves us back. And so, Emma showed me that not only can expectations not be met, but they can be faulty. My error was believing that I couldn't love what I perceived was an imperfect child. My faulty logic was that because I was broken and imperfect myself, those soul-deep cracks within me would keep me from fully loving Emma.

WE HAD OUR SPECIAL GAMES that we played each time we were together. The nurse would be gone, Hanna and Josh would be going about their business, and Emma and I would position ourselves on the living room couch and play "Yehali Preeyehali." This required her sitting on my lap perpendicular to me, in a sideways position. I would bounce her up and down and sing, "Mi yehalli, mi yehalli ee v yamoo mi preeyehali"—"we were driving along and fell into a hole in the road." At the last words, I would part my legs, and Emma's bottom would sink into the gap created as she folded in half. She flapped her arms in excitement in anticipation of the ending. Sometimes I'd attempt to trick her by prolonging the song and delaying the ending. She would have none of this. She commandeered the game and threw herself back, knowing and fully trusting that I would catch her.

Then we would move onto my bed. There, I would lie on my back with Emma positioned perpendicular across my stomach, with her also on her back—in a plus sign configuration. She rocked herself back and forth, pushing off with her feet for a few counts. Then in a loud and worried voice I would say, "Where is Emma? I can't find Emma." She'd immediately hoist herself up, flipping and slightly rising onto her side with some effort so she could reveal her face to me. "Oh, there you are! I didn't see you over there!" I would feign surprise and make an exaggerated production of this. Emma's body shook with laughter—she left a trickle of drool on my shirt as a parting gift, then resumed her starting position for the act to be repeated another twenty times, or as many as I could sustain.

Other times I would sit next to her and just talk baby talk to her, because I could. "Who's my yummy girl? Mama loves Emma this much." I would bring my arms out far to my sides and sing the "Mama loves Emma and Emma loves Mama" song that I made up. She rewarded me with a long string of "mamamamama" sounds—the best two syllables. I don't even think she was calling me; it was more of an attempt at a reciprocal conversation, as if those two letters voiced repeatedly contained the secrets of the universe, her life story, and the lessons I needed to learn.

"What's your name, big girl?" I would prompt her to say the only other word she could, and with a breathy "eh" sound, she would exhale a barely audible "Ehmma." "That's right, your name is Emma." I clapped in praise while she folded in half, laughing. It didn't escape my notice that she only said those two words—not *dada*, not *baba*, not *papa*, nothing else—nothing but *mama* and *Emma*. I told myself that this was her way of forgiving me for giving up on her, for giving her up those years ago before she had a chance to prove her specialness and absolute place in our family.

Sometimes I'd watch from my seat on the couch as she made her way toward me. Emma's movements were clunky and jagged, but to me, she was art in motion, a musical piece played in staccato. I would attempt to go unnoticed as I'd try to sneak in yet another episode of the Real Housewives of NY, or Orange County, or Atlanta—my one guilty pleasure. Determination was engraved on her face as she considered the two hardwood steps that led into our sunken living room. Then she'd close her eyes in anticipation of the not-so-soft landing and bounce on her diapered tush down each step. Once at my feet, she pulled herself up onto the couch by planting her forearms and elbows into the cushion of the couch and, with nothing less than sheer superhuman strength, threw her body up while pivoting it 180 degrees so that she could land with aplomb on her padded behind next to me. The next movement involved her reaching for the remote control I'd be hiding behind my back, retrieving it, and triumphantly and with a deliberate gesture, placing it in my hand again so that I could comply with her wordless command to change the channel to Sesame Street. "Okay, okay, big girl," I'd say in capitulation. It was an impressive battle of wills and one that I invariably lost—secretly happy that I did.

I MARVELED AT HER PHYSICAL uniqueness. The fullness in her cheeks never seemed to have abandoned her, so as a teenager, she still had the roundness of face and baby fat of a toddler. Her skin was like milk in a porcelain cup, un-assaulted by years of the sun's damaging rays. A chin dimple gifted to her and only her by her father became more pronounced and leapt to life when she smiled.

Her hands were the epitome of softness—delicate, round pillows of cloud. With no visible evidence of knuckles, you only knew that they existed when she rapped the back of her hands on her table tray in imitation of me. Her fingers ended in ladylike fingernails that would have looked great in a manicure if she were to ever appreciate or allow one. Sometimes I would take my wedding ring off and pull it down over her ring finger. She would immediately lift her hand to eye level, twist her wrist briskly to the left and to the right as if admiring the ring's beauty, laugh her silent laugh, and proceed to remove it with her lips. I allowed myself briefly to imagine her a healthy young woman with prospects of marriage.

It was easy to love Emma. I watched how her school therapists and teachers doted on her. Her teachers and school nurses sang to her. Her therapists' quarterly reports stated "what a pleasure" Emma was to work with. She rewarded them by actively participating, by her smiles and silent laughter, by the kisses she blew by putting her lips together and effecting a pop. When I had occasion to bring her or pick her up from school, I would be privy to the extent of her rock star status. "Hi, Emma girl," we'd get from all directions as I pushed her wheelchair down the school's corridor. "Hey, Emma, where you going?"

"It's like she's the mayor of the school," I would brag to Tolya in the evenings. "Everyone knows her!"

One school nurse in particular would call us at home to report or remind us of something—to bring in extra cans of formula or clothes—and in the process, dive into an entire matchmaking scenario, telling us how one of Emma's classmates, Danny, kept "giving her these looks like he really likes her. And he's very handsome and comes from a very nice family. I met his parents. They're lovely." It was all I could do not to burst with laughter, knowing as I did that poor Danny could barely hold his head up on his own, and those googly eyes she was referring to were the result of his lack of motor control and inability to focus. And here was this well-intentioned though kooky nurse planning a wedding.

To know Emma was to love her, I saw with each person whose life she entered.

When she was about fifteen, Colleen, a new nurse, swept into our lives. Seventy-nine and not five feet tall, this Irish spitfire of a lady took over in the best possible way. Though feeble looking at first glance, she lifted Emma up at every opportunity and made her walk, barking orders like a drill sergeant: "Left foot, Emma, right foot. That's right. Good girl!" Emma usually happily complied, delighting in the attention.

While most other nurses chose not to leave the ease of home even on lovely warm days, Colleen would strap Emma into her wheelchair and walk, sometimes as far as two towns over, a mile in each direction. Then upon returning home, she would join Emma on the couch and sing,

Sing a song of sixpence, a pocketful of rye,
four and twenty blackbirds baked in a pie.
When the pie was opened, the birds began to sing.
Now wasn't that a dainty dish to set before a king?

This was followed by a little disciplining, to show Emma who was boss. "If you don't do (such and such), I'm going to knock knuckles," she warned. The first time I witnessed this, I was alarmed at the force with which she took Emma's wrist and tapped her hand against her chair tray, effecting an audible sound from bones that I probably never realized were there in Emma's pillowy hands. "Colleen, please don't do that. That sounds painful," I pleaded, even though Emma didn't wince or evidence any discomfort.

"Eh, she's fine. It doesn't hurt," she said dismissively. "Builds character." And she knew firsthand about building character, having grown up on a farm in Ireland, the oldest of eight or ten kids; hard labor and a little pain did not faze her—it was what made her. She raised her son as a single parent. Then buried her child.

She knew suffering but suffered with grace.

Looking at Emma through Colleen's eyes, I could witness the competence she engendered in her: the expectations laid out and summarily met by my daughter, who lived for the attention and, if she favored you, aimed to please. Colleen approached Emma at her fullest potential and lifted her up, physically and emotionally, to meet a level of skill and depth of character that most could not glimpse, but she could.

We felt fortunate to know this remarkable woman—a powerhouse of a lady, strong willed and determined. But in Emma, I believe, she found her match. Which is why I suspect she adored her as she did. Because Emma was no wallflower, she sometimes left souvenirs of black-and-blue marks when she wordlessly grabbed Colleen's arm and squeezed—her body shaking with the effort of inducing pain, in protest to something or other. Hence, the knocked knuckles. It was a battle of wills, glorious to see, which often ended in a draw of silent and boisterous laughter (Colleen spoke and laughed loudly because she was partially deaf in one ear), followed by both ladies falling backward onto the couch—Emma in Colleen's embrace.

The days that Colleen worked had me running home. With her, I didn't feel my home forcefully occupied. She brought heart and energy and Entenmann's Pecan pies for Josh and Hanna, which we all polished off in no time. But as

Emma got bigger, over the course of the three years that she was with us, Colleen became more and more frail. I didn't think it helped that her only form of sustenance seemed to be a Danish and tea in the morning and nothing else until dinner.

Toward the end, I watched horrified sometimes as she stood Emma up to walk and herself wobbled, almost losing her balance. Until one day she did, and she and Emma went toppling onto the mat, without injury. It was a wakeup call.

"She gave us the last three years of her work life," I said to Tolya one day, weeks after she had retired. We were standing and looking at the portrait her cousin had painted of her in 1961 and which Colleen gifted us, saying, *I have no use for it.* In the two-by-three-foot frame, twenty-five-year-old Colleen is turned sideways and looking over her shoulder, channeling a young Lucille Ball with fire-red hair and matching lipstick, which popped like a Warhol against an azure background. Her sky-blue eyes and shamrock-green sweater completed the image. On the bottom, *Colleen Susan O'Connor* is written in small neat script.

We hung it right outside Emma's room, in the space between her bedroom door and ours, so that each time I pass it, I feel her vibrant energy radiate off the canvas. Colleen left an indelible mark on our hearts, as I know Emma did on hers. Even after she retired, each year around Emma's birthday we could expect a card in the mail. They were always, of course, those musical cards that when opened played a little song and which Emma loved so much that after a day of repeated opening and closing, they would invariably stop working.

Though Emma loved most everyone, no one could compete with the infatuation she had for her grandfather, my father, Fyodor—known as Fred at work, Deda Fedya to his grandkids. The feeling was wholly mutual. It went like this: My father would come into our apartment and from the doorway yell, "Emma! Look who's here!" If Emma was on the living room sofa at the time, she would lean over and turn to the source of the sound. Thrilled with what she saw, she would smile, nod with half her body, and proceed to gingerly slide off by rolling her back down the sofa's edge, then proceed to scoot on her behind in the direction of the foyer. When she reached the two steps that separated the sunken living room from the other spaces, she forcefully pivoted onto her knees and planted her elbows onto the top step. With half of her body in the foyer, she somehow pulled herself up and rolled herself over to where my father stood waiting for her.

"Let's go, Emma," he prompted as she positioned herself on her back, on the hardwood, and lifted both legs in the air. No one could predict what followed unless you had witnessed it before. My father grabbed one of her legs at the ankle and spun her so hard that she often made two full rotations before coming to a stop. Watching this circus, I was reminded of the break dancers on the streets of Washington Square Park, who drew crowds to watch them perform their difficult feats of body in unusual motion. "Again?" my father would ask after Emma stopped laughing. Emma would sign for "more" and raise her legs in the air, and the act would be repeated another half a dozen times. I watched my father get completely lost in the back and forth with this little girl, who laughed so easily, who may never have been able to score a 99 on a test. And that was okay.

It made complete sense that my father would be Emma's favorite, just like he was my most devoted playmate growing up. A favorite memory: When I was little, my neighbor friends would come over to play hide and seek in our small one-bedroom apartment. While they counted, with their faces buried in their palms, my father would grab me, carry me to the closet, lift me high over his head, and place me on a large shelf, deep in its recesses. Then he would quickly cover me with a blanket and close the door behind him. My friends could never find me. He took me out after they'd grown weary and given up with defeat and when they weren't looking, so that we could reenact the hiding again next time.

In the same way, my father came to Emma—met her on her level—then elevated her to his, where *life was beautiful* and meant to be enjoyed. And she willingly went along.

By the time Emma turned sixteen, I realized that she had blossomed into herself, a person with thoughts and feelings and her own unique ways of expressing them. She reached people emotionally and affected them, orchestrated relationships with them, and in her small but significant way, became a force to be reckoned with.

To watch Emma engaging with those she cared for was to witness a circle of love, all inclusive, all encompassing. To watch her was to witness what she did best—give love and receive it. In that respect, she was more emotionally evolved than most, me included.

But I was learning. I was falling head over heels.

CHAPTER 28

ONCE, WHEN EMMA WAS ABOUT fifteen years old, I went to an astrologer for a reading. A close friend told me about having seen him herself and described it as an "interesting experience." I was easily convinced, as I was open to such things—ludicrous as Tolya considered them.

I think I also wanted to believe that someone had their finger on the pulse of the future, could predict the unpredictable. Because we had so little to no control of things, I irrationally hoped that someone could offer me an intimation, a clue as to what I could expect, a direction I should consider so that I may be better prepared, equipped for such events.

I watched as Richard, the astrologer, plugged in the dates and times of birth of Tolya and the kids into a fancy computer program with planet names and alignments. About Hanna's and Joshua's future love lives, Richard said, "They will be like Italian operas." Hanna was going to be "well traveled" and financially very secure. "She's either going to marry rich," he said, "or make her own money, but she'll be very comfortable financially." I loved the sound of that, envisioning her the Hollywood starlet that everyone was predicting her becoming, considering the acting and main roles she had landed in her school plays. In Joshua's chart, he saw a science career, but when asked if Josh had a favorite subject or interest in school, I drew a blank, as he was an all-around good student and had not shared any preferences with me or his father previously. (Six months later, Joshua would announce that he wanted to study astrophysics.)

"An older person, close to your husband, will pass," Richard continued, "but not soon, not for another year or more." This *was* disturbing information and sparked thoughts of Tolya's ailing father, who had recently experienced a few health scares. I wondered at the conviction in what Richard was saying, to be able to state such a troubling prediction—a death—without reservation. *How strong must you believe in this arbitrary, almost mythical, unsubstantiated endeavor*, I thought, *to speak such words out loud?*

And then I asked him about Emma. "Her chart indicates that she was born under Saturn and Pluto. But Pluto is the dominant here. It signifies loss, death, unfairness of life. It's the god of trauma. There is a palatable connection to you, as there is a moon on top of her chart, which means *mother*. Pluto gives her understanding of the mysteries of life and death. There's also a moon in Sagittarius, which is a statement of life, the joy of life, the magic, the beauty of life. Wanting to live life as fully and richly as possible." He went on, "Sagittarius believes in a positive outcome, a better future. Sagittarius believes in a tomorrow, and Pluto reminds us of death, which is a remarkable contrast—Sagittarius is youthful and optimistic, and Pluto is what corrupts, what contaminates, what destroys. And she's born with both. It's a remarkable chart that she's born with. Pluto reminds us that life is beautiful but also that, essentially, life is unfair."

I then shared with Richard Emma's condition and her limitations through choking tears that, to my own surprise, found their way out. After all these years, why was I still crying when telling her story, our story? Did my heart ache for my daughter's lot or for my own? The truth was perhaps somewhere in the middle—for both our fates. Richard listened quietly, his empathic eyes telling me that he was

sensitive to my pain. Then he made another ominous statement in which he warned us to be careful whose care we left
Emma in. Shortly thereafter, the older nurse burned Emma's
hand trying to curl her hair for my sister's wedding.

"Will she live a long life?" As soon as I spoke the last
word, I devolved into tears and regret at having asked. Guilt
and shame of feeling like a bad mother resurfaced.

His answer decimated me: "No." He paused. "She will
not live a long life," and my tears turned to sobs.

Why was I moved to ask? I wondered. Because I wanted
to be told the future, as if his pronouncements were carved
in stone? Because I didn't want to imagine a world where we
would no longer be able to care for her, protect her, because
she would have outlived us? Which children must do—outlive
their parents. Because I couldn't, didn't want to imagine her
old, neglected, forgotten in her wheelchair in some facility
with aides who didn't give a damn whether she was comfortable or not, in pain or not, hungry or not.

It was a future I did not allow myself to envision.

Three months later, my grandmother Baba Manya, died.
This was the older person close to Tolya that Richard was
referring to, I told myself. After twelve years under a shared
roof, she succumbed to pneumonia—an all too common
threat to the ailing elderly. In her absence, it felt like an era
ended. Undeniably the matriarch of our family, she left a hole
in our home and our hearts—where she lived.

The night before her funeral, I walked outside in the dark
and cried. I don't know if I believed I could reach her, but I
tried and spoke to her—aloud. "Babulya, watch us tomorrow
when we say goodbye to you. Please watch us. Please."

The next morning Hanna and I stood atop the raised
podium of the funeral home, filled with the people that
remembered her a giant presence of a woman, and sang the
Sabbath Prayer song from *Fiddler on the Roof* while Joshua

accompanied us on the violin from below. I knew she would have loved that. After all, she began with song with me, so it was only fitting that our singing accompanied her to the "better place" that everyone euphemistically referred to.

Shortly after her passing, I had a disturbing dream in which I answered the doorbell and found Baba Manya standing there. She didn't say anything, but assuming she wanted to come in, I said, "Babulya, you don't live here anymore. You have to go back to Allachka and your sisters and grandpa and your parents. They're waiting for you." Then I woke up sobbing.

My mother's spirituality and beliefs had started to rub off on me.

"How could I not let her in?" I later cried, telling my mother the disturbing dream. A shadow of a belief, I realized, was born: the notion that there was something after this life, after our physical bodies died. The idea of a soul and an afterlife that so many hold on to, religious or not, which I hadn't reconciled with before, was now seeping into my dreams and having me talking aloud to the dead.

For some time after her passing and before we gave her room to Joshua, I would walk Emma to her great-grand-mother's bed, sit ourselves down on it, and repeat the hand game and song Baba used to sing: "Saroka varona, kashkoo vareela . . ." Then, because we were alone, I would list off everyone that wasn't there with us. We played this game often. "Where is Papa?" I would ask in a high-pitched voice, raising my hands, palms up in wonder. "Not here," I would answer my own questions in an exaggerated sing-song tone. Emma folded in half laughing, and I'd repeat this, naming Joshua and Hanna and grandparents and nurses and finally ending with Baba Manya.

"Where is Baba Manya?" Pause. "Not here," I'd finish, with tears streaming down my face while Emma laughed.

I pushed Richard's predictions about Emma aside and threw myself heart-first into bonding with Emma. Her personality blossomed; she seemed to be more self-aware and took more notice of others around her. When traveling in an elevator, she worked to be noticed, and we could expect her to reach for the stranger sharing our ride, tapping them with her curled fingers or grabbing a skirt or pant leg. "Look at me," she seemed to be saying. "See me. Talk to me." I marveled at her comfort in the company of others. *So unlike me,* I thought. As painfully careful as I was in choosing who to engage with, Emma's attitude was in complete contrast. She seemed to live by embracing the saying, *What others think of me is none of my business.* She didn't care what people thought as I speed-rolled her down the street in her wheelchair while she chewed pensively on her bib, or opened her mouth and stuck her tongue out to catch the breeze, or folded in half laughing, sending drool onto her legs.

One of my favorite authors, Tom Robbins, wrote, "The human ego is a treacherous apparatus, best kept at a safe distance from the self." This is precisely where Emma lived; there was no self-consciousness in the way she went about her life. Because of her cognitive limitations, vanity did not impose on her. She was blissfully unaware that it was socially inappropriate to pull her wet, chewed-on shirt over her head in class, for instance. Even so, her teacher asked us to have her wear a tank top or bra for just those occasions, though there was still nothing to "support" other than what looked like baby fat. Only at sixteen did she begin to show the beginnings of puberty. Her awareness of her body and the subtle pleasures that it was capable of became apparent each time we changed her diaper. As soon as she felt freedom from the bulky cotton, her hand quickly found its way down below— to between her legs, where she would linger briefly before someone removed it.

Nowhere was her growing maturity more pronounced than during our favorite pastime—bath time. All it took was for me to run the water of the tub, and Emma would assume a speedy scoot on her bottom in the direction of our bathroom. I began by sitting her on the edge of the tub, then swung her legs over and into the water, unstrapped her diaper, and slid it out from between her legs. Then I lifted her up and slowly lowered her in. I would get in and recline with my back against the faucet side. Mercifully, it was a nice-sized Jacuzzi tub. Even so, it was designed to accommodate one adult-sized person. I had to sit upright to fit myself, while Emma reclined against me with her back on my chest and her feet just about touching the other end of the tub. Because her legs never fully extended but always stayed slightly flexed, we fit relatively well, with not much discomfort.

Emma would raise her arms and bring them down into the water—duplicating the splashing movements I taught her. She did it with such gusto—indifferent to the water covering her face and getting into her eyes. Then she would move her legs in a jerky manner on my command to kick her feet. For a moment, it felt like I was watching a toddler; I had to remind myself that she was a teenager, on the precipice of womanhood, though what that meant for her would be very different. But for now, she was following the course leisurely, on her own timeline. Sixteen but not having begun to menstruate—and maybe never would. Little buds of breasts that seemed to be deciding to grow or not—certainly nothing bra-necessitating. Stray wisps of pubic hair that screamed she was no longer a toddler.

I imagine she felt a freedom of weightlessness in the water that she did not experience outside of it, where gravity held her down. Sometimes she would get quiet and still in that reclined position, the same one we would assume going down the park slide together, and take in the sensation of the water softly caressing her normally uncooperative body. These were

rare instances—Emma being still—a serenity typically asso-
ciated to her only when she slept, prone as she was to being
in constant motion, if only with her hands.

But then the trance would break, or perhaps to enhance
the pleasurable experience, her hand would find its way down
again. I let her linger there but only briefly. Even as I removed
her hand, I felt unsettled and guilty about denying her basic
pleasures of the body—her clothes and diaper protecting her
from herself. I worried that outside of the bath, it would
become her default activity, and we'd have to field new calls
from her school. Emma wasn't aware of her sexuality, but
she knew primitively, like we all do, what felt good.

The closest I ever came to that sense of freedom and
acceptance of my body was when Tolya and I traveled to
St. Martin with another couple—Tolya's childhood friend
and his girlfriend. Lounging on the beach, I watched topless
European women glide across the water's edge in oblivious
comfort. I admired their indifference to onlookers of both
sexes. I envied them—not their perky breasts, but the ease
with which they moved through space. It had been three
months since we'd given Emma up, and I viewed my body
differently. This body, my body, that had nurtured and delivered life was suddenly something other than an object of lust.
And in a wave of reckless abandon, I reached for the string
of my bikini top and, in one brisk motion, pulled it over my
head and flung it to the side. Then, I just as quickly reclined
back onto my lounge chair in half hiding. And for the five
long minutes that I lay exposed, my eyes shut to block out
others' glances, I felt a blissful liberation I never felt before
and I suspect would never feel again.

I had forever struggled with weight, always beating
myself up for not being skinny enough, frequenting the gym
regularly, watching what I ate. I equated size and weight with
love and value. I should have been grateful for my healthy

body; instead I lived in self-criticism. I imposed, unwittingly, my hang-ups on Hanna, and Holly when she was younger. Emma, however, would not be imposed upon by me. She recognized the body for what it was: a vehicle for getting around, for getting things done, for pleasure. While Hanna in her adolescence locked the door to her room to change clothes and would never let me into the bathroom while she showered, Emma was most comfortable in her naked glory and cared little what others thought.

If Tolya was cognizant of the physical changes his oldest daughter's body was moving through, he did not acknowledge it with his actions. This became disturbingly apparent whenever we visited friends. Accustomed to assuming the responsibility of her feedings and diaper changes, he thought nothing of changing Emma in whatever area of people's homes she happened to be. So the floor of the playroom where Emma hung out, surrounded by our friends' children watching the big-screen television or playing video games, would morph into a makeshift changing table. One day, when Emma was already in full-blown puberty, I walked in on one of these diaper changes. Kids and some adults were seated on the massive sectional sofa, and Tolya was—arena style—on the floor, hunched over Emma on her back, pulling her pants off.

"Stop!" I yelled. "What are you doing?" He responded with a puzzled look and genuine surprise at the interruption.

"What?" he answered, raising his eyebrows with the same innocence with which he still viewed his growing daughter. "You can't do that in front of other kids and adults," I answered. "It's not appropriate," I continued. "Don't you get it?" Tolya shook his head in response, and that told me everything.

"I don't get what the big deal is," he concluded. Not many things were big deals for him. I envied his equanimity. Emma was his daughter in that sense. Neither very much cared what others thought.

When healthy, the body works like a well-oiled machine, all parts fitting into the right grooves, all gears in proper motion. As Emma matured, the external changes were easy to spot, but the internal story played itself out imperceptibly until it broke out onto the scene like a dark movie mystery, and we were left to follow the clues in solving it. This is how Emma came to be diagnosed with Crohn's disease.

For months, Emma, who was chronically constipated and needed external help with her bowel movements, suddenly began having bouts of explosive diarrhea and precipitously losing weight. The school nurse would call to report that Emma was having such bad episodes that her stool would escape her diaper and clothes and land on her feet, covering her orthotics in its path. In a month's time, her already slight body that weighed all of seventy-five pounds inexplicably relinquished ten hard-won pounds of precious weight.

As Tolya and I sat across from the gastroenterologist naming yet another assailant on Emma's already battered body and detailing the new hypoallergenic formula that would have to substitute the Ensure I felt was barely sustaining her, all I could hear was the internal voice in my head stifling a suffocating scream, flooding my sensibilities with the realization of the injustice of it all for this little girl who was already contending with so much. And now, a new diagnosis to add to our collection of so many.

And then there were her legs. Thin and spindly, they tapered off into virtual sticks of bone from below the knees, where what muscle she ever had there had atrophied into nothingness from lack of use. Her feet never grew past the size of a toddler. At fifteen she was still wearing child's-size-thirteen sneakers, and that was only to accommodate the length and width of the orthotics that encased her feet from her toes up to almost her knees.

When I imagined her upright and possibly independently ambulatory, I didn't consider that it was her "faulty" wiring that kept her brain from communicating with her joints and muscles, allowing her to move forward, vertical, through the world. I only saw her little four-inch feet and thought that even if her internal circuits were working properly and her gears were sufficiently oiled and operating, how could she possibly balance all that weight and height on two such small surface areas? It was like standing a pyramid on its head and expecting it to maintain itself without toppling to its side.

Gradually, stealthily, her feet began to turn, the right more pronounced than the left, and to point away from her body as if in rejection. Her tiny, unused feet seemed to be moving away from her, from her uncooperative body, limbs that refused to "play nicely" with each other. And so, her lower extremities degenerated such that she looked like she was born with club foot. She was losing that barely established ninety-degree range of motion, and I worried about how long it would take, if unchecked, for it to become uncomfortable or impossible for her to stand flat on her feet.

"Her right foot requires surgery before it gets any worse." We were seated in the orthopedist's, Dr. F's, examination room after he had attentively and gingerly examined Emma. I loved Dr. F for the way he handled her. A charming and charismatic man, with an air of achievement and aptitude, with Emma he was all "pretty girl" and "sweet girl." He addressed her in the gentlest of ways, almost reverent of her specialness. "The corrective surgery would require that we break the bone and reset it," he continued. "She will be in a cast for three to four months while it heals."

Eight years prior, Emma had tendon/Achilles heel release surgery, but this was serious, this was breaking bones—intentionally. My darn tears again made their appearance on the stage of my face. Dr. F put his hand on my shoulder.

"She'll be okay, don't worry," he reassured me. I almost asked him if he'd done this type of procedure before, but my senses returned to me just in time.

The surgery went well. Four months later her cast was removed but not without leaving her with temporary reflex sympathetic dystrophy. This caused her foot to become tremendously sensitive to touch. Each time we placed the lightest of pressure on the surface that had been shielded from external stimuli for all those months, she recoiled and wailed in pain. It was as if her neurons fell into a deep sleep, then were assaulted into life again. The physical therapist showed us how to massage the offended skin to desensitize her again so that we could don her socks and braces and test drive her newly reconstructed limb. She had to use it or lose it, and Emma was no quitter. Patched up, she resumed her drive to move and even initiated. When she'd see me approaching her while she was sitting on the couch, she would stand up sometimes seconds before I even reached her, forcing me to lunge in her direction, then grab my hands and walk me.

As Emma grew and her physical needs and the addition of new diagnoses further complicated her life and created extra layers of care, I worried that these restrictions and limitations would be difficult to manage and that any situation could potentially spiral into a crisis. Hurricane Sandy sent us into panic mode, as it did so many others, in fear of the fuel shortage. What if Emma had to be driven to the hospital for one emergency or another, and we didn't have gasoline in the car to get her there? The same fuel shortage could prevent her supply company from delivering her life-sustaining formula and feeding equipment. How would she survive? What if the pharmacy could not receive her seizure medication, and we couldn't keep her seizures at bay? What if there was a power outage or fire?

We would make do, figure it out, and adjust course, as we always did. And not just with Emma but with everything life threw at us.

Quotidian events were somewhat easily dealt with, but what if your building management decided to redo the elevator on the side of the pre-war building that you occupied, because it kept breaking down, as happened to us? And what if you lived on the top floor, the sixth floor, and had an adolescent in a wheelchair? Well, that made for creative thinking and enlisting help wherever we could find it. In the almost two months or so that we had no access to the elevator, we relied on the kindness of our superintendent, Jose. The super was strong, towering upwards of six feet in stature. Each day after school, Jose would meet the nurse and Emma off the school bus and take the working elevator on the other side of the building up to the sixth floor. There, he would lift Emma up and carry her the dozen steps to the rooftop, push open the emergency door that he left open for just this purpose, place Emma in her wheelchair that the nurse pulled up the same staircase, and take her across to the other side of the building, our side, where he would reenact the entire enterprise in reverse, down the stairs.

Then there was the year some apartments in our line became infested with bedbugs. The neighbor just below us complained loudly, reached out to us for help, and ultimately sued the management for money spent ridding her apartment of the critters. We watched, holding our breath, praying that the bugs didn't reach us, travel up the walls, through floors. Finally, it appeared that we had escaped the disaster, until a year later when Tolya suddenly began waking up with an itchy rash. Rocco, the bedbug-finding Beagle, was summoned. We looked on as the dog spiritedly scratched at Tolya's side of the bed and the couch, where he sometimes fell asleep watching television. And then the nightmare ensued.

The entire apartment was packed in large heavy-duty black garbage bags, and furniture was thrown-out. A thousand-dollar cleaning bill later, for those articles of clothing that couldn't be washed and dried on high heat, we evacuated. Tolya, Emma, and I crashed in my parents' two-bedroom apartment, which was in three-block proximity to ours, and Josh and Hanna went to sleep at Tolya's parents', three blocks from us in the other direction. We had managed to live very strategically situated between the two sets of grandparents, which was immeasurably helpful when the kids were little. I claimed my parents couch while Tolya and Emma shared the daybed in the smaller bedroom. Tolya was kind enough to suggest this arrangement, knowing what a light sleeper I was and how rambunctious Emma was in her sleep. He later grew to regret a month of being slapped awake by his big girl, who delighted in finding a playmate next to her. But this was our normal, the physical and emotional closeness of family. It grounded us and elevated us at once, forcing us to improvise as we went along.

CHAPTER 29

TOLYA'S FATHER GIFTED ME HIS Russian Zenith SLR camera shortly after we married. He saw me running around with a point and shoot, photographing skyscrapers, flowers, and anyone willing to pose for me, and decided to encourage my budding interest. It was a film camera, and I was obsessed with it. I taught myself to shoot reading everything I could about the craft, then going out and applying the information, until the day our apartment was robbed and the camera went the way of my wedding ring into the thieves' pockets. I was devastated but didn't quit. I returned to photographing with a point and shoot until digital cameras came out and I transitioned to that.

Around the same time, Facebook assumed its place in my life, and the two events conflated to create a new reality. I began posting pictures of the kids, and Emma especially became more public than she'd ever been before. I saw Facebook as a vehicle for introducing her to others, most of whom had never met her. Until that juncture, I harbored a sense of her being in hiding, unlike Josh and Hanna, who were out there in a bigger realm, acting out their lives, being "real."

On Emma's sixteenth birthday I posted a picture of her and shared with the "Facebook world" her story. In three poignant paragraphs, I summarized sixteen years of our lives with her, consciously omitting the adoption months. Tolya, who was vehemently opposed to anything social media related because it left an electronic footprint, scolded me. "Why do you have to do that?" he asked me, with judgment in his tone.

"Why can't I do that?" I railed, angry. "She's my child. I'm proud of her. I want to show her off to the world." I was a different person from the one that once hid her daughter in the stroller so I wouldn't have to deal with others' curiosity.

I had been posting beautiful photos of Josh and Hanna and acutely felt Emma's exclusion. I don't know what I expected, but the response wasn't overwhelming, partly because I didn't have that many "friends" and mostly utilized Facebook as a platform for showcasing some of my amateur photos taken with my point and shoot.

To celebrate our twentieth wedding anniversary, Tolya and I booked a week-long trip to Amsterdam. We strategically scheduled it to be around the time that Emma would be in a three-week sleepaway camp in New Jersey. This was her second returning year, the first time having been an amazing experience with counselors from all over the world doting on her and charmed by her silly ways of engagement, attention seeking, and showing love.

With my Canon DSLR, purchased on a whim at our local Costco shortly before the trip, with its "kit lens," the cheaply made starter lens that came in the camera bundle, I could not have been happier as I aimed it at the seventeenth-century canals with the overarching trees that framed the bridges and tunnels. Bicycles leaning languidly against time-weathered brick, resting on cobble-stoned streets with flowers weaved into the openings of their baskets, seemed to breathe their own personality, as if without a driver they could effortlessly take off in the direction of their choosing whenever they pleased. These found their place in front of my lens, as did the picturesque multicolored Dutch canal houses that stood like tall soldiers, erected to serve the merchants that carried out business there centuries ago. And the windmills and clog-clad walls of the clog and cheese factories—all these landed in my viewfinder, and I was a girl on a psychedelic trip of the senses, my camera only leaving my face long enough for me to inhale the charged air, orient myself, and focus on the next object of scenic attraction.

Amsterdam assumed its position on the podium of my favorite cities, above Paris, Barcelona, Rome. Not for its grandeur or history, but for precisely the opposite qualities—its understated modesty, ease, and beauty. It was the tulip to the narcissus of Paris. If Emma were a flower, would she be the tulip, confident in her serenity and self-love, and I, the narcissus—reaching for my reflection in the pond, worrying about how I presented to the world? Was it sheer coincidence that tulips were my favorite flowers and made up my wedding bouquet? Was it coincidence that I felt more at home in this city, as detailed in the "Welcome to Holland" letter that I reread each year, than in any other? Not flashy and exciting like Italy, but with its own simple, demure gifts of Rembrandts, tulips, and windmills?

And even though we were continents away, Emma managed to find us. Toward the tail-end of our trip, we received a call from the counselor at Emma's sleepaway camp. "Emma fell out of her bed this morning," she said. They found her uninjured, quietly sitting cross-legged, chewing on her shirt, waiting to be collected. "She's fine. The beds are low, as you know, but we had to report it to you," she concluded. The low plastic bed railing did nothing to detain her or prevent her from exiting the bed when she chose to. But she was safe—as safe as I felt in this city. Because of this incident, a new realization bubbled up to the surface. Here we were, living our lives the way I had envisioned, traveling, collecting experiences. And there was Emma, temporarily being cared for, loved by other good people. Could our separate, unique experiences be reconciled? Could we exist together and still lead full, happy, rewarding lives? The answer was yes! I could no more part with Emma than I could with myself. I understood then that we were forever intertwined and that as long as I could take care of her and keep her safe, she would not leave me.

When we returned home, I posted an image of Emma on her last day of sleepaway camp, surrounded by a half a dozen counselors, some squatting near her wheelchair, some standing behind her with smiles on their genuine, open faces. Just before snapping that image, I noticed a counselor swipe a finger over her eye, and when she looked up, her eyes were liquid pools of what? Sadness? I was taken aback. Could Emma have had such an impact on her? Was she crying because she was saying goodbye to her? Because my silent, silly girl touched her heart, like she had touched and rearranged mine? That's what I told myself. It wasn't unbelievable. Emma, I knew, had the ability to do that to people.

I had once wondered what people thought when they saw her chewing on her bib with that faraway look on her face as I sped her down the block in her wheelchair, singing our repertoire of songs. But I no longer cared. I recalled with shame wishing they knew her beyond the way she presented with little apparent agency over her body and mind. Because her character, her interior beauty was luminescent, and it was that inner light that extended itself out and swept people in. Unless you were one who did not see past her outer appearance and into her soul, and you were "unevolved," as Vivian Gornick's mother used to call people who lacked emotional intelligence—"*ne razveetiy*," as we said in Russian—then you missed out, were excluded from the inner sanctum. But if you were lucky enough to be invited in, if you were a beloved nurse or doting teacher, a long-term therapist, then you were rewarded. Emma made people love her and, in that process, made those same people love themselves for recognizing the crystalline pureness and uniqueness of her. She became the tour guide to their deepest inner emotional landscape that is often so difficult to reach.

Something else happened upon our return from Amsterdam. I emptied my memory card of the foreign sights and posted a dozen or so images from the trip onto my Facebook page. These garnered lovely compliments.

Then someone private-messaged me, asking me how much I charged. *Charge for what?*

"Someone is willing to pay me for my photos." I laughed, showing Tolya the inquiry. "Can you believe that? It's unreal," I said. And it did seem ludicrous, a joke someone was playing. Still, I propelled my energies in the direction in which the winds were moving, telling myself I had nothing to lose and that I owed myself at least an exploration.

I borrowed my friends' children to create a photo portfolio and started booking weekend photoshoots. After my very first newborn shoot fiasco in my home, in which I attempted diaper-less images with a sweet two-week old baby girl who promptly proceeded to pee on my couch between prop changes because we forgot to put the diaper back on, I swore I would never again attempt newborn photography. But then after all, I did, and soon enough I earned the flattering title of "baby whisperer." I had surreptitiously found a creative outlet in photography, and Facebook and word-of-mouth referrals began to come in faster than I could sometimes handle. And as a bonus, I had a legitimate excuse to replace the ugly brick orange sectional that I'd grown to hate. A win-win, as I saw it.

Emma finally had great nurses who provided consistent coverage. There was Marie, an older nurse from Haiti, and a younger one, Shandell, who took her around the neighborhood and would sometimes venture into stores and buy Emma clothes, just because she loved her and because she had two younger daughters of her own, so she felt a motherly kinship toward Emma. Josh and Hanna were old enough to fend for themselves and get to classes and appointments on their own and were mostly hanging out with friends, and I found myself working seven days a week. Except that it didn't feel like work at all. I was getting to hold, rock, and photograph other peoples' babies, then give them back and go home to my three.

Life was becoming more hectic in some ways and less in others. We were managing and not just scraping by, but actually doing it well.

As the photography took off and more people came to know my story, Emma's story, I often heard from other parents, "I don't know how you do it. I don't know if I'd be able to do the same." I was flattered but sensed a tinge of underlying pity in those words. This was an image I labored hard to avoid. I intuited that Emma presented to others as a burden and that my life seemed difficult to manage.

That's when I would realize that the life I had feared most, encumbered, dark, marginalized and imperfect in its otherness, was not that at all. It was luminescent, inclusive, and imperfectly perfect. I was seeing things from a different lens. And I would answer peoples' queries in as lighthearted a way as I could muster: "It's not as hard as it seems. Emma is a very low-maintenance and happy girl. We're not so special. If you had to, you could make it work too."

I recalled a television documentary in which parents of a severely autistic girl were praised and called special. The reporter made a subtle reference to the parents being "chosen," because they possessed the qualities of great, selfless love and dedication. Their answer was striking. "Special parents are not born, they're made." They took no personal credit, acknowledging instead that their special child was the "raison d'etre"—their reason for being—and the reason for them being the way they were.

We had carved out a family culture that described us. We didn't look or function like your typical family but created our own normal, one that worked for us. I recalled the time when I couldn't imagine Emma fitting neatly into our lives, but now I realized how absolutely perfectly she not only fit into our world, our family, but shaped it, created the outline, the template for our existence. She was the missing link.

Tolya and I both worked while raising three kids, traveled, and even found time to train and run the 2014 New York City Marathon. We were inspired by Emma. Emma who pushed her uncooperative body to its limit every day. Surely, I told myself, I could push my healthy one through a 26.2-mile run. And so, I watched bemused and not a little frustrated as an eighty-seven-year-old repeat marathoner, whom I had overheard talking at the start of our run, passed me on mile twenty-two. But I was also moved and in awe of what our bodies could do.

Along with the pictures from the marathon, I posted these words: "Most important reason for running the marathon was for kids like our Emma, who can't run or walk." The underlying message was to live your best life. Count the blessings, not the cracks in the road. If you can walk, run. Heck, run a marathon.

I took inventory of the lessons Emma taught us in her silent yet wise way: that life is hard but worth fighting for, to be heard; to be seen; to appreciate the gifts you have, the ability of speech, ambulation, sovereignty over your thoughts, actions.

A shift in me took place. I stopped researching residential programs for Emma to transition to when she aged out of her high school at twenty-one, and began exploring day programs that would pick her up in the morning and return her after five. She would continue to live with us. This was an affirmation that seemed to have snuck up on me, when in truth, it was probably always there—the knowledge that when the time came, I would not be able to part with Emma like I did before, ever again.

You don't always get what you want, but you get what you need. I needed Emma to grow, to teach me to love with my full heart, to appreciate all of life's gifts.

CHAPTER 30

"THIS IS EMMA, EVERYONE" began the video I recorded and posted on Facebook on Emma's eighteenth birthday. Hanna was holding the smart phone and recording as I introduced Emma in real time to the thousands of followers I now had on my Facebook page. "This is what Emma has learned in the past eighteen years . . . ," and I proceeded to demonstrate all she knew: her body parts, how she crossed her legs like a lady when asked, how she lightly slapped me when I pretended to cry. She happily displayed all her hard-won skills: the way she folded in half when she laughed, how she said *Emma* and *Mama* in her breathy, barely audible way. She brought her hand to my lips when I asked her to let me kiss her hand. She nodded yes with her whole body when asked if Emma was a good girl, shook her head no, vigorously, when asked if she wanted to go "beddie bye," and much more. We ended the video with Emma blowing everyone a kiss, by putting her lips together and affecting an audible pop.

I attached the video to this text:

So, this happened eighteen years ago today. The doctor handed me a tiny little baby girl, a special little girl, who according to the doctor's predictions, at best "would be a vegetable" and at worst "wouldn't live very long."

I won't lie. I cried . . . a lot. I spent many nights wondering, "Why me? Why us?" We were young.

We were healthy. We had no family history. The chances were like one in one hundred million. I now realize that we won the lotto. Hit the jackpot. I no longer wonder why me, why us. I now know that everything happens for a reason . . . whatever your beliefs . . . God's will, the stars and planets lining up . . . Emma chose us to be her parents, to nourish her, to love her, to help her reach her full potential, to prove the doctors wrong. Not because we're great or wonderful or because we were the best choice. No. Because I, we, had something to learn . . . and Emma was here to teach us. I'm still learning. We are all a work in progress. It took me many years to get to this point, and it was not an easy, smooth journey. No. I fought it . . . I was weak, selfish. I felt sorry for myself. Emma spent the first five months of her life in a hospital . . . in intensive care, being monitored, tested, operated on. And then we gave her up. And we took her back. Unlike most people who make this difficult decision, we were one of the few fortunate ones who got a second chance. I have not forgiven myself for the five months I lost with Emma, for her returning to us sicker than when we gave her up . . . on oxygen. I have spent every day since her return asking for her forgiveness, for my weakness, my selfishness. And I will spend the rest of my life trying to make it up to her. Among the things that Emma has taught me, us, over the years is that life is precious. Life is fragile. Life is beautiful. Happy eighteenth birthday, baby girl. I'll keep learning . . . as long as you'll keep teaching.

And this time, the response was overwhelming—hundreds of likes, birthday wishes, and dozens of shares. Three years after starting my photography journey, I had friends and families—my photography clients—who cared to hear my story, Emma's story.

"Again, you're posting her?" Tolya asked in his disgruntled way.

"Again, I'm telling you, I'm proud of her," I said.

So many commented on how lovely Emma was, and she was—lovely—and doing so well. Medically, she was stable and had been for a long time. I prided myself on her not having to have been hospitalized for anything nonelective since her life-threatening spells with pneumonia and RSV virus in Pennsylvania those seventeen years ago. I secretly aimed a declarative middle finger at the doctor in St. Luke's hospital that predicted that she wouldn't live past her first birthday.

And then she got sick.

One day I came home from a work meeting to find Emma already in bed. I touched her head, and my hand burned from her heat. The thermometer read 103. She was lethargic and not herself. With ibuprofen hastily administered, I prayed the medicine would work quickly.

The next morning, we awoke to a still raging temperature. "Can you take her to the pediatrician?" I asked Tolya. "I have meetings in the field all day." I felt a pang of guilt at delegating to Tolya, but my absurd work ethic was again kicking me in the gut.

Two hours later Tolya called to say that Dr. I was sending them to the ER, that she didn't like the way Emma's lungs sounded or how she looked.

"Emergency room?" I bellowed into the phone. "My god, it's that serious?" I scanned my memory, quickly trying to remember the last time we were in the ER with Emma, and it took me back to the night she swallowed the medical tape that secured the oxygen cannula to her cheeks. That was seventeen years ago! Then to her first seizure episode in the psychologist's office when she was three. And then

I recalled an incident just two years ago when a new home nurse called the ambulance after Emma had a seizure with her and we weren't home to intervene or explain that this was not an ambulance-necessitating situation, that she had "breakthrough" seizures a couple of times a year, that we handled it ourselves, that it was not an emergency. That this was our life. That the ER was no longer the big bad wolf, and we were no longer easily bullied into fear.

"I'll meet you there soon," I said, hanging up the phone. I felt a ludicrous sense of responsibility to finish my work, especially knowing that Emma was in good hands.

The service coordinator, who knew Emma's story and who was also a mother, suggested that I drop everything and go immediately, that the meetings could be rescheduled. *She must think I'm crazy*, I thought through a panicked fog. *What kind of mother . . . ?* she may have even wondered. The kind that was used to dealing with emergencies, the kind that had an extraordinary husband and father to her kids, the kind that managed a chaotic but full and rewarding life with many balls perpetually in the air. That kind.

When I got to the emergency room of our small community hospital, I found Emma in a state I hadn't seen in a long time. Oxygen cannula, machines beeping, numbers on a screen flashing—screaming their presence. And Emma, so pale, her breathing labored and shallow. But her demeanor was what struck me the most. I had seen her in discomfort, especially during stomach virus episodes when she'd be nauseous and not be able to vomit to relieve her pain, but this was different. The light in her eyes seemed so dim, her lids at half mast. She moaned when she saw me as if to tell me how she was feeling, and I brushed her bangs back to kiss her burning forehead.

"What's going on, big girl?" I said, pasting a weak smile on my face so as not to register the worry that was building up in my chest. "Emma has a boo-boo?" Another moan.

Just then a nurse walked in to take her temperature, and I pounced on her with questions.

"We're still running tests, but it's looking like pneumonia," she said. "Has she been sick the last few days?" she continued.

"No. She was perfectly fine yesterday morning . . ."

"No cold?"

"No," I said, feeling inexplicably vexed at her questions. Instinctively, I heard judgment in her inquiries, even though I should have known better. They were collecting a history. This was vital information.

I told myself I needed to be helpful, so I explained. "This is really out of nowhere," I said. "Last year, yes, she had walking pneumonia that evolved from a cold, but literally she was fine yesterday." The look of confusion on the nurse's face told me that she wasn't necessarily convinced by the information I was relaying, and a frustrating sensation of implied negligence crept up on me.

The fever was not budging. It had been hours since she was admitted to the ER, with no sign of a hospital room. Even though it was Christmas Eve, the ER was packed, like any other day. Sickness did not recognize holidays or special occasions. It was disrespectful of your plans. It crept up on you or landed on those unsuspecting, like an unsecured air conditioner dropping from a six-story window just as you're passing underneath it. Emma was rendered so weak by the fever and whatever was causing it that she didn't even attempt to remove the oxygen mask that had replaced the nasal cannula that wasn't efficient at keeping her oxygen levels up.

I posted my location at the hospital on Facebook, telling myself that we'd probably have to stay the night but that we'd be home soon. It was an easy way to dispense information without texting all our friends individually. I received well wishes and for Emma to get better soon. It made me feel less alone and offered an invisible net of support that promised to hold us up.

She must be so scared, I thought as I stroked her hair. I had to comfort her, bring the familiar to her, normalize this unnatural situation. So, I sang to her, the songs I made up with her name in each. The ones that made her smile and laugh before, when she felt good. Her eyes fluttered open and then closed periodically. She was trying to engage, to give me the expected response she had always given me whenever we'd do this dance. But I could see that she was struggling under the weight of whatever was ravaging her body.

"Who's my yummy girl?" I whispered into her ear. She moaned. I continued, "Emma hooliganistaya, devochka paganistaya." And there it was! Her body shook with laughter for just a second, almost involuntarily, at the words she recognized calling her a hooligan—just like she had always done before. That tremendous, silent laugh, so unique to her, found its way out, past the fever, past the weight of illness, despite the circumstances. It exploded to the surface like a small earthquake that rankled her insides with delight, then settled just as quickly. I was encouraged, telling myself that this was a great sign. If she could muster a laugh, she was going to be okay. *We are strong. We are survivors.*

Shortly thereafter, the test results came back, and the diagnosis of pneumonia was confirmed. Emma was started on antibiotics, and her temperature began to drop. A room became available, and the hospital was keeping her overnight. Even with the diagnosis, I wanted to believe that things were looking up, because now we knew what was going on and were attacking it with the gift of medicine. I recalled all the ways it had saved us in the past. Tolya told me to go home to Josh and Hanna and he would stay with Emma. He could fall asleep anywhere, so the reclining chair of a hospital room was as good a surface as any.

I returned to the hospital in the early morning to find Tolya sitting on Emma's hospital bed and Emma attempting to lunge out of it. Her eyes were wide and her mouth gaping as if gasping for air. She was thrashing and throwing her body in all directions.

"Oh my god! What's happening?" I yelled, having never seen Emma in such a state of distress.

"She can't breathe," Tolya answered, visibly anguished at not being able to help her. The nurses milling about asked us to leave the room so that they could sedate her. We did as we were told and stepped out into the hallway.

"They're asking our permission to intubate her," Tolya said. "Is that bad?" I looked at my almost fifty-year-old husband, and I'd never seen him so vulnerable, so scared.

"It must be serious if we have to sign, giving permission," I said. "Let's hear them out. I know as much about it as you do." I needed the facts. I needed to hear reason. Knowledge was power, I reminded myself. "We need to find out if it's a temporary measure that they're recommending. But if they're suggesting it, they must feel it necessary," I concluded. I went back to the place of following the rules, coloring inside the lines. If we could do that, Emma would be okay.

She was on the ICU floor of the hospital. We had graduated from NICU, lost a letter, gained eighteen years of life, but again fallen back on needing intensive care. The resident doctor met with us to discuss the implications of intubation. We were assured that it was reversible if Emma's lungs stabilized and she could breathe on her own. He pointed at the old man across from Emma's bed, who shared the room with us and was also intubated. "You see that patient? He is battling alcoholism, and this is not his first visit here." This was to say, as we understood it, that intubation was reversible and, hopefully in our case as well, an extreme but temporary option.

We signed, deferring to the knowledge of those better equipped to help Emma. This was new, uncharted territory and one we never expected to find ourselves in. The doctor went to work on the intubation, and within several minutes, which felt like a lifetime, we could return to her room.

The image of Emma sedated into sleep with an offensive plastic tube snaking out from between her tiny lips, her arms secured at her sides as if she were a criminal that posed a danger to others if she were not restrained, IVs and other lines emanating from her like more vipers attacking her defenseless body, was more than I could take. I sank into the chair beside her and wept.

"She's oxygenating better," the nurse caring for her on that shift said. "That's good."

"What does that mean for her prognosis?" I asked.

"It means there is more oxygen in her bloodstream."

I allowed myself to feel a bit more encouraged by this information. I even took a picture of Emma in this hideous state, telling myself that when she was all better and back home, I would post the before and after of this warrior girl. I would yell from the proverbial rooftops that this was what a fighting spirit could do.

But the next day brought with it bad news. Emma was not oxygenating well at the original settings, and the doctor was forced to increase the oxygen levels being pumped into her lungs. "We're playing around with the numbers, trying different things," the resident doctor stated. I didn't like the sound of that. It sounded too experimental. *What do you mean you're playing around?* I wanted to ask, but instead I decided to probe further and pick his brain.

"Can you tell us what's going on with Emma's condition?" I asked. He went on to say that things weren't as terrible or serious as we might think and that there are worse conditions to be afflicted with, like diabetes, which his niece suffered from.

"Are you kidding me?" I blurted before I could filter my thoughts. I felt my blood pressure shoot up like the hammer game at the amusement park. "Are you actually comparing Emma's situation to a person living with diabetes, which, by the way, my grandmother lived with until way into her eighties and didn't die from?" I must have gotten too loud or too close in my outrage because he started hemming and hawing, raising his palms up as if to push me away or calm me or both. I had the unsettling feeling that this doctor was being lackadaisical toward Emma's care. I suspected that because of her limitations, he wasn't placing as much value on her life, on saving her, as he would on a normally healthy patient. Eighteen years of fighting for her perhaps left me sensitive, wound exposed, and I was not having it. This quack of a doctor would prove to be an obstacle and a thorn in our side in future dealings with Emma's care, and this was just a preview.

By the Friday after Christmas Day, I had all but lost track of time. There was no evidence that we'd be going home anytime soon. Emma was unstable and not responding to the increased oxygenation. "We've never had to resort to such high numbers before," the resident said. "We have to keep her sedated, because the amount of pressure her lungs are being subjected to would otherwise be very uncomfortable, if not painful, if she were awake."

How did we get here? I thought. *How did everything unravel so quickly?*

This uncertainty surrounding what exactly was happening with Emma's lungs prompted me to seek out answers. I demanded to speak to a pulmonologist familiar with Emma's case so he could explain to us the course of treatment they were pursuing and what they had gleaned so far from her symptoms and test results. In plain speak, I needed to know what the hell was going on.

The pulmonologist had kind eyes and a softness to his voice, useful for practiced delivery of bad news, I imagined. And bad news was what we got. Tolya and I found ourselves staring at X-rays of Emma's lungs, which the doctor held up to the putrid light of the hallway outside Emma's room. And we heard words, unintelligible and foreign, not unlike the first time with the geneticist when she was born and *chromosomes*, *anomaly*, and *mutation* circled our heads like Hitchcock's birds.

This time it was ARDS—acute respiratory distress syndrome. This was the bully battering Emma's lungs. This time a new army of words paraded in the air around us—air that we could breathe but Emma no longer could. "Water in the lungs . . . pneumonia . . . survival rate low . . . her condition . . . damaged lungs . . . organ failure," the doctor seemed to be mouthing. But the words had abandoned their source, just like Emma's lungs on X-ray seemed to have extricated themselves and abandoned her body, jumped ship and into the waters—the waters that were drowning her lungs and denying her breath.

I want to die. I want to die, I thought eighteen years ago when given the diagnosis.

She's going to die . . . she's going to die! screamed a voice in my head that day. I turned a desperate gaze on Tolya, but his eyes stayed fixated on the charcoal silhouette of his daughter's broken lungs, behind which we knew beat a pure, perfectly undamaged heart.

And then it occurred to me; in our hypervigilance with her other medical issues, the more pressing, visibly life-threatening ones—her Crohn's, the seizures, her feeding, her feet—we had inadvertently shifted focus off her lungs.

But where had this come from? Last year, her "walking pneumonia" resulting from a cold was successfully treated with antibiotics. How was this pneumonia different? It had surfaced out of nowhere, without warning. I imagined bacteria like silent legions of warring soldiers, inexorably living, thriving, making a home in Emma's lungs—festering, unwelcome squatters—until one day they overwhelmed her lungs, took her hostage. But I was guessing. Because no medical professional could know the answer with certainty. Not that it would have made a difference.

We were so distracted by the many other organs and body parts we struggled to heal—her eyes (probing), her ears (tubes and mild hearing loss), her hands (splints), her feet (orthotics and surgeries), her eating (G-tubes), her brain and nervous system (seizures), her bladder (vesicostomy), her colon and intestines (Crohn's)—that we lost sight of her lungs, the original player. Because once she came off the oxygen for when she slept those fifteen years ago and the pulmonologist cleared her and deemed that part of her healed, we looked away and reoriented our attention.

The single organ we never had to concern ourselves over was her heart. It was whole and pure and massive. It never needed to be repaired, healed. It was never broken. It was perfect the way it was. Always.

Still, I could not accept this. I needed another opinion. I did not trust this little community hospital with its rude residents and its small-minded, limited thinking and experimenting. They didn't have a children's division that specialized in kids like our Emma. I was convinced that Schneider's Children's Hospital of Long Island Jewish, where she had been born and spent two months, her first home, would surely know better—could save her, as they had before.

I turned to friends for help. My friend Luba connected me with Dr. Y, the head of some department at Northwell Health. "He's great," Luba said. "He may be able to help at least get some answers."

I called and we spoke briefly. He graciously offered to talk to the resident overseeing Emma's care, and the next day he surprised us by showing up at the hospital unsolicited, unannounced, even though he had been told that Emma was not transferable, that the risk of her dying in transport was too great and that neither hospital was prepared to chance it.

He showed up to see for himself. To meet us and Emma and offer some comfort, if possible. "That's what you call a mensch," I said to Tolya.

"I wanted to come and make sure they're doing everything they can," he reassured us, "and they are. They would do the same in Northwell, rest assured." This gave us a small measure of comfort in knowing that we were giving Emma the best care, doing everything in our power, leaving no stone unturned.

But the prognosis remained. I didn't want to believe it, even as I stared at Emma's now swollen body, from the steroids, from the fluid retention—her face appearing twice the size, her tongue protruding large and invasive between her crimson lips. A catheter was inserted to help drain her bladder of urine, because she could no longer do it on her own, and to monitor its production. And the oxygen battering her tired, weakened lungs continued to assault.

What did they do to you, baby? What did they do to you?

With everything going on, I remembered at the last minute that I had four photoshoots scheduled for that weekend. Two on each day. I emailed or texted a hurried message to each family explaining that my daughter was critically ill, and I was sorry but I had to cancel. Each family responded with understanding and words of compassion, because they had children and I was raising to their hearts a parents' worst unspoken fear.

I posted a new status that day that said, "Emma has taken a turn for the worse. Please continue to keep us in your thoughts." Suddenly, it was as if I were pleading with a pagan religious body of the Facebook community—a temple of my own creation, whose members knew me and cared what happened to me and mine. For all its faults and my questionable belief system and healthy skepticism, I convinced myself in that moment of desperation that if I put out there, into the universe, a plea asking for good thoughts and prayers, that all that good energy would unite into a positive force that would shift the earth back on its axis and make things right again.

Then I left the hospital to walk around the block and cried. But with each step I took, I became convinced that this was a test. That my commitment to, my love for Emma, was being questioned. Because I strayed too far away from my responsibilities to my family, my children—Emma most of all. I was being punished for my hubris, my arrogance. For exhaling. So, I prayed to a god I didn't believe in, just in case, because there are truly no atheists in the foxhole: *If you help Emma get through this, I will give up the photography business. I will devote all my time to Emma, and I will believe in you*, I said out loud. As if God needed my belief. As if bad things didn't happen to good people, even those that believed.

It had been more than a week since Emma was admitted. Our days bled one into another. We descended to the hospital cafeteria like zombies to put something in our mouths, or our parents would bring us food, and we would sit there grimly trying to push nourishment down and share the latest developments about Emma's condition. But the reports got progressively worse. She had now developed sepsis, which we learned was an infection in the blood, and her extreme swelling and fluid retention was the result of organ failure.

A new pulmonologist, Dr. P, came to speak with us. She said Emma's condition was grave. I asked if there was brain damage from the insufficient oxygenation, and she said that the damage that was more concerning was that to her lungs. With the high levels of oxygen being forced on them, there was risk of lung collapse. I asked for a prognosis. She responded with gentleness and compassion, probably more than any previous doctor had afforded us since this nightmare began.

"Once extubated, there is very little, if any, chance that she will recover. Her lungs are no longer viable. I'm very sorry."

There it was. The death sentence for the second time in her life.

Desperation seized me, and I asked, "Isn't there anything else that can be done?"

And perhaps in part to appease me, she mentioned a tracheostomy, which I knew was an egregious surgical opening in her throat to which a tube delivering oxygen would be permanently attached. In the time that I imagined with horror Emma in a medical facility, arms restrained, because surely she would attempt to extricate the tube from herself—*No, I will not punish her with that kind of existence, that kind of suffering*—the doctor was already saying that there was no guarantee that measure would work because her lungs were so broken.

There was no corrective action to take, no mistake to undo.

We had broken the news individually to our parents, Josh and Hanna, Holly, who was then three months pregnant with her first child, and our friends.

"They don't think she's going to make it," we said, because we couldn't bring ourselves to say the word *dying*.

When we were alone, Tolya posed what did not seem that obvious a fact until he said it out loud. "You understand they're keeping her alive artificially, don't you?"

This realization led to the next steps we would be forced to consider: to keep Emma attached to machines until her body gave up on her eventually, or to mercifully withdraw the extreme intervention of the tube forcing prolonged suffering, as we saw it, and let nature take its course and afford her a dignified exit.

We found ourselves faced with having to make end-of-life decisions for Emma. A heinous, agonizing place for anyone to find themselves in, but for us as parents having to make it for our child, well, it was no less than residing in Dante's rings of hell.

The stark, ugly truth was that there was no way for us to change the course or the outcome of this story. "You know that story?" Joshua's three-year-old voice resonated in my head. I didn't know this story, and I didn't want to know it. I realized that our family was now part of a new narrative, another atypical drama. First, we were parents raising a disabled child; now we were those likely burying that child.

Emma lived her eighteen years with grace and beauty, and we owed her the dignity of an easy death. Everyone deserved that. Just as soon as our decision was made, someone handed us the DNR to sign. The DNR is a "do not resuscitate" directive that disallows heroic measures to prolong life if no improvement is possible. Shortly thereafter, Dr. G, the director of hospice, approached us. I knew about hospice and the purpose it served: to allow terminally ill people to live out their lives in dignity, but I always assumed it was a separate facility that housed such patients. Dr. G told us that the hospital had their own hospice division and that a room had just become available. We wouldn't have to transport her out anywhere, and this gave us some peace. Dr. G was a lovely bear of a man. An Orthodox Jew, he could have been our rabbi, dispensing sage advice or offering an empathic ear, if we were to belong to a temple and believed in his comforting truths. I was immensely grateful for his tender broaching of the subject. He even took time to speak kindly with our parents and compare stories of origin.

But as with all things in life, it is sometimes only a matter of time before an undetected tidal wave overcomes you, just when you felt it was safe to resurface from under the dark expanse of the ocean because someone had thrown you a life raft.

When the attending doctor, the same one who undermined the severity of Emma's condition in the shadow of his niece's life-threatening diabetes, got wind of our decision, he promptly requested an ethics committee meeting to "explore" all our options.

We were outraged. What the hell was going on? "Why is he doing this now that we've made this wrenching decision?" we asked each other. We learned that the hospital ethics committee consisted of persons assigned by a hospital to consider, debate, make recommendations, or report on ethical issues that pertained to patient health.

This doctor was questioning our decision to extubate, we concluded, and we were being forced to relive our soul-crushing choice. According to his assessment, Emma had some days where she was oxygenating slightly better than others, and so he didn't want to be "rash" in the decision to extubate, as if a decision like that could be made rashly, as if all the other things going on—her sepsis and organ failure—were nonexistent, as if the right dose of insulin could bring our child back.

The next day we found ourselves sharing a large conference table with Dr. G, a head nurse, the kind female pulmonologist, the hospital director, the doctor who called this, and one or two other people we'd never met.

I felt on trial.

Through choking tears, we pledged our love for Emma to these virtual strangers, who we felt were trying to tamper with our parental rights to decide in the best interest of our child, and gave them space to make their case. In the end, it was explained to us by Dr. G that the purpose of the meeting was not to tell us what to do but to make sure we understood all our options, that this was fairly standard procedure in end-of-life decisions, and that the meeting would ensure everyone was on the same page when it came to patient care.

I appreciated his explanation, and we left the meeting agreeing to transfer Emma to hospice, but wait a few days to "see what happens," to give Emma a chance to pass on her own, as we understood.

The hospital room on the hospice floor of the building was the opposite of that in St. Luke's, where Emma was also the only occupant. This room lacked the sterile feel of the white walls and floor so typical to hospital rooms. This room was spacious as well, but breathed warmth with its muted tones and colors and possessed an almost reverent quiet about it. It could have passed for a bedroom of a home where a healthy child resided in the surrounding comforts of family.

Emma had stopped producing urine, confirming organ failure. Her swelling was even worse than days prior. She had been removed from all interventions other than pain medication, sedation, and the tube that was keeping her heart beating. A day had passed since the ethics committee meeting, and we were looking for comfort to help us get through "seeing what happens."

Dr. G was mercifully there again to offer support.

"She's holding on," I said to him when I met him in the hallway outside Emma's room. But he already knew that because he'd been checking up on her. He nodded with understanding. "I'm not surprised," I continued. She's always been a fighter, a survivor."

And then he said something that took my breath away with its beautiful sentiment: "Maybe she's negotiating."

I laughed at this through my tears. At that moment, I loved that man with all my broken heart as I said, "I'm sure she is."

In the meantime, we had all but moved into that room that could hold all of us with our emotions swirling and bouncing off one another. My parents and in-laws, friends, Hanna and Josh, and Tolya's sister Marianna all took turns saying goodbye, some quietly as their sadness slowly meandered down their cheeks, others loudly, like Josh and Hanna, who sobbed with abandon as they kissed their sister's face. *What is this doing to them?* I thought. *How scarred will they emerge from this, how scathed?*

My mother sang to her the war ballads that were her agreed-upon music genre, and once she even exclaimed that Emma opened her eyes briefly. I didn't believe it until I saw it for myself.

One moment I'm talking to her and singing, and suddenly I see her heavy lids lift ever so slightly, almost imperceptibly, past the strong sedation, past the capitulation of her body on herself, and her eyes meet mine. And in that harrowing moment, she seems to be asking, "What's happening to me? Why can't you help me?" and I fall on her, weeping, and *I'm sorry, I'm sorry, I'm sorry.*

Two weeks had passed since Emma's admission, and the director of the hospital came to speak with us.

"Please don't take this the wrong way," he began, "but we need to admit people to this room, so we're letting you know that this will no longer be a private room. I hope you understand."

Perhaps I misunderstood then and believed him to be telling us to vacate, because I remember asking, "But she's not suffering, is she?" as if I was looking for permission to let her linger and "wait and see" a little longer.

His response leveled me. "She's suffering because she's not home with you, healthy like before." And then to solidify his point, he shared with us his very personal story about how he went through a similar experience with his young disabled son. Maybe, it was meant to give us strength to go through our initial decision to not prolong Emma's suffering, or to give us comfort in knowing we were not the only ones to have faced such demons. We thanked him for sharing his story because we recognized it as well meaning.

After he left, we decided we'd wait out the night in hopes that we wouldn't need to take any actions, that we'd be spared being haunted by our choice.

I made my way to Emma and stroked her porcelain cheeks, which now felt taut from the fluid that had built up and was pushing under the surface of her babylike skin. I kissed her forehead and whispered this: "It's okay to go now, baby. It's okay to go."

Did I really believe she was waiting for my permission to let go—this determined, spirited little girl who laughed her annihilating silent laugh in the face of anyone trying to tell her what to do when she was well? She was hardly going to start caring now.

I was trying to shield my conscience from future guilt that I knew would never leave me. But she was suffering and so were we, to see her this way. These last days in hospice, we had been straddling two universes, the present one we occupied and the one we tried to prepare for but never truly could, realizing that with artificial life support, this torture could go on for days, perhaps weeks. But to what end? To only one.

We had shared with everyone our dilemma about whether to extubate or not, except with our parents, Tolya's and mine. We weren't sure they would understand our decision and agreed that we were protecting them from having to grapple with the same guilt, doubt, remorse—whatever emotions came to settle on our conscience as a result. Not wanting to burden them, we kept them ignorant of our thoughts. Whether they suspected as much or not, we did not know.

That night Tolya and I slept in Emma's room, where the hospital set up two recliners for us next to each other. I took Tolya's hand and prayed for dreamless sleep as I swam on tears into oblivion.

It was a sleepless night, punctuated by the nurses walking in and checking Emma's stats. The soft muffled whirring of the oxygen machine served as white noise, a backdrop to our sleep.

I remembered the white noise app I used during my newborn shoots, the ones that made shushing sounds or simulated sounds the baby heard in utero. I relied on these to help me lull the baby into a deep sleep as I walked and rocked in preparation for the next prop pose. And when the baby would finally be asleep, the parents would say to me, "Wow, could you come at three o'clock in the morning to us and do this?" and "You're so patient."

And I would laugh and think, *I've had so much practice with Emma. This is nothing. A healthy baby doing what they're supposed to? This is cake. So much to be grateful for.*

Now I think, *We're back where we started, on oxygen, listening for breath. Full circle completed.*

The morning brought with it no change. The kind pulmonologist, Dr. P, came in and gave us info on what would take place next and what to expect. We would be asked to leave the room while they extubated, then return immediately after.

And that's what we did.

It was so good to see Emma minus the offensive tube between her lips, though she was still sticking her tongue out at us. I touched and kissed her face all over.

We didn't know what to expect. Would we know when she had gone? I had the urge to climb into bed with her, curl my body around hers one last time so she wouldn't feel alone. But I didn't. Instead I sat on a stool next to her, leaned in so far that I was practically on the bed with her, and caressed her arm, her full cheeks. *I love you, baby, and I'm so sorry. I'm so sorry.* And then suddenly, a sharp intake of breath so deep that I saw her chest rise and then fall. It looked like she was trying to hold on to life and to breathe on her own. My own breath caught. It was so startling and I cried so loud that the pulmonologist rushed in to see if everything was okay. Through heaving sobs, I tried to tell her, "I think she's trying to breathe. I think she's trying to live. What's happening?"

We are strong. We are survivors.

The pulmonologist checked Emma's pulse and turned to us. "She's gone."

CHAPTER 31

"EVERY CHILD CHANGES YOU IN different ways," wrote Lauren Slater in her memoir, *Playing House: Notes of a Reluctant Mother*. Hanna was my artistic muse. She manifested my dreams of performing to an audience whose approval and praise I inherently sought, ever since my grandmother Manya took me around to sing and collect sweets that would be responsible for my teeth-decayed smile. I lived vicariously through my youngest child, collecting accolades as if they were my own, because they were a product of my relentless encouragement to nurture her natural talents.

Joshua was my sweet boy, tender of temperament, generous of his love and unconditional acceptance of me even as I struggled to reign in my perfectionist tendencies. He was smart, witty, funny, and perpetually happy, with confidence that I could only recall nostalgically before it shattered in adolescence.

Emma was the fulcrum upon which I teetered. She was my perfectly imperfect child, my teacher, my sage, and I loved her more for it. She elevated to the surface my worst fears and perceived flaws and shed light on them so that they no longer had the power to possess me, to threaten my existence. By casting the focus on her care and well-being, Emma relieved me of the burden of self-obsession, to be perfect and lead a perfect life. I was less a prisoner to others' judgment and no longer succumbed to the anxieties that so mercilessly plagued my psyche in years past. It was as if by taking on my pain, she freed me of my existential wounds, just as I had wanted to do for her all those times she hurt.

From Emma, I learned there is beauty in the unspoken words, in the actions of implied determination. In all the ways that she had communicated her wants and needs, the unconditional love her uncooperative body housed, which I had first seen as not whole and now saw for what it was, a concerto of desires, a lightness of being I could only dream of, an existence dictated by a connection that surpassed body and spoken language, that surpassed all that limited her. She was freer than I would ever be: free from judgment, free from psychic pain, free from all the suffering I imposed on myself in a world of rules, conditions, and expectations.

Emma helped me navigate the tangled pathways of my heart and rearranged it. From her I learned that sometimes you find beauty where you least expect it. In her, I found beauty and wisdom and grace. This little girl, who in my youthful ignorance I believed was broken, had healed me. Because it was me that was broken all along. She was always the whole matryoshka, at the center of the nesting dolls. My mission, once I chose to accept it, was to move through the extra layers of myself, through the other matryoshkas nested in different versions of myself, to get to the heart, the soul, the epicenter of everything that was perfect and forgiving and whole about me. And that was Emma. She lingered patiently until I found her, found myself.

But why did she have to leave so soon? I wanted to know. I was still learning, still had so much evolving to do. Was the lesson distributed, and I had homework to complete? How was I to make sense of this? Was her purpose fulfilled once I realized that I fully accepted her and loved her enough to stop looking to live separately from her?

These thoughts did not arise until much later.

But on this day, I was still reeling from coming home without her, forever.

We went straight home from the hospital the morning that Emma took her last great breath, and I crawled into her bed—which had been unoccupied and unmade for two weeks, as if preparing for her return there—and I buried my face in her pillow, trying to inhale what remained of her scent, and I cried.

I recalled our nightly ritual in which she raised her arms to receive the blanket I dropped from my hands. As it landed just under her arms, she would lower them around it with an exaggerated hug, then turn to her side and rock herself a few times back and forth, inviting in sleep.

That night Tolya and I lay in a darkness that felt much darker than ever before. We sobbed into our blanket to muffle the sounds that escaped from the deepest recesses of ourselves, fearful of alarming the kids if they were to hear.

I had never heard Tolya so distraught, and it scared me a little, maybe because it competed so fervently with my own wailing. I recognized my cries; these were the cries that seized me the day she was born. That day we were in a different home, in a different bed, but next to the same person. That day she was alive in a hospital struggling to live, and I was grieving her birth. This day she was probably still in the hospital, but she was no longer struggling, and I was grieving another improbable loss. I realized that if someone had asked me then, eighteen years ago, what the worst day of my life was, I would have said the day Emma was born. Now, I would answer the day she died.

The next day, everyone descended on our house. Without invitation, armed with the knowledge of our grief, our friends paraded in with food and alcohol to dull the pain and relieve the senses. Someone set the dining table, and we found a dozen friends around us. We found ourselves sitting *shiva*, a

Jewish tradition of seven days of mourning following a loved one's death, without intending it.

I was reminded of every New Year for the past decade. Because we couldn't celebrate outside our home, needing to be with Emma, we threw crazy end-of-the-year parties where sometimes as many as fifty people celebrated with us. The walls burst at the seams with love and merriment, and we felt insanely fortunate that our lives were this full and our friends so devoted that they would forgo other plans so that we wouldn't be alone on this day.

We had built this, and it was a wondrous thing.

But now, the party was over. I knew we would never welcome in the New Year this way ever again. With Emma gone, it lost its purpose.

Prepared food packages began arriving at our doors, friends brought bags full of groceries, condolence cards piled into a tower of sympathy accumulated on the credenza, and trees, so many trees, were planted in Israel in Emma's memory by friends, photography clients, my old bosses. This was a lovely tradition that we learned of on our trip to Israel twenty-five years ago, in which a tree is planted to honor the memory of a loved one. I was convinced Emma had a miniature forest created just for her.

I posted this on Facebook:

It is with broken hearts that we say goodbye to our beautiful Emma girl. She was the bravest little angel we have had the privilege of calling daughter, sister, granddaughter, cousin, niece, friend. She touched everyone's lives. She was our hero. She wasn't to live more than a year, as per doctors, but she almost made it to her nineteenth birthday. Emma wanted me to thank everyone for the outpouring of love, support, prayers, and kind words and sentiments from

people she never even met. She was not of this world.
Rest in peace, baby. ♥♥♥. *Emma will be laid to rest*
this Sunday at 10 a.m. Everyone welcome.

Condolences poured in, poems and sentiments from
hundreds. People that knew her recalled her brilliant smile.
Those that never met her wished that they had, but felt like
they knew her from my conversations about her. This was
the greatest gift. It affirmed that I didn't hide her from the
world as I once worried, that she didn't live in the shadows
but inhabited the universe as much as we all did. Many spoke
of her beautiful soul, her reasons for choosing us to be her
parents, the impact she had on so many—those she touched.
"Perfection comes in many varieties," wrote my old boss,
Ruth Meyers Sprintz. Many alluded to the specialness of her
spirit. Emma's first occupational therapist, Wendy Goldstein
from first grade, wrote this:

> *Fifteen years ago, I took my first job as an OT and*
> *had the pleasure to work with this little girl at P811Q*
> *along with her speech therapist, Kathy Nemeth*
> *Tilden. Emma was the sweetest girl, with so much*
> *love to give and a spunky personality. Fifteen years*
> *later—this photo has traveled with Kathy and I to*
> *the Bronx, where we display it in our office to remind*
> *us every day of the true meaning to be respectful, to*
> *always be patient, and to always smile.*

She attached a picture of six-year-old Emma in the classroom that hung on her wall above her desk. I bawled when I
saw this and showed it to Tolya. He shook with grief. "Look
at her reach," I said. "I had no idea." Strangely, all this made
Emma feel alive to me, if only for a moment, until I was
stunned back to the devastating truth.

My friend Luba set up a fundraiser, with donations going to Cohen's Children's Hospital of LIJ, where Emma spent the first two months of her life, and we raised $10,000. We also created a Facebook page called Emma's Laugh, where we added pictures and videos, the fund information, people's beautiful words of comfort and condolences, poems, and later eulogies.

The video I recorded the day of her eighteenth birthday made it onto the page ("I'm glad you recorded Emma's birthday video," Tolya had said to me), as well as one we found serendipitously. It was recorded by my father, one day while we were vacationing and he was babysitting with overnights. In it, he and Emma are in her room on the couch, her television playing the *Hairspray* DVD on repeat, my father in just his underwear with his hairy torso, encouraging Emma to dance.

"Let's go dance," he grabs her, still sitting, into a tango embrace. "Let's dance, Emma. Acha, chacha, chacha, cha. Emma gonna dance with deda." Emma, with a wet bib in her mouth, shimmies and laughs, grabbing at him as if to hug him, falling backward onto the couch amid laughter and loss of control. More of "Let's go, Emma. La-la-la-la-la-la-la, look at the camera, don't touch my glasses. Good girl, Emma, chacha chacha chacha cha." Emma beams happiness. The video ends with a "Brava, bravissima," and I think: *This is everything.*

The day of the funeral, before everyone's arrival, Tolya and I stood over an open casket. Emma occupied the child-sized box made of warm-stained wood, in a white gown and a white head covering reminiscent of the kerchiefs that her great-grandmother may have worn decades ago in a small village in Ukraine. With her swelling gone, her lips able to come together and touch once again, her porcelain skin as unmarred and flawless as ever, I recognized her and then I didn't.

Most startling of all was the soft smile that graced her face. The ladies that prepared her for burial must have taken care to do this, and I was grateful for it because it intimated a peacefulness so much in contrast to the last image we had of her at the hospital. But then an inexplicable anger gripped me at the falsehood of the pretense, at the memory that in life, Emma's smile was never a conservative demure suggestion of contentment but a lips-parted, tongue-protruding, drool-decorated production that radiated beams of light and love and only belonged to one.

A memory found me: In coming to this country, my grandfather had traded in his tailoring to work as a *shomer*. According to Jewish tradition, from the moment of death until burial, when it's believed the soul hovers in a sort of liminal space, the deceased may not be left alone. This ritual is called *shmira*. When I was younger, I was told that my grandfather, Yefim, worked as a night watchman in funeral homes—a security guard of sorts—and I would wonder what there was to protect but a dead body, and who would want to steal a dead body anyway? Now I know what he did could be considered a *mitzvah*, and it gave me peace to know that Emma was not alone.

We had chosen the smaller of the funeral home rooms that was said to accommodate 150–180 people, mostly because it felt warmer of the two, more intimate. When we returned after meeting with the rabbi in a separate part of the chapel, where we took part in another ritual of mourning, that of tearing our garments (this is symbolic of recognizing the loss—that our hearts are torn—but also that the body is only a garment that the soul wears), we found ourselves walking into a room full of people. Wall to wall people, standing huddled in close proximity to one another, hugging the walls around the perimeter of those seated.

I froze.

Who were all these people? Surely, we did not know everyone here, just like at a wedding where people are expected to bring a plus one, a date, a companion, and the guest list invariably doubles. But when I stood up at the podium to read my eulogy, my eyes spanned across the room, and I saw all my coworkers, old bosses, current bosses, childhood and high school friends with whom I'd lost touch, Emma's teachers who came out of retirement to pay their respects, Hanna's and Joshua's friends and their parents, old nurses and current nurses, therapists, Dr. Y and his wife, and my photography clients, some half a dozen moms whose babies and children I photographed.

I believe my father was the first to speak. He delivered his eulogy in his broken English and broken tear-stifled speech. Grandma Tamara followed. My friend Luba stood next to her husband, Gary, and read, choking up but not stopping. Then Josh and Hanna shared their memories of their older and wiser sister, making observations of lessons taught and learned. My heart swelled with pride. We had done this right. We had nurtured—somehow—three beautiful souls.

Tolya and I were the last ones to speak. I asked him to let me have the last say—as always in our marriage—and he read this:

> It is hard to think and write about Emma's life, as she is always so present in our heart and mind.
>
> Emma was given one life to live, but she transformed so many.
>
> She used her own gifts to touch us all, to redeem us, to bring us together, to love.
>
> Emma is our family's lifeblood, our nucleus.
>
> Our inspiration comes in many forms, from our environment, from individuals, from groups.
>
> To refer to Emma as an inspiration is to minimize her impact on our own lives.
>
> Ever-present, Emma, taught us to live beyond our own everyday lives.

We have spun folklore around Emma's accomplishments.

Her possibilities and promises have always increased with every new step, with every new exploit.

Even though we try to enumerate Emma's talents, as we lovingly call them, on her own terrain, on her own terms, one by one, we forget that there is a more nuanced portrait—that when you add two or three or four raindrops together, you do not obtain an itemized list of raindrops but a loving sun-shower.

With Emma as our rudder in our lives the focus was always what was possible and never what seemed impossible.

My every memory and the memories that we all have of Emma are filled with epic and poetic stories but, importantly, also with our own tales of transformation of who we are, who we want to be, and who Emma changed us into.

At the moment, I feel lost at sea without my adorable Emma, the pilot of my life.

Each memory of Emma's passing is a tidal wave that brings me under the surface of the water, gasping.

How easy at times it seems to let go and go under.

I take solace in the presence of all of you with us and those that reached out with prayers, poems, and kindhearted words.

Your loving messages give us strength to stay strong, Your sympathetic voices guide us to continue one day at a time.

Emma will always be our celestial and mystical force, directly and immediately exerting her presence upon our minds and our souls.

Emma's angelic presence is with us now and forever. Rest, my love.

This from a college English-as-a-second-language student, I thought when he finished. I was impressed and surprised by his many references to the soul, the mystical and angelic. My husband the skeptic, the scientist, the self-proclaimed atheist suddenly morphed into a preacher, a rabbi, and a Buddhist monk all rolled into one. I witnessed something spiritual overcome him, even if he denied it later, when he spoke of his otherworldly child. I was especially relieved that he remained standing to the end, as he shook like a leaf, his voice aquiver, so much so that I feared he would collapse.

When it was my turn, I gathered my strength and bulldozed forward. I was determined to tell Emma's story in the clearest of ways. I thought my voice would waver, but it held steady. My heart did not gallop away. It trotted alongside me like a trustworthy friend, making sure I hit every note, left nothing out, did not falter, did not fail. Did not cry.

The day was frigid and overcast, our drive to the cemetery accompanied by a blanket of cloud threatening snow. Upon our entering the cemetery, though, the clouds suddenly parted, and the sun's rays pierced through the steely sky. Later, our friends Michael and Betty would send us a picture they took of that moment that I would not have believed unless memorialized. A long streak of blue split the clouds, and it was as if the heavens opened to show Emma the way.

As I walked to her gravesite, the cold air pierced my nose and pricked my eyes. The ground under my feet felt solid, unyielding, and I wondered how loose the soil would be for throwing and covering the casket with, another ritual that dictated mourners pick up a handful or shovel full of soil and fling it into the opening the casket filled, symbolically burying the dead. According to one custom, mourners use the back of the shovel at first, to demonstrate reluctance. I refused to actively partake in burying Emma as I watched others do and as the thud, however soft, reverberated like a hammer on my head. Then I heard the rabbi say something about tucking a child in bed, and I lost it. Gut-wrenching sobs overtook me, and my legs gave way just in time for someone to catch me.

In that moment, I felt my heart a carpet-bombed town, and my grandmother Manya's words echoed in my ears. *It is not the order of things. Parents should not bury their children.*

LIFE AFTER EMMA PRESENTED AS an alternate universe. The world became *before Emma* and *after Emma*. I did not know how to navigate it without the quotidian worrying about nurse coverage, school bus, feeding supply delivery, seizure medication refills. I saw Emma in every corner of the house—scooting on her bottom down the sunken living room steps, sitting in her room watching *Hairspray*. I continued to wake at night to listen for the sounds of her tossing around from the discomfort of a soiled diaper. I even considered moving. But that wasn't the answer, I knew. Waves of sorrow overwhelmed me and left me in a pool of tears. And after I was spent, I would see the image in my mind's eye of Emma reaching over and gently slapping me, like she did when I fake-cried.

Grief forces us to remember, and I never wanted to forget. I opened myself up further to spirituality. I turned to titles like "Do Dead People See You Shower?" and others that spoke about the soul and what happens after death. I began talking to Emma in my head, looking for signs, for proof, however anecdotal, that this was not the end for us, that there had to be more.

I recognized that I did not have the luxury of capitulating to my grief. We still had two children to finish raising. Josh was accepted to McGill University in Canada, and it would only be a short three years before Hanna would leave for college. I would have what I thought I always wanted—an empty nest.

But sequestering within the walls of the apartment proved agonizing, so I returned to work, prematurely. My coworkers looked at me with surprise to see me back so soon. Of course, physically I was present, but my head was in the past, and my eyes became wet in each meeting in which a child's medical concerns remotely resembled Emma's. I was a mess. The first day after returning to work was particularly annihilating. *What am I doing here?* I thought.

I did not know where else to be.

As I walked into the lobby of my building, at day's end, something took hold and I mentally said this: *Emma, let me know you're okay. Just please let me know. I need to know.* Two minutes later, after entering the apartment, I found a package from Emma's school. Immediately, I assumed it was the extra change of clothes we'd sent in for her—to change a chewed-on shirt or soiled pants.

With heavy hands, I ripped the package open to find Emma's face staring at me. She was in a beautiful large gold-trimmed picture frame, and in it, her mouth was poised for a kiss, the kiss that she blew by putting her lips together and effecting a loud popping sound. I lowered to the floor, pressing my lips to the glass, and sobbed.

Emma had sent me a sign. And in that moment, I could hear her—her breathy, quiet laugh—and I felt something close to elation.

HOW DO YOU GO ON after loss? It's the same question we asked ourselves when Emma was born. The answer is, like the marathon we ran, you put one foot in front of the other, and you look around to appreciate the scenery, to find loved ones among strangers cheering you on, holding up signs that tell you, you can do this. You got this. And it's not about winning; it's about getting to the finish line—if not running, then walking or crawling—and if you can't do that, then scooting on your behind to where you need to go, the way Emma taught us.

"How are Josh and Hanna coping?" many asked. I would always answer with "They're strong. They'll be okay." But the truth was I didn't know much about how they were dealing with their sister's death. Shortly after Emma's passing, in anticipation of having to return to school, Hanna tearfully shared with me that just weeks prior, when Emma was still alive, she brought in a picture of her to share her special sister with the class in a "show and tell" assignment. "How can I go back now?" she cried. "What am I gonna tell people, when I just spoke about her?"

My heart ached for my children. They were not new to death, having had to say goodbye to their beloved great-grandmother. But this was different. My grandmother had lived a long life. Emma was a child. They were learning that death was part of life, but were they understanding it the way I was even struggling to understand it myself?

It has taken five years, but I know now life prepares you for what will come, like the training wheels of a bicycle. Taking Holly in and raising her gave me practice for when my own children arrived. Witnessing my grandmother bury her own daughter before I would bury my own, paved the way for dealing with unimaginable loss. Choosing social work as a profession, with a focus on children with special needs, was a fortuitous path.

In my research on dealing with grief and death, I came across a book written by a Danish author, Glenn Ringtved, called *Cry, Heart, but Never Break*, an illustrated children's book that tries to explain death to four children who are faced with having to say goodbye to their ailing grandmother, whom Death comes to collect. The children try to stall their grandmother's death by plying Death with coffee, hoping that it will leave. But as we know, death can be delayed but not avoided.

In this story, Death is not angry or spiteful but compassionate and empathic, as he explains his job as necessary, for "*What would life be worth if there were no death? Who would enjoy the sun if it never rained? Who would yearn for the day if there were no night?*"

This is what they needed to understand. This is what I needed to understand.

So, we continued to live, and I continued to collect signs. Two months after Emma's passing, we took the kids skiing to Utah, a trip we had planned before Emma got sick. On top of a ski slope, thousands of feet above ground, on the other side of the country, we bumped into Dr. F, the same Dr. F who operated on Emma's feet. "I heard," he said. "I'm so sorry for your loss. She was a very special little girl." *Yes*, I think. *I hear you, baby.*

Emma's Laugh Facebook page, the one we created in memory of her, began playing tricks on me. Without fail, after every particularly difficult night in which I'd cry myself to sleep, I'd get a morning message telling me to "keep up the good work with Emma's Laugh." I'd show it to Tolya as proof of my certainty that she was with me and sending me these words.

"It's a computer program, nothing more," Tolya would say. "It's a coincidence. You're talking superstition."

"There's no such thing as coincidence," I insisted.

I'd point out every "sign" as I perceived it: me driving in the car, crying because a memory found me and grief struck, and my tears would be interrupted by a radio ad for an email marketing company called Emma, and immediately, my tears would turn to laughter. Or I would be driving with directions home plugged into my phone GPS, accidentally make the wrong turn, and find myself in front of Emma's school. *I hear you, baby.*

Two weeks after Emma's passing, my friend Joanna saw me struggling and shared: "There's a medium on Long Island. No, not the Long Island medium," she said suppressing a chuckle. "Why don't you see him?"

By then, I was even open to this and felt I had nothing to lose. That hour irrevocably, fantastically changed my life. I was connected to Emma, briefly to my grandmother, and even our cocker spaniel, Jules, who died while I was pregnant with Emma, made an appearance. I was told things no one could have known had they Googled me and read every Facebook post I ever made. "Life is like a play," explained the medium. "We each have our roles to play. Your daughter's role ended, and she left the stage. But you still have a part to play until your time comes. And when you walk off, she will be waiting for you backstage." I left with nothing less than a spiritual awakening, recharged and brimming with hope.

But I was selective with whom I shared this experience, acutely aware as I was of people's differing beliefs, not to mention that I felt not a little insane, as if I were detailing an alien sighting. To my surprise, many did not find me crazy but instead nodded their heads with an air of wisdom or long-held knowledge to which I was a neonate and just becoming privy.

Emma continued to exist as a screensaver on my phone; on the pink bib I saved and transferred from purse to purse; on videos recorded; in the collage of pictures I hung in her room, which became my writing and editing space; and in the occasional dream that felt too real to want to wake from, in which she was reclined full body on top of me, and we were playing our old game of "Where is Emma? I didn't see you" as she rose up to give me the kiss that I asked for. When I opened my eyes and still felt the weight of her on me, I knew that she was there.

I returned to photographing families and babies, but before doing so I worried. "What am I going to tell people now when they ask me how many kids I have?" I asked Tolya—a question not very distinct from Hanna's desperate query of me.

The time came, and the questions invariably arose. "You're so patient," the mom would say. "Do you have children?"

"Three," I answered without hesitation.

ACKNOWLEDGMENTS

THIS BOOK WOULD NOT HAVE existed were it not for the many individuals that took part in its creation. A huge thank-you to Marion Roach Smith, who taught me the fundamental art and craft of memoir writing. In her no-nonsense yet uplifting and inspiring way, she helped nurse and midwife this labor of love into the world. I owe a debt of gratitude to all the editors and talented authors who helped shape the manuscript into its present form: Elizabeth Cohen, Jeff Ourvan, Emily Rapp, Maria Kuznetsova, and Heather Siegel. To David Lavie for generously offering to read and edit many pages. My gratitude to the community of fellow workshop writers who walked the path alongside me and encouraged me to keep writing and rewriting.

My parents; my in-laws; my sister, Holly, and her husband, Mike; my sister-in-law, Marianna, and her husband, Leonid; and Baba Manya have been by our side from day one and have showered us with love and revealed their strength. To my nieces, Zara and Olivia, and nephews, Edward and Matthew, for making me laugh and giving me hope.

To our friends who have embraced us and our unique family and made us always feel welcome in their homes and in their lives. I am grateful for my best girlfriends: Luba, for always being my first reader (after my husband) and cheerleader, and my friend Joanna, for helping me connect with

Emma after her passing. Without this revelation and new-found belief, I doubt this book would have ever been written.

To the teachers, therapists, doctors, and nurses who gave Emma the care and quality of life that allowed her to blossom into her best self.

To my husband, for giving me the greatest gift—our three children. My mother was right; I *was* the lucky one. Thank you for listening to my early chapters and crying. I know it was not easy to relive the years. Thank you for saying you thought I portrayed you better than you were in real life and gave you more credit than you deserved. That only speaks to your humble character and proves me right. I am indebted to my children, Joshua and Hanna, for inspiring me to be a better mother, a better person.

And finally, to Emma—for choosing me.

Most names, appearances, and places have been changed to protect identities.

AUTHOR BIO

DIANA KUPERSHMIT holds a Master of Social Work degree and works for the Department of Health in the Early Intervention Program, a federal entitlement program servicing children from birth to three years with developmental delays and disabilities. She has published online in the *Manifest Station, Power of Moms, Motherwell Magazine, Her View from Home,* and *Still Standing Magazine.* On the weekends, she indulges her creative passion working as a photographer specializing in newborn, family, maternity, and event photography.

Author photo © Diana Kupershmit

SELECTED TITLES FROM SHE WRITES PRESS

She Writes Press is an independent publishing company founded to serve women writers everywhere. Visit us at www.shewritespress.com.

Loving Lindsey: Raising a Daughter with Special Needs by Linda Atwell. $16.95, 978-1631522802. A mother's memoir about the complicated relationship between herself and her strong-willed daughter, Lindsey—a high-functioning young adult with intellectual disabilities.

Edna's Gift: How My Broken Sister Taught Me to Be Whole by Susan Rudnick. $16.95, 978-1-63152-515-5. When they were young, Susan and Edna, children of Holocaust refugee parents, were inseparable. But as they grew up and Edna's physical and mental challenges altered the ways she could develop, a gulf formed between them. Here, Rudnick shares how her maddening—yet endearing—sister became her greatest life teacher.

Make a Wish for Me: A Family's Recovery from Autism by LeeAndra Chergey. $16.95, 978-1-63152-828-6. A life-changing diagnosis teaches a family that where's there is love there is hope—and that being "normal" is not nearly as important as providing your child with a life full of joy, love, and acceptance.

Expecting Sunshine: A Journey of Grief, Healing, and Pregnancy after Loss by Alexis Marie Chute. $16.95, 978-1-63152-174-4. A mother's inspiring story of surviving pregnancy following the death of one of her children at birth.

Blinded by Hope: One Mother's Journey Through Her Son's Bipolar Illness and Addiction by Meg McGuire. $16.95, 978-1-63152-125-6. A fiercely candid memoir about one mother's roller coaster ride through doubt and denial as she attempts to save her son from substance abuse and bipolar illness.

Breathe: A Memoir of Motherhood, Grief, and Family Conflict by Kelly Kittel. $16.95, 978-1-938314-78-0. A mother's heartbreaking account of losing two sons in the span of nine months—and learning, despite all the obstacles in her way, to find joy in life again.